TRENDS IN DEEP LEARNING METHODOLOGIES

Hybrid Computational
Intelligence for Pattern Analysis
and Understanding Series

TRENDS IN DEEP LEARNING METHODOLOGIES

Algorithms, Applications, and Systems

Series Editors

SIDDHARTHA BHATTACHARYYA

NILANJAN DEY

Edited by

VINCENZO PIURI

SANDEEP RAJ

ANGELO GENOVESE

RAJSHREE SRIVASTAVA

ACADEMIC PRESS

An imprint of Elsevier

Academic Press is an imprint of Elsevier
125 London Wall, London EC2Y 5AS, United Kingdom
525 B Street, Suite 1650, San Diego, CA 92101, United States
50 Hampshire Street, 5th Floor, Cambridge, MA 02139, United States
The Boulevard, Langford Lane, Kidlington, Oxford OX5 1GB, United Kingdom

Notices
Knowledge and best practice in this field are constantly changing. As new research
and experience broaden our understanding, changes in research methods, professional
practices, or medical treatment may become necessary.

Practitioners and researchers must always rely on their own experience and knowledge
in evaluating and using any information, methods, compounds, or experiments
described herein. In using such information or methods they should be mindful of
their own safety and the safety of others, including parties for whom they have a
professional responsibility.

To the fullest extent of the law, neither the Publisher nor the authors, contributors, or
editors, assume any liability for any injury and/or damage to persons or property as a
matter of products liability, negligence or otherwise, or from any use or operation of
any methods, products, instructions, or ideas contained in the material herein.

Library of Congress Cataloging-in-Publication Data
A catalog record for this book is available from the Library of Congress

British Library Cataloguing-in-Publication Data
A catalogue record for this book is available from the British Library

ISBN: 978-0-12-822226-3

For information on all Academic Press publications visit our
website at https://www.elsevier.com/books-and-journals

Publisher: Mara Conner
Editorial Project Manager: Gabriela D. Capille
Production Project Manager: Swapna Srinivasan
Cover Designer: Victoria Pearson

Typeset by TNQ Technologies

Working together
to grow libraries in
developing countries

www.elsevier.com • www.bookaid.org

Contents

Contributors

Leo Adlakha
Department of Computer Engineering, Netaji Subhas University of Technology, New Delhi, India

Rangel Arthur
Faculty of Technology (FT) — State University of Campinas (UNICAMP), Limeira, São Paulo, Brazil

S. Bagyaraj
Department of Biomedical Engineering, SSN College of Engineering, Chennai, Tamil Nadu, India

Vishal Bharti
Department of Computer Science and Engineering, DIT University, Mussoorie, Uttarakhand, India

Dinesh Bhatia
Department of Biomedical Engineering, North Eastern Hill University, Shillong, Meghalaya, India

Ana Carolina Borges Monteiro
School of Electrical Engineering and Computing (FEEC) — State University of Campinas (UNICAMP), Campinas, São Paulo, Brazil

Akash Dhiman
Department of Computer Engineering, Netaji Subhas University of Technology, (Formerly Netaji Subhas Institute of Technology), New Delhi, India

Neha Dohare
Department of Information Technology, Maharaja Surajmal Institute of Technology, New Delhi, India

Reinaldo Padilha França
School of Electrical Engineering and Computing (FEEC) — State University of Campinas (UNICAMP), Campinas, São Paulo, Brazil

Vagisha Gupta
Department of Computer Science and Engineering, National Institute of Technology Delhi, New Delhi, India

Kanishk Gupta
Department of Computer Engineering, Netaji Subhas University of Technology, (Formerly Netaji Subhas Institute of Technology), New Delhi, India

Yuzo Iano
School of Electrical Engineering and Computing (FEEC) — State University of Campinas (UNICAMP), Campinas, São Paulo, Brazil

P. Vigneswara Ilavarasan
Information Systems Area, Department of Management Studies, Indian Institute of Technology, Delhi, India

B. Janakiramaiah
Department of Computer Science & Engineering, Prasad V. Potluri Siddhartha Institute of Technology, Vijayawada, Andhra Pradesh, India

G. Kalyani
Department of Information Technology, Velagapudi Ramakrishna Siddhartha Engineering College, Vijayawada, Andhra Pradesh, India

Arpan Kumar Kar
Information Systems Area, Department of Management Studies, Indian Institute of Technology, Delhi, India

S. Arun Karthick
Department of Biomedical Engineering, SSN College of Engineering, Chennai, Tamil Nadu, India

Jatinder Kaur
Department of ECE, Chandigarh University, Mohali, Punjab, India

Sarabpreet Kaur
Department of ECE, Chandigarh Group of Colleges, Mohali, Punjab, India

Pardeep Kumar
Department of Computer Science and Engineering, Jaypee University of Information Technology, Solan, Himachal Pradesh, India

Amit Kumar Kushwaha
Information Systems Area, Department of Management Studies, Indian Institute of Technology, Delhi, India

Amit Malviya
Department of Cardiology, North Eastern Indira Gandhi Regional Institute of Health and Medical Sciences, Shillong, Meghalaya, India

Amit Kumar Mishra
Department of Computer Science and Engineering, DIT University, Mussoorie, Uttarakhand, India

Animesh Mishra
Department of Cardiology, North Eastern Indira Gandhi Regional Institute of Health and Medical Sciences, Shillong, Meghalaya, India

Nitin Mittal
Department of ECE, Chandigarh University, Mohali, Punjab, India

Shweta Paliwal
Department of Computer Science and Engineering, DIT University, Mussoorie, Uttarakhand, India

Sandeep Raj
Department of CSE, IIIT Bhagalpur, Bhagalpur, Bihar, India

Shelly Sachdeva
Department of Computer Science and Engineering, National Institute of Technology Delhi, New Delhi, India

Deepak Kumar Sharma
Department of Information Technology, Netaji Subhas University of Technology, New Delhi, India

Rajshree Srivastava
Department of CSE, DIT University, Dehradun, Uttarakhand, India

Bhanu Tokas
Department of Computer Engineering, Netaji Subhas University of Technology, New Delhi, India

Preface

In recent years, deep learning has emerged as the leading technology for accomplishing a broad range of artificial intelligence (AI) tasks and serves as the "brain" behind the world's smartest AI systems. Deep learning algorithms enable computer systems to improve their performance with experience and data. They attain great power and flexibility by representing more abstract representations of data computed in terms of less abstract ones. The age we are living in involves a large amount of data and by employing machine learning algorithms data can be turned into knowledge. In recent years many powerful algorithms have been developed for matching patterns in data and making predictions about future events. The major advantage of deep learning is to process big data for better analysis and self-adaptive algorithms to handle more data. Deep learning methods with multiple levels of representation learn from raw to higher abstract-level representations at each level of the system. Previously, it was a common requirement to have a domain expert to develop a specific model for a particular application; however, recent advancements in representation learning algorithms (deep learning techniques) allow one to automatically learn the pattern and representation of the given data for the development of such a model. Deep learning is the state-of-the-art approach across many domains, including object recognition and identification, text understanding and translation, question answering, and more. In addition, it is expected to play a key role in many new areas deemed almost impossible before, such as fully autonomous driving. This book will portray certain practical applications of deep learning in building a smart world. Deep learning, a function of AI, works similarly to the human brain for decision making with data processing and data patterns. Deep learning includes a subset of machine learning for processing the unsupervised data with artificial neural network functions. The development of deep learning in engineering applications has made a great impact on the digital era for decision making. Deep learning approaches, such as neural networks, deep belief networks, recurrent neural networks, convolutional neural networks, deep autoencoders, and deep generative networks, have emerged as powerful computational models. These models have shown significant success in dealing with massive amounts of data for large numbers of applications due to their capability to extract complex hidden features and learn efficient representation in unsupervised settings. Deep learning-based algorithms have demonstrated great performance in a variety of application domains, including e-commerce, agriculture, social computing, computer vision, image processing, natural language processing, speech recognition, video analysis, biomedical and health informatics, etc.

This book will cover the introduction, development, and applications of both classical and modern deep learning models, which represent the current state of the art of various domains. The prime focus of this book will be on theory, algorithms, and their implementation targeted at real-world problems. It will deal with different applications to give the practitioner a flavor of how deep learning architectures are designed and introduced into different types of problems. More particularly, this volume comprises 12 well-versed contributed chapters devoted to reporting the latest findings on deep learning methods.

In Chapter 1, recent advances in the increasing usage of biometric systems using deep learning are presented. It basically focuses on theory, developments in the domain of biometric systems, and social implications and challenges in existing systems. It also highlights the need for customers and deep learning algorithms as an alternative to solve state-of-the-art biometric systems. Future insights and recommendations are summarized to conclude the chapter.

The role of deep learning in this analysis of data and its significance in the financial market is highlighted in Chapter 2. Applications of deep learning in the financial market include fraud detection and loan under-writing applications that have significantly contributed to making financial institutions more transparent and efficient. Apart from directly improving efficiency in these fields, deep learning methods have also been instru-mental in improving the fields of data mining and big data. They have identified the different components of data (i.e., multimedia data) in the data mining process. The chapter provides some recent advances and future directions for the development of new applications in the financial market.

In Chapter 3, a convolutional neural network-based deep learning framework for classifying erythrocytes and leukocytes is presented. A novel architecture is presented for white cell subtypes in digital images that fits the criteria for reliability and efficiency of blood cell detection, making the methodology more accessible to diverse populations. The proposed method is developed in Python. Experiments are conducted using a dataset of digital images of human blood smear fields comprising nonpathological leuko-cytes. The results reported are promising and demonstrate high reliability.

Chapter 4 proposes a deep learning framework to predict information popularity on Twitter, measured through the retweet feature of the tool and algorithmically created features. The hypothesis involved is that retweeting behavior can be an outcome of a writer's practice of semantics and grasp of the language. Depending on the understanding of humans regarding any sentence through knowledge, word features are created. A long short-term memory framework is employed to grasp the capability of storing previous learnings for use when needed. The experiments are conducted to classify a tweet into a class of tweets with high potential for being retweeted, and tweets with a low possibility of being retweeted.

Chapter 5 presents insights into recent advancements in the field of healthcare technology by employing Internet of Things (IoT) technology and deep learning tools. IoT has tremendously transformed and revolutionized present healthcare services by allowing remote, continuous, and safe monitoring of a patient's health condition. The chapter focuses on such technologies, their adoption, and applicability in the healthcare sector, which can be productized and adopted at a larger scale targeted at the mass market.

In Chapter 6, an overview of deep learning in the domain of big data and image and signal processing in the modern digital age is presented. It focuses particularly on the significance and applications of deep learning for analyzing complex, rich, and multidimensional data. It also addresses evolutional and fundamental concepts, as well as integration into new technologies, approaching its success, and categorizing and synthesizing the potential of both technologies.

Chapter 7 presents a deep learning framework for the detection and classification of adenocarcinoma cell nuclei. The challenges involved in examining microscopic pictures in the identification of cancerous diseases are highlighted. The chapter presents an approach, i.e., region convolutional neural network, for localizing cell nuclei. The region convolutional neural network estimates the probability of a pixel belonging to a core of the cell nuclei, and pixels with maximum probability indicate the location of the nucleus. Experiments validated on the adenocarcinoma dataset reported better results.

In Chapter 8, a deep learning model for disease prediction is envisaged. The architecture developed can be helpful to many medical experts as well as researchers to discover important insights from healthcare data and provide better medical facilities to patients. To demonstrate the effectiveness of the proposed method, the deep learning architecture is validated on electronic health records to perform disease prediction. The experimental results reported better performance for state-of-the-art methodologies.

Chapter 9 unfolds the brief history of deep learning followed by the emergence of artificial neural networks. It also explains the algorithms of deep learning and how artificial neural networks are combating security attacks. Furthermore, it describes the recent trends and models that have been developed to mitigate the effects of security attacks based on deep learning along with future scope. The impact of deep learning in cyber security has not yet reached its maximum but is on its way to creating possible new vectors for the mitigation of modern-day threats.

Chapter 10 focuses on decision trees in the data mining stream. A novel decision trees-based stream mining approach called Efficient Classification and Regression Tree (E-CART), which is a combination of the Classification and Regression Trees for Data Stream decision tree approach with the Efficient-Concept-adapting Very Fast Decision Tree (E-CVFDT) learning system, is presented. The proposed E-CART approach mines the streams on the basis of its type of concept drift. A sliding window concept is used to hold the sample of examples and the size of the window is specified by the user. Experiments are performed considering three types of drifts: accidental, gradual, and instantaneous concept drifts. The results reported using the proposed approach are compared to CVFDT and E-CVFDT.

Chapter 11 explores a model based on deep convolutional neural networks to automatically identify dementia using magnetic resonance imaging scans at early stages. Dementia is a disorder signified by a decrease in memory and as well as a decline in other cognitive skills like language and vision, and is a widespread problem in older people. The pretrained model, Inception-V3, is retrained for that purpose. The experiments are validated on the Brain MRI DataSet, namely OASIS-1, where a higher accuracy is reported on the testing dataset.

In the final Chapter 12, the primary aim is to propose a method for the classification of hand symbols. There are different stages that serve this purpose. Initially, preprocessing is applied to the hand symbols to remove the noise associated with the images. Preprocessing includes the smoothening, sharpening, and enhancement of edges of an image. The preprocessing step is followed by the segmentation stage. In this stage, a specific region or an area of interest is extracted from a hand image using thresholding. Furthermore, different features are extracted such as color features, geometric features, and Zernike moment features. These features for a hand image are applied to a set of different classifiers such as support vector machine (SVM), K–nearest neighbor, decision tree, and native Bayes in which the SVM classifier achieves a higher accuracy.

This volume is intended to be used as a reference by undergraduate, postgraduate, and research students/scholars in the domain of computer science, electronics and telecommunication, information science, and electrical engineering as part of their curriculum.

May 2020
Vicenzo Puiri
Sandeep Raj
Angelo Genovese
Rajshree Srivastava

CHAPTER 1

An introduction to deep learning applications in biometric recognition

Akash Dhiman[1], Kanishk Gupta[1], Deepak Kumar Sharma[2]

[1]Department of Computer Engineering, Netaji Subhas University of Technology, (Formerly Netaji Subhas Institute of Technology), New Delhi, India; [2]Department of Information Technology, Netaji Subhas University of Technology, (Formerly Netaji Subhas Institute of Technology), New Delhi, India

1. Introduction

The dictionary definition of biometrics by Merriam-Webster [1] describes it as "the measurement and analysis of unique physical or behavioral characteristics (such as fingerprint or voice patterns) especially as a means of verifying personal identity" From this definition, it is easy for us to infer that the key advantage and major use of biometrics is to uniquely identify a person. For a long time, humans have thought of utilizing the very specific traits that make a person unique to describe the identity of a person, as is evident by many records from the early cataloging of fingerprints dating back to 1881 [2]. But only in the past few decades have we reached the point of developing technologies advanced enough to satisfy the requirements of a practical biometric utilization system, and advancement in new machine learning algorithms in recent decades has a major part to play in these advancements.

The technology continues to improve and is also sufficiently refined now that official government organizations have accepted its use [3], given its substantial advantages. One of the major advantages that biometric security brings to the table is that not only does it ensure that the person accessing a system has the authorization to do so, but it also ensures the identity of the user in question, which cannot be done with the traditional methods of username and passwords as this simply gives access to anyone who has access to the given credentials. In other words, it does not depend on "what information you possess" but "who you are." This added layer of protection has helped to make significant strides in the field of security, which is essential in today's world with increasing threats to society via

Trends in Deep Learning Methodologies
ISBN 978-0-12-822226-3
https://doi.org/10.1016/B978-0-12-822226-3.00001-5

terrorism, illegal migration, financial frauds, and infringement of personal privacy and data.

There has been significant progress in the different areas of biometric recognition such as iris, face, fingerprint, palmprint, and even nonconventional areas, including handwriting recognition, gait recognition, voice recognition, and electrocardiogram.

Before understanding the motivation of deep learning in biometrics we must first understand the motivation of machine learning in biometrics. Biometric recognition is not the only domain of security that machine learning has been instrumental in; it has immense application in all kinds of security domains, for example, vast automation in governing opportunistic networking protocols [72] and so much more. The simple reason for incorporating machine learning here is a generalized problem statement, i.e., to match an input biometric feature with what we have inside a database. For this problem statement, a clear and simple algorithm cannot exist by the very nature of the problem. Furthermore, there exist many hurdles along the way like the variability of input, noise in data, and poor quality of input. Such problems can even cause difficulty for simple machine learning architectures [4]. Hence, we tend to seek a deep recognition architecture as much as we can because of its characteristic robustness and tolerance toward noise. The need for identification and prediction from millions of datasets comes under the forte of deep learning networks. It can effectively segment a biometric dataset from noise in the background. The nature of end-to-end deep learning that connects direct input to final output [5] can disentangle the input biometric data in the process and understand the more intricate features that help determine the identity of a person and help handle large intraclass variations. Traditional machine learning algorithms that do not utilize deep learning often require a predefined set of features to work with, and the task of defining them lies under the expertise of the biometric recognition system creator. This implies that the system is as good as the features it is programmed to operate on, since careful selection of features is an essential part of defining the efficiency of any machine learning architecture. On the other hand, a deep learning algorithm is said to develop its own feature set to maximize performance. This is better because there can be a multitude of hidden features impossible for a human to define.

The field of deep learning is just starting out and in the last three decades we have been introduced to recurrent neural networks (RNNs) and many of the biometric recognition algorithms proposed are the derivatives of

RNNs. The other prominent architecture heavily utilized in biometric recognition is a convolutional neural network (CNN), which is the basis for any algorithm employed in the area of image recognition, and models trained on the architecture of a CNN are extremely common whenever a biometric input is image based, like an iris scan or a fingerprint. Newer optimization techniques and noise reduction techniques are also making their way into the deep learning trend with an algorithm like generative adversarial networks to enhance the features of a given input for noise reduction and better recognition output [6].

But the most impactful event that triggered heavy utilization of deep learning algorithms in the past 5—7 years was high-performance computing via machine learning using Graphics processing unit (GPU) and Tensor processing unit (TPU) modules [7,8], and a large amount of high-quality labeled data [9] that became accessible because of advancement of technologies in the domain of data mining, data accessibility, and data storage. Such advancements have been instrumental in opening a vast area of applications, ranging from innovations in healthcare [60] to successful research in emerging areas such as opportunistic networks [64], and the current trend of machine learning seems only to be going forward in the near future.

The chapter begins with an explanation of the motivation for integrating different biometric modalities for robust and improved security systems. It then goes on to make us familiar with the deeper concepts of biometrics, what they are, and what role they play in the current socioeconomic life of humans. Next, it describes the theoretical aspects of deep learning and its application in the domain of increasing biometric recognition accuracy and strengthening security countermeasures and mitigation methods. The chapter draws parallels between the current methods employing deep learning in biometric security and protection. Finally, the chapter talks about the future prospects of how modern upcoming technologies like data fusion will revolutionize the field even further. The scope of potential areas with research opportunities is also discussed in this chapter.

1.1 Biometric recognition

In this subsection, we analyze the process of a typical biometric recognition system and the requirements that make it efficient and reliable. It will further explain the need for deep learning and how it is operational in providing such capabilities.

1.1.1 Overview

The process of biometric recognition has two stages as shown in Fig. 1.1. First of all, the user is enrolled into the system, and the characteristics to be used for biometrics are taken as input and the important features are extracted; this is followed by storing them in a template database for recognition processes later on. Now, during the recognition process, the user provides their biometric input and the features are extracted again; this time the template database is referenced for matching and the individual in question is verified or identified accordingly. We will see the difference in identification and verification in the next section.

A biometric recognition system has essentially four components [10]: a sensor module acquires the biometric input that needs to be processed. This is followed by a feature extraction module that processes the biometric input acquired by the sensor module and a specific feature set relevant to the recognition process is extracted. For example, the feature extraction

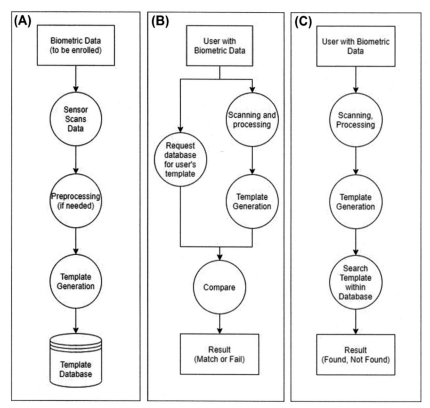

Figure 1.1 (A) Enrollment steps. (B) Verification steps. (C) Identification steps.

module is used to extract the position and orientation of ridge bifurcations and ridge endings from fingerprints. This is followed by a matching module that matches the obtained extracted feature set against the template database, and the result is generated, which provides a matching score. The final component is a decision-making module that uses the matching score to establish successful or failed verification and identification.

1.1.2 Identification versus verification

Both identification and verification are recognition methods; their usage depends on the context of their application. Verification methods are a 1:1 matching protocol where only a single individual's biometric data is stored in the template database and the recognition is done to confirm whether the user who tries to gain access is that particular individual or not. Identification methods provide a 1: n matching protocol where the identity of a user is cross-referenced with multiple biometric identities in the template database; this enables the biometric recognition system to perform negative recognition.

1.1.3 Expectations from a biometric security system

While there are multiple methods of biometric recognition employed in various different applications in the current scenario, efficient biometric recognition systems need to match basic security and recognition standards:

- Intraclass variations [11]: In conventional key-password methods, a 100% matching score is required, which is not a feasible expectation from a biometric system. The decision-making module does not make a binary decision on the basis of a perfect match. This discrepancy is due to variability in sensing conditions, such as the presence of noise in the recognition process, or variation in characteristics of the user itself, for example, a sore throat could affect voice recognition. Other circumstances that could affect the process are based on user interaction with the system, such as impartial fingerprints. Such variability in the user input is called intraclass variation. A biometric recognition system needs to use a probabilistic approach to make sure that a user stored in the template database is able to access the system at all times despite these variations.
- Data integrity: While biometric recognition systems can be highly efficient in dealing with intraclass and interclass variations, a threat is posed in a biometric system that can be easily dealt with in traditional user-password methods, i.e., in the case of a biometric recognition system,

if an individual is able to obtain the template database, the individuals enrolled into the template database are at risk because that information can be further used to access other biometric systems that use the same trait. Hence, these systems need to provide the highest degree of protection for the biometric databases and also tackle different spoofing methods and attacks against the biometric system.

- Accuracy: A biometric system's recognition accuracy is of grave importance. Biometric systems can pose two essential errors when operated: a false match where a user who is not enrolled in the template database is verified and granted access to the system via matching the user with an identity that is not theirs, and a false nonmatch where the user enrolled in the template database is not verified when they try to access the recognition system. These further define the false match rate (FMR) and the false nonmatch rate (FNMR) [12], and there remains a tradeoff between the FMR and FNMR. Both can be considered interdependent of each other and the feature set presented. The optimal feature set yields the same value for these and is termed the equal error rate (EER), which conveys the accuracy of a biometric system quantitatively [13]. The performance of a biometric recognition system depends on numerous factors and does not remain static. It depends on factors such as:
  - Size of the template database
  - Algorithms employed in feature extraction and classification
  - Ambient conditions such as temperature, humidity, and illumination
  - Quality of sensed biometric input

2. Methods

This section details the various deep learning algorithms that are employed across various biometric modalities. The purpose is to give sufficient insight into the theory of these algorithms. It further helps outline how they are applied in the recognition process.

2.1 Prominent deep learning algorithms

While currently there are a plethora of algorithms with minute modifications that are being employed and experimented on for their use in precise biometric recognition, it becomes essential for us to talk briefly about some of the crucial algorithms that play a fundamental role in defining the more specialized algorithm. These include:

- Convolutional neural networks
- Recurrent neural networks
- Autoencoder networks
- Siamese neural networks

2.1.1 Convolutional neural networks

The initial idea of a CNN came into existence around 1980 [14] but it was properly proposed around 1998 [15]. They are predominantly used for the analysis of image-based data because of their unique property of preserving the spatial structure of an image [16]. They are specialized deep neural networks (Fig. 1.2) that take advantage of built-in kernel convolutions [15] in the convolutional layer. Convolutional layers convolve input images with convolutional kernels. Typically for an image analysis via standard deep learning, the image is first required to be preprocessed, as raw pixel data is superfluous and often contains noise and wasteful data. This pre-processing would typically be done to reduce the total amount of data to work on, but not necessarily the total amount of information. This is done with the help of techniques such as Gaussian blur, mean blur, Sobel edge detector, and other related algorithms. Once this is done the processed input is fed into a deep learning algorithm to gather useful inferences.

A CNN is different to a standard deep learning network since it allows for the direct image input to be fed into the system. This input is passed through various convolutional layers similar to the preprocessing step in standard deep learning, but the advantage is that here the neural network itself defines how the convolutional layers are going to behave to best extract the features to best classify the input. This method has shown

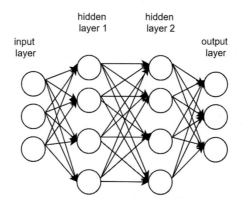

Figure 1.2 A typical deep neural network (for comparison purposes).

significant new applications in computer vision opening new arenas, such as unique as smart agriculture [69] and so much more. We will further see how essential CNNs are in the field of biometric recognition. We analyze what happens step by step in a CNN.

A CNN is end to end, meaning it takes direct input and produces direct output, learning about the appropriate features along the way. First, it takes up an image and runs a random kernel convolution operation on it. A kernel convolution operation takes up a local receptive field, i.e., a subset of adjacent pixels of the original 2D image, and generates one single point output for this kernel. Then it slides this local receptive field such that it centers another pixel and generates another single point output for this kernel. It keeps doing this until it exhausts all possible local receptive fields and the final result is a feature map for that one particular convolutional operation (Fig. 1.4). This process is done for a number of random convolution operations to generate their own feature map, and finally all these feature maps are stacked among themselves as can be seen in Fig. 1.3. Now we downsample all the feature maps generated in a process called pooling, where we take $N \times N$ adjacent nodes and based on their activation generate one output node. Doing this for all feature maps generated we obtain a new set of downsampled feature maps on which we again run the multiple convolutions. This process is done multiple times to finally obtain a set of feature maps that has lost its spatial integrity data but contains the information in multiple feature maps. These feature maps are then fully connected to the output. Training a CNN is similar to any other deep learning network with backpropagation of error. CNN is predominantly used for image data analysis, making it perfect for utilization in scanned biometric data, namely fingerprints, face, iris, etc. [17].

2.1.2 Recurrent neural networks

Simple deep neural networks are considered as "feed-forward networks" in which input data is being mapped to output data. The architecture is made so that only the nodes in the nth layer are connected to the $(n + 1)$th nodes in a forward data propagation manner. An RNN modifies this architecture by adding a feedback path, thus allowing the properties of a feedback network to influence the learning process [18]. The feedback network in an abstract sense allows the deep neural network to learn the temporal dependency of the data being analyzed. The feedback network allows data from the same nodes at a previous point in time to influence its data in the present time; this is illustrated in Fig. 1.5. Their use case is in the analysis of

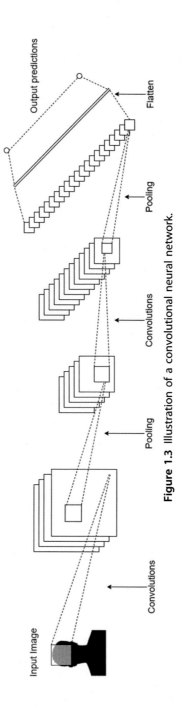

Figure 1.3 Illustration of a convolutional neural network.

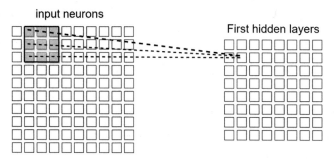

Figure 1.4 Convolution operation to create the first hidden layer, a visualization.

time-dependent functions and/or unsegmented tasks. An RNN also has some well-known modifications that further amplify the memory aspect of the architecture. We have long short-term memory (LSTM) architecture that has special nodes to store temporal information and gates that control when to store information and when to forget it [19]. Another derivative is gated recurrent network, which is similar to LSTM but more efficient and less complex as it has fewer parameters than LSTM [19]. Their application in biometrics involves the analysis of behavioral biometrics such as signatures and gait recognition biometrics.

2.1.3 Autoencoder network
Autoencoder networks are deep learning networks that consist of two deep neural networks, one termed an encoder and the other a decoder. The job of an encoder is to create a compressed feature set called latent space representation, based on the input image, and the job of the decoder is to recreate the input data based on the features it is presented with. But autoencoders can do more than that; their specialty comes from the fact that they can be trained to recreate relevant input data without the accompanying noise that was present previously [20] and therefore they have the potential to be used in a preprocessing stage of registering biometric data.

2.1.4 Siamese neural network
Siamese architecture has been used for recognition or verification applications especially for one-shot learning tasks where the number of training samples for a single category is very small [21]. The main goal of this architecture is to learn a similarity index from data, minimizing a discriminative cost function that drives the similarity index high for similar pairs of input. Fig. 1.6 shows how a Siamese network is used; the network has two

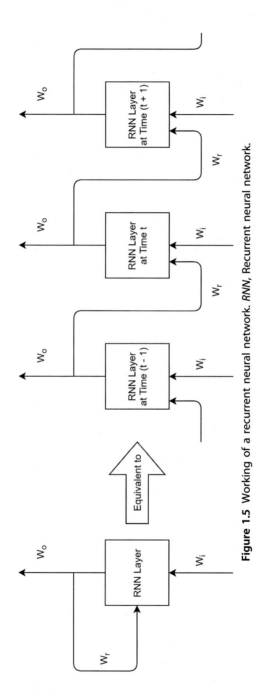

Figure 1.5 Working of a recurrent neural network. *RNN*, Recurrent neural network.

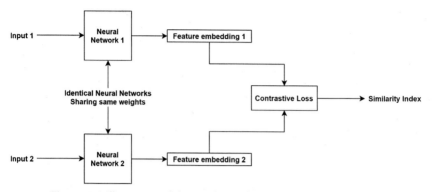

Figure 1.6 Illustration of the working of a Siamese neural network.

separate branched deep neural networks that have the same weights and architecture. The fully connected output layer calculates contrastive loss in the output of the two sample inputs and adapts the weight accordingly to classify correctly. They are used in conjunction with CNN or RNN architecture to compare an enrolled biometric with a scanned biometric [22].

2.2 Deep learning methodology for precise recognition

In this section, we discuss deep learning methodologies that are currently being used in or have been researched for their effectiveness in biometric recognition systems. Biometric recognition systems can be realized via multiple biometric traits that vary from the extent of recognition as well as the characteristic trait of the user taken as a biometric input. To that end, biometric recognition can first be classified into hard and soft biometrics.

2.2.1 Hard biometrics
Hard biometrics consists of physiological traits assumed to be unique and ubiquitous. Hard biometrics is predominantly used in a biometric system. Hard biometrics can be further categorized on the basis of the nature of characteristic traits as physiological or behavioral biometrics. Physiological biometrics concerns with unique physiological traits exhibited by a person. Behavioral biometrics concerns the behavioral traits exhibited by a person, such as a person's movement, writing style, speech accent, etc.

2.2.1.1 Face recognition
The first step toward achieving the goal of recognition is identification, and Viola–Jones algorithm [23] or hog face detection [24] is used for this

purpose. Then, face landmark estimation is used to normalize the face, i.e., to anchor each characteristic point like iris, nose, and eyebrow into 68 specific locations [25]. These are the preprocessing steps that are done during both the enrollment process and verification process. The major challenge to ponder at this point is how to train the algorithm to match biometrics with only one image provided during the enrollment process; this is called one-shot enrollment. This is resolved by what is stored in the database. The methodology is to generate a random binary code of length 256−1024 bits and train a deep CNN to map the enrollment image with the binary code generated. The idea is that during the verification process, the same deep CNN (DCNN) is run on the face image provided with the objective that it will map this image to the same binary sequence; if it does so, the face is recognized. To create more robust security, the system uses a truly random sequence of bits without any correlation to the enrollment image and also generates SHA-512 cryptographic hashing of the sequence of bits, which is what is eventually stored in the database. To improve the efficiency even further, the system performs data augmentation via a Keras image data generator application programmimg interface [26] or autoencoder networks [20], which extrapolate the enrollment image data.

The CNN network can distinctly be seen to be composed mainly of two stages [26]: the system first utilizes VGG-Face CNN to extract 4096 features, and then finally in the fully connected phase of the CNN network these features are used to generate the final binary encoding. Analysis of a CNN model indicates that it works by minimizing the differences of images of the same face and maximizing the differences of images of different faces, i.e., the final feature set generated by the model, which will be used to predict the binary code that is similar when considering the image of the same person; however, it is vastly different for faces of different people. Fig. 1.7 illustrates the identification process and Fig. 1.8 illustrates the block diagram for the enrollment process itself.

2.2.1.2 Fingerprint recognition

Fingerprints are composed of a pattern of ridges and valleys; the ridges are distinguished by many important points, known as minutiae. The spatial configuration of these minutiae is unique for each individual. The degree of uniqueness can be understood by the fact that even identical twins do not have the same fingerprint. This can be further made more secure by taking into account multiple fingerprints for recognition. While the matching scores provide a very good result for fingerprint-based recognition, a

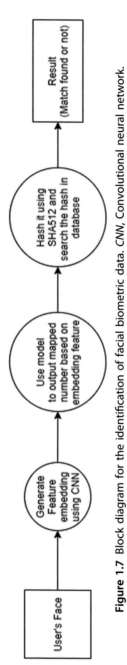

Figure 1.7 Block diagram for the identification of facial biometric data. *CNN*, Convolutional neural network.

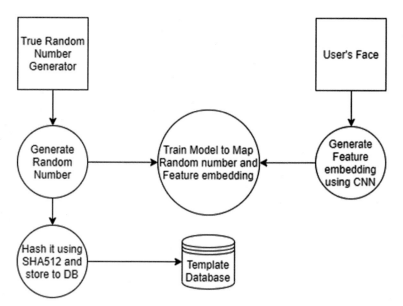

Figure 1.8 Block diagram for the enrollment of facial biometric data.

problem that might arise that would need tackling is the computational complexity generated while matching when the template database stores millions of users.

Many fingerprint recognition systems utilized today depend on minutiae and delta recognition machine learning models like the multidimensional artificial neural network [27] rather than deep learning architecture; even so, there has been substantial research done on the subject concerning deep learning methodologies. More importantly, deep learning is used to effectively extract fingerprint features of importance, namely minutiae, deltas, ridges, and pores. Most of these utilize CNNs. Some examples include DeepPore model [28], Wang's u-net model [29], and Labati's model [30]. Finger pore detection is a task well handled by a CNN. The paper referenced at [31] discusses exactly this by cleverly incorporating logical operation to ease out computation and make the system more feasible. The research discusses utilization of Bernsen's binary method [32] to take the fingerprint images and derive a so-called binary image, which is a combination of ridges and pores of the fingerprint (eliminating all the other noise); it then uses an image enhancement method [33] to extract an image containing only the ridges. These two images are passed via an XOR operation to obtain an image containing only pores of the fingerprint. Up to this point, preprocessing the fingerprint is complete and the new image obtained is fed into a judge-CNN architecture, which consists of a VGGNet-based algorithm (Fig. 1.9).

Another methodology [12] discussed utilizes ResNet architecture with a transfer learning approach, i.e., it uses a pretrained ResNet50 model and repurposes it for the similar task of recognizing fingerprints. Utilization of ResNet helps to avoid the vanishing gradient problem here, as ResNet skips chronologically hidden layer connections creating a direct connection between distant hidden layers. The research suggests that the proposed algorithm has an accuracy rate of 95.7%, which is comparable to the Gabor-wavelet method at 95.5% [12].

One research paper [34] also explores the potential of deep learning in minutiae pattern recognition by the proposal of minutiae extraction network (MENet). This works on a similar principle as a convolutional function selecting a small kernel out of a given image and predicting if the kernel's central pixel is part of a minutiae point; if yes, then it marks it as a positive. This creates a map of specific minutiae points for a given finger-print, which can be further utilized for authentication purposes. The architecture is relatively simpler containing five convolutional layers and two layers at the end, which are fully connected, each having 1024 nodes and ReLU activation, which are connected with SoftMaxBoolean output. The concern here is the requirement of a large set of training data for better performance.

2.2.1.3 Palmprint recognition

The surface of the palm contains ridges and valleys just like fingerprints. In recent years, palmprint recognition has come to light because its template database is increasing. Palmprints pose certain advantages over fingerprints, such as the provision of additional features like wrinkles and principal lines, which can be easily extracted from images of slightly lower resolution. Palmprints provide more information than fingerprints, hence palmprints can be used to make an even more accurate biometric system.

For palmprint recognition we will be exploring two methods: the first one [35] utilizes convolutional neural network-fast (CNN-F) architecture. It has eight layers: five convolutional and three fully connected ones. An experiment concerning the same over a PolyU palmprint database can be found in [35].

Another method for palmprint recognition comes from the research provided in [36]. This research utilizes a Siamese network model, and can

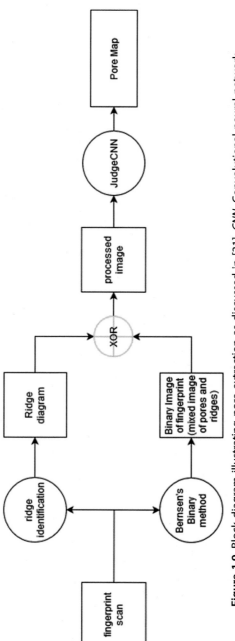

Figure 1.9 Block diagram illustrating pore extraction as discussed in [31]. CNN, Convolutional neural network.

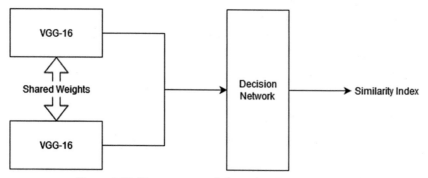

Figure 1.10 Siamese network for palmprint recognition.

be seen in Fig. 1.10. As explained earlier a Siamese network consists of two branch networks with shared weight. For the purpose of palm recognition, the two methods employ CNN networks, both with the VGG-16 model. Finally, instead of a simple fully connected network, we have a decision network that combines the layers in both branch networks. The architecture is composed of a dual five convolutional layer and three fully connected layers at the end, followed by a SoftMax.

2.2.1.4 Iris recognition

The iris is the colored annular ring that surrounds the pupil. The color, texture, and pattern of each person's iris are as unique as a fingerprint. In this case as well, identical twins have different iris patterns, just like fingerprints. The iris is extremely difficult to surgically spoof. It is also secure because artificial irises can easily be detected. Iris recognition has been integrated into large-scale applications such as the Iris Recognition Immigration System [37]. It has good FMR but its FNMR can be very high.

Feature-based machine learning is currently employed for iris recognition in the majority of systems; nonetheless, many newer ways have been proposed in recent research with the potential to augment or replace feature-based recognition. One such method of augmentation discusses better feature collection in the process of iris segmentation in [38]. The paper proposes two modified CNNs. The first is the hierarchical convolutional neural network (HCNN) in which we create more than one input from one input image. Taking different patches of the original image, say the original is 256×256, we take three pixel sets, 256×256, 128×128, and 64×64, fixing the center of all these at the center pixel. Then we run CNN on each of these patches and fuse the final output

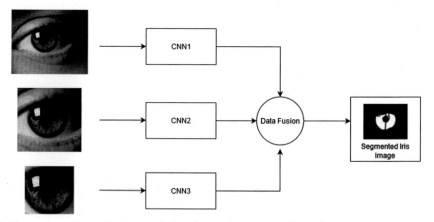

Figure 1.11 Hierarchical convolutional neural network (HCNN) for iris segmentation.

answer. This is done to capture finer local detailing, but the drawback is multiple calculations for the same pixels near the center, as illustrated in Fig. 1.11. The second is to use a multiscaled fully convoluted network (MFCN) [38]. An MFCN is a special type of CNN that does not contain fully connected CNN but rather connections made in stages; this helps as we can include upsampling layers in between, which allows us to handle the data faster and much more accurately. The CNN layers connected in segments calculate their own respective output, forwarding it to the next segment as well as the fusion layer, which makes sense of data passed onto it from each segment. The end result is faster and more accurate classification, especially for dense classification as is expected from a biometric recognition system. Another method discussed in [39] utilizes deep sparse filtering to aptly perform the recognition. A deep sparse filtering network learns the number of features rather than finding a cluster between different input data; this process avoids hyperparameter optimization and thus converges to a solution quickly. A simple modification of CNN is to create a DCNN with many layers, dropout learning, and small filter size, as discussed in [40]. This gives us DeepIrisNet, which currently performs just as good as the state-of-the-art algorithms while also generalizing over new data.

2.2.1.5 Vein recognition

Dorsal hand vein structure allows us to look at biometrics in a unique way and significant research has been done in this direction. One of the methods is to use SqueezeNet and multibit planes [41]. The dorsal hand image is scanned in grayscale format with each pixel having a value between 0 and 255. Each pixel comprising the image is then represented as its 8-bit representation:

$$\text{pixel} = b_7 * 2^7 + b_6 * 2^6 + b_5 * 2^5 + b_4 * 2^4 + b_3 * 2^3 + b_2 * 2^2 + b_1 * 2^1 + b_0 * 2^0$$

Using this formula, each pixel is distributed into eight planes; it is present if there is a 1 in the corresponding plane's place value and absent if there is a 0 in the corresponding plane's place value. After this, redundant planes (with very few pixels present) are eliminated, thereby making the system resilient toward noise. Finally, the selected planes are passed into a SqueezeNet architecture, and their output combined to produce the final recognition result, as can be seen in Fig. 1.12.

2.3 Voice recognition

Voice recognition is often considered as a combination of both behavioral and physiological characteristics. The weak links in the voice recognition security can be external environment noises or recorded voice. Another limitation is that it is not too distinctive to be employed for large-scale verification.

Deep learning has found plenty of use cases and research in the area of speaker recognition. A 2017 paper [42] talks about a simple deep learning architecture with an input layer consisting of Mel frequency cepstral co-efficient (MFCC) of audio chunks and output of an enrolled speaker. The input audio is distributed into small audio chunks of 20−40 ms with an overlap of 10 ms between consecutive frames. MFCC is computed for each of these chunks individually and a matrix is constructed with rows denoting individual frames and columns denoting different MFCC coefficients for each frame; these are then fed into a deep support vector machine to construct a matrix of enrolled users, which are utilized during the matching process (Fig. 1.13).

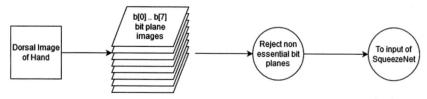

Figure 1.12 Dataflow for vein recognition.

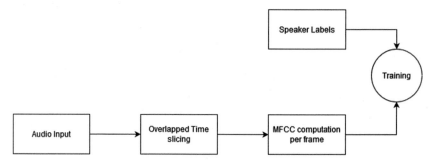

Figure 1.13 Preprocessing flowchart for voiceprint recognition. *MFCC*, Mel frequency cepstral coefficient.

Another approach would be to go ahead with Siamese networks as discussed in [43]. The Siamese network would take up two input samples and calculate the distance between hidden features between the two samples provided. It then reduces this distance if the samples belong to the same class and increases the distance if the samples belong to different classes. This may seem familiar to the discussion on face recognition, but the difference is that here Siamese networks are being utilized instead. It therefore shows how it will help in recognizing a person with the help of voice features.

2.4 Gait recognition

Gait analyzes human movement and contains an ensemble of time and spatial configuration information of the body. Gait recognition is not highly unique; hence, its application is currently in low security systems. It has advantages that become relevant despite its low security, that is, it can observe the biometric input in a nonintrusive way as gait analysis can be done using cameras from a distance. It may vary with time due to changes in body weight and injuries. It can also be influenced by choice of footwear and clothing. Robust algorithms are required to deal with these varying situations. Gait analysis uses video sequence footage for the recognition procedure and hence is computationally expensive.

The first process is discussed in [44] and is illustrated in Fig. 1.14. The process takes each frame from the input video and performs a silhouette extraction using any edge detection algorithm, which is then used to calculate the "local direction pattern (LDP)" for each pixel (it assigns an 8-bit value based on the direction the pixel moves in subsequent frames). These LDPs augment the optical flow data associated with a person in the

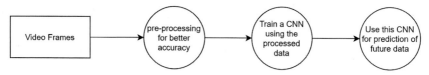

Figure 1.14 Working of the gait recognition biometric system. *CNN*, Convolutional neural network.

video and after principal component analysis of this data, it is passed through a simple CNN; the preprocessing allows us to extract the mobility information of each frame, which results in greater accuracy. The experimental results can be seen in [44]. Research given in [45] discusses a different approach. As we have learned, RNNs are typically good at temporal variant tasks and gait is a temporal process; it should follow then that we try to use it to augment our CNN networks. This is exactly what the proposed research tries to do. The input video is used to train a CNN model similar to the previous one and an RNN model independently, and is followed by performing an information fusion operation on the two to obtain the real final identification.

2.4.1 Signature recognition

The method by which individuals sign is a behavioral characteristic of the signer, which may change over time due to the emotional state as well as the physical conditions of the signer at varying points in time. Signatures have been accepted into various legal, governmental, and commercial transactions. Further advancements are being made as dynamic signatures are being introduced, which requires a pressure-sensitive pen-pad. Dynamic signatures improve the verification as it adds features to analyze such as speed, pen pressure, and order of strokes, while the user signs it onto the pressure pad. Signature-based recognition may be at risk due to professional forgers who may be able to recreate the signature and spoof the recognition system.

The current signature recognition system is based on Siamese-LSTM (see Fig. 1.15 for a block diagram of the data pipeline). This is a Siamese neural network used in comparison-based tasks along with a distinguished modification of the RNN architecture known as LSTTM (which consists of forget gates for better memory function). The LSTM memorizes distinct characteristics of a signature, and verification is the result of Siamese architecture. Experimentation regarding this process is given in the research cited at [46].

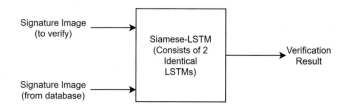

Figure 1.15 Data flow for signature recognition. *LSTM*, Long short-term memory.

2.4.2 Soft biometrics

Soft biometrics has recently being used to enhance traditional biometric recognition and allow human identification using verbal descriptions. Soft biometrics can include characteristics such as hair, height, age, gender, and more. These can be obtained from large distances without subject cooperation; hence, they become beneficial in the case of mass surveillance of public spaces. These are physiological and behavioral features that can be described using human labels. They are not unique but can be aggregated to provide discriminative biometric modality. They can be used for supplementing hard biometric features as seen in multimodal biometric modalities, as well as fast retrieval from huge template databases.

2.5 Databases

Deep learning methodologies go hand in hand with the database that is used to train them, since a deep neural network architecture after it has been built requires data to train it. The research papers discussed in this chapter make use of various data sources depending on their concerned modalities. Some of them along with other potentially benefiting databases are collectively discussed here. The PolyU database [47] provides us with a fingerprint dataset (1690 images, 320*240 px, 1200 dpi) and palmprint dataset (from 230 users, 800*600 px), which are also used for evaluating the models prepared fingerprint recognition and palm print recognition. It also has other biometric datasets, including iris and variation of fingerprint/palmprint datasets. The dataset for the face recognition model comes from three sources, namely CMU-PIE [48] (with 41,368 images of 68 subjects), FEI [49] (with 2800 images of 200 subjects), and Color FERET [50] (with four images of 237 unique subjects each) databases. The model for iris segmentation previously discussed is tested on Ubiris.v2 [51] and Casia.v4 [52] iris databases. For voiceprint the data comes from LibriSpeech [53] with over 800+ h of English speech.

There are many other databases currently made available either under open-source license or noncommercial license. These include the AR Face database [54], currently having 4000+ face images under various lighting conditions and expressions. For fingerprint datasets one might consider the FVC2002 [55] (eight prints of 100 unique subjects), FVC2004 [56] (eight prints of 100 unique subjects), and FVC2006 [57] (12 prints of 150 unique subjects) datasets. A dataset for gait recognition has been developed by the National Laboratory of Pattern Recognition available in four classes [58]. For voiceprint, Mozilla has created "common voice" [59] with 30 GB+ worth of open-source speech data along with its soft biometric features. Other popular online resources that are maintained regularly include Google dataset [61] and Kaggle dataset [62]. Research institutions and organizations are also a potential source of noncommercial biometric datasets.

2.6 Deep learning methodology for spoof protection and template protection

While the field of biometrics has seen great contributions from machine learning in increasing recognition accuracy, its continued growth and wide-scale application pose a new class of hackers aiming to infiltrate the systems and jeopardize the security of the users of the biometric access system. To that end, all biometric recognition systems are made of generalized components that can be attacked by hackers; different attacks on the basis of point of attacks on the system are shown in Fig. 1.16.

While many of the attacks shown in Fig. 1.16 are generalized and applicable to other information systems, spoof protection and template database protection are specific to biometric systems. We shall discuss spoofing and template database protection via applications of deep learning in the following sections.

2.6.1 Spoof protection

Spoofing refers to the process of presenting fake biometrics to the sensor. These can be generated by gaining possession of the biometric data of a registered user via false means, such as the process of lifting fingerprints from objects touched by the person. Spoof protection is rapidly becoming a necessary attribute in biometric systems. At the center of spoof protection lies liveness detection, which could help determine if the biometric input is a static image or presented by a live human being.

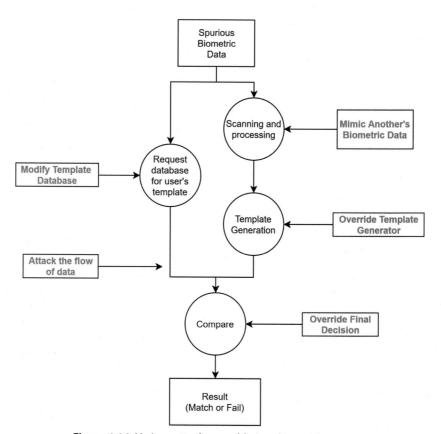

Figure 1.16 Various attacks possible in a biometric system.

Many advancements have been observed in the field of spoof protection using deep learning. Jung and Heo proposed a CNN architecture [63] to solve the problem of liveness detection, which is a sturdy framework for detection and training. Squared error of regression line is applied for every accepting field in the proposed architecture and the training is carried out directly using every fingerprint. The performance index exhibited by the system is controlled by biasing the value in the squared error layer.

Xia and others developed Weber local binary [65], a local descriptor with applications in fingerprint liveness detection. The proposed model contains two modules, the former being the local binary differential excitation module and the latter being the local binary gradient orientation module. The outputs from these modules produce a discriminative feature vector that is processed as input into a support vector machine.

Yuan and others [66] introduced a backpropagation neural network that detects liveness in fingerprint biometric modules. The image is preprocessed to obtain the gradient values that act as input to the neural network, then hyperparameter optimization is carried out to obtain better accuracy. Koshy and Mahmood [67] applied nonlinear diffusion to the captured images. The diffused images were fed into a CNN architecture, Inception v4, to extract complex and deep features to help classify images as live or fake images.

All these proposed methods have been presented recently, meaning that spoof protection using deep learning is a new field and will see further advancements in the future.

2.6.2 Template protection

Biometric recognition is carried out by matching the extracted features with the template database, an essential component of a biometric system that cannot be replaced. Template protection is of utmost importance for many reasons; however, one cause of concern may be that if the template is stolen, the person in possession of the biometric template has access to all other biometric systems where the individual is enrolled using the same biometric modality.

There are a few requirements from a template protection scheme [68]:
- Diversity: Matching different templates should be done keeping in mind not to destroy the data integrity of the template.
- Cancelability: If a biometric template is jeopardized, the option to nullify that template and reinstate a newly generated template should be available.
- Security: Template creation should be a one-way process, and it should not be possible for someone to recreate a complete biometric data based only on its template.
- Performance: Performance should remain practical and protection should ideally have no effect on the accuracy of detection.

There are several methodologies available for biometric template protection; primarily, two of them see the application of deep learning: cancelable biometrics and biometric cryptosystems.

2.6.2.1 Cancelable biometrics

Cancelable biometrics gives emphasis to the cancelability part of the template protection scheme. The idea is to introduce methodical noise into the biometric features before creating a template out of them. In case the template leaks, the noise signature is changed and the same biometric trait can again be used to create a new template. The main element (biometric trait) is never compromised because of the noise added in between, which also ensures privacy of the trait as it becomes more difficult to retrieve the original biometric data based on the noisy compromised template.

Recent advances have been made in the field of deep learning in cancelable biometrics. Abdtellaf and others proposed a CNN architecture with the utilization of such an idea within a facial recognition system [68]. It was formed using deep concatenation and a ResNet architecture. Multiple CNNs worked independently on different localized regions of the image. Afterward, a fusion network mixed all the features extracted from the local CNNs into a data-rich output, and finally, it was passed through a bio-convolving function, which in essence is a one-way convolution function that ensures privacy and security of biometric templates while not hampering the recognition accuracy. Talreja and others provided a different way to implement cancelable biometrics in their paper [70]. Here, they used the extracted feature sets to generate a binary vector, from which particular values were selected, based on a user-dependent key (stored local to the user). This was passed through an error-correcting decoder to generate a multibiometric sketch whose hashed output was finally stored as a template in the database. At the time of verification, the user presented both the biometric trait and the stored dependent key. A combination of them in a similar fashion to that during enrollment allowed a hash to be generated, which was matched to what was stored in the database for verification.

2.6.2.2 Biometric cryptosystems

Biometric cryptosystems associate a cryptographic key with the biometric data presented during the enrollment process, which simplifies aspects of a biometric system with regards to security. Due to the variability of biometric data, direct key extraction is rather difficult and henceforth a system utilizing a biometric cryptosystem allows the existence of partial data of enrolled biometrics (enough not to compromise the system); this is termed helper data and it assists in key extraction during the authentication process. There are a few instances of deep learning methods employed in biometric cryptosystems. The model discussed for facial recognition earlier utilizes concepts of biometric cryptosystems. Xiulai Li proposed a deep learning-based method [71], where the iris dataset was normalized and used to train CNN architecture-based deep learning neural network models. The encryption side collected the iris image and inputed the trained deep learning model to extract the feature vector that was passed through the Reed—Solomon encoder that encoded the given feature vector. Albakri and others [73] proposed a CNN-based biometric cryptosystem for the protection of a blockchain's private key. Here, the biometric input of users other than the training input was taken, its features were extracted, and a vault was created to mix these features along with a key for protection.

2.7 Challenges in biometric recognition and security

While biometric recognition is being increasingly employed for the sake of the security perspective, there remain challenges that still need to be addressed for the next step in the integration of biometrics into more institutions. One disadvantage of biometric systems is the need for extra equipment, such as high-resolution cameras required for iris recognition and fingerprint readers for fingerprint recognition. The extra equipment also makes the recognition expensive and difficult to scale. In the context of deep learning's application in biometric recognition, the challenge faced is the lack of a sufficiently large training sample available for a particular biometric modality. The factors that influence the accuracy of deep neural networks are the depth of the network, the extent of pretraining, and the data augmentation performed by random rotations and cropping of the datasets. There is still no well-established methodology that involves deep learning helping or replacing many popular and classical recognition methods developed in the past few decades, like the popular code-based iris recognition or minutiae matching-based fingerprint recognition successfully deployed today.

3. Comparative analysis among different modalities

A biometric system takes advantage of unique biometric data for the purpose of authentication of a person, the idea being that it is hard to replicate or use brute force to compromise this type of security. But as we have seen, by using the same deep learning technologies one can try to create fake biometric data just as easily. Hence, the most favorable approach for security would be two-factor authentication where biometrics and password-based authentication are used, or perhaps a multimodal approach where multiple identification criteria make spoofing much harder to perform.

In the context of deep learning applications, although it is proven to be effective, in use cases such as these they are often more than what is needed;

hence, there also exist methodologies that can more accurately be considered as feature-based machine learning where the designers of the architecture have a clear idea of what to include in a feature set and the outcome is also quite robust and resilient, such as in the case of current iris recognition methods that are better at identifying individuals when compared to face recognition.

Table 1.1 shows parameters that can be used to compare and contrast methods of biometric authentication among themselves. When considering the practical socioeconomic aspect of the whole system, not only is the technology used of concern but also the cost and practicality of the entire system, which is roughly compared in the table.

4. Further advancement

The application of deep learning in biometric recognition and security is still at its budding stages and the opportunities of the integration of deep learning in biometrics are increasing rapidly. This is highly evident from the fact that a majority of the antispoofing and template protection systems discussed in the previous section have been proposed in the past few years. Similarly, biometric recognition has seen a surge of deep learning integration in recent years.

Deep learning displays potential for significant strides in biometrics for a variety of reasons:

- Identification in a large user base: Deep learning provides the appropriate framework required to support identification among millions of users with efficiency, which requires a large dataset, complex models, and computational power.
- Data noise: Deep learning provides the ability to tackle data noise while receiving biometric input. It has the capability to learn and sort many factors while learning distinguishing features.
- Biometric aging: Biometric recognition has an inherent intraclass variation, which is aging. Deep learning can be potentially employed to tackle this intraclass variation by generating synthetic extrapolated biometric data.
- Multimodal biometrics: Multiple biometric modalities can be integrated for better protection by jointly training the architectures of the modalities.

The different instances of deep learning in the field of biometrics mentioned in the previous sections have influenced the scope of research in

Table 1.1 Characteristics of common modalities.

Features	Fingerprint	Palmprint	Gait	Iris	Face	Vein	Voiceprint
Ease of use	High	High	Low	Medium	Medium	Medium	High
Best true recognition (%)	95.7	99.62	98.5	97.7	98.19	99	98
Cost	High	Very high	High	Very high	High	Very high	Low
Remote authentication	Available	Available	Available	Available	Available	Available	Available
Sensor technology used	Optical/ultrasonic sensor	Optical/ultrasonic sensor	Video camera with large storage space	Laser/infrared scanner	CMOS image sensor	Laser/infrared scanner	Microphone and acoustic analyzer
Deep learning method used	DeepPore, binarization + CNN, ResNet with transfer learning	CNN-F, VGG-16 Siamese	CNN on specifically preprocessed data, RNN	Hierarchical CNN, DeepIrisNet	VGGnet + fully connected network	SqueezeNet + multibit plane	Deep support vector machine

CMOS, Complementary metal–oxide–semiconductor; CNN, convolutional neural network; CNN-F, convolutional neural network-fast; RNN, recurrent neural network.

a multitude of ways. Proposal of MENet [34] for the purpose of fingerprint minutiae extraction acknowledges hardware requirements for computational speedup, which would further increase its utility; until then it stands as a proof of concept. The utilization of high-performance hardware among other options is considered to be the next step for its implementation. Further considerations in the pipeline include optimization in post-processing operations for inputs of substandard quality. It is also under consideration to build protective systems against fingerprint masking. The implementation of a Siamese network in palmprint recognition is presented in [36]; future scope for the methodology is to further reduce the EER by optimizing the network structure. The CNN-F structure proposed in [35] aims to improve further performance via a data preprocessing and data augmentation approach to achieve higher accuracy.

Many of the methods discussed such as deep learning for iris segmentation are only partly usable in a complete biometric system, since they lack the whole recognition pipeline, and therefore they are yet to be used in practicality. Development of software and fully fledged systems with such proof of concepts at their center might allow us to build more robust biometric systems. Also, a worthy topic of discussion is augmenting the biometric recognition process by the combination of various preprocessing steps, databases, and architectures as discussed in this chapter and arriving at new results.

5. Conclusion

There are many things to consider when it comes to the analysis of biometric data and its use to establish an authentication system. Each biometric domain provides its own benefits and disadvantages that are rooted in the data itself and the deep learning algorithms have to work with them to achieve the goal of maximum credibility. Therefore we see many types of biometrics involved, each with a unique deep learning architecture behind it. Some are good at low-quality processing, some are good at one-shot learning, while others are good because of the very nature of the data itself, like RNN-based architectures for behavioral biometrics and CNN-based biometrics for visual biometrics. We also observe that development in the field of protection of biometric systems is still at the primary stages when we talk about the application of deep learning in the domain; most research mentioned in spoof protection and template protection is relatively new compared to the work done in biometric recognition. The field is successful in gathering the interest of many researchers and as more and more deep learning algorithms are being discovered along with more computation speed and newer technologies being integrated, the trend will naturally lead to the increasing involvement of deep learning methodologies in the domain of biometric recognition.

References

[1] Biometrics | Definition of Biometrics at Dictionary.com. Retrieved December 20, 2019. https://www.dictionary.com/browse/biometrics.

[2] The History of Fingerprints — Onin. Retrieved December 20, 2019, from: http://onin.com/fp/fphistory.html.

[3] Biometric Lock/Unlock — Unique Identification Authority — Uidai. Retrieved December 20, 2019, from: https://uidai.gov.in/925-faqs/aadhaar-online-services/biometric-lock-unlock.html.

[4] Deterministic Noise — Wikipedia. Retrieved December 20, 2019, from: https://en.wikipedia.org/wiki/Deterministic_noise.

[5] End-to-end Learning, the (Almost) Every Purpose ML Method, 2019, May 31. Retrieved December 20, 2019, from: https://towardsdatascience.com/e2e-the-every-purpose-ml-method-5d4f20dafee4.

[6] J. Chen, J. Chen, H. Chao, M. Yang, Image blind denoising with generative adversarial network based noise modeling, in: Proceedings of the IEEE Conference on Computer Vision and Pattern Recognition (CVPR), 2018, pp. 3155—3164, https://doi.org/10.1109/CVPR.2018.00333.

[7] Cloud Tensor Processing Units (TPUs) | Cloud TPU | Google. Retrieved December 20, 2019, from: https://cloud.google.com/tpu/docs/tpus.

[8] Deep Learning | NVIDIA Developer. Retrieved December 20, 2019, from: https://developer.nvidia.com/deep-learning.

[9] Statistics — ImageNet, 2010, April 31. Retrieved December 20, 2019, from: http://image-net.org/about-stats.

[10] A.K. Jain, A. Ross, S. Prabhakar, An introduction to biometric recognition, IEEE Trans. Circ. Syst. Video Technol. 15 (1) (2004) 4—21.

[11] G. Echterhoff, E.T. Higgins, J.M. Levine, Shared reality: experiencing commonality with others' inner states about the world, Perspect. Psychol. Sci. 4 (2009) 496—521, https://doi.org/10.1111/j.1745-6924.2009.01161.x.

[12] S. Minaee, E. Azimi, A. Abdolrashidi, FingerNet: Pushing the Limits of Fingerprint Recognition Using Convolutional Neural Network, 2019. ArXiv.:1907.12956s Full text.

[13] P.T. Higgins, A.H. Choi, Y. Chen, J.-C. Fondeur, P. Li, J. Tian, X. Yang, S. Zhou, D. Day, C. Busch, G. Canon, M. Swayze, C.J. Tilton, D. Setlak, E. Tabassi, P. Grother, E. Tabassi, P. Grother, D.J. Buettner, et al., Biometric and user data, binding of, in: Encyclopedia of Biometrics, Springer US, 2009, pp. 69—76, https://doi.org/10.1007/978-0-387-73003-5_282.

[14] K. Fukushima, Neocognitron: a self-organizing neural network model for a mechanism of pattern recognition unaffected by shift in position, Biol. Cybern. 37 (4) (1980) 193—202, https://doi.org/10.1007/BF00344251.

[15] Y. Lecun, L. Bottou, Y. Bengio, P. Haffner, Gradient-based learning applied to document recognition, Proc. IEEE 86 (1998) 2278—2324, https://doi.org/10.1109/5.726791.

[16] W. Zhang, Shift-invariant pattern recognition neural network and its optical architecture, in: Proceedings of Annual Conference of the Japan Society of Applied Physics, 1988, p. 734. https://drive.google.com/file/d/1nN_5odSG_QVae54EsQN_qSz-0ZsX6wA0/view?usp=sharing.

[17] K.S. Itqan, A.R. Syafeeza, F.G. Gong, N. Mustafa, Y.C. Wong, M.M. Ibrahim, User identification system based on finger-vein patterns using convolutional neural network, ARPN J. Eng. Appl. Sci. 12 (2016) 3316—3319.

[18] A. Sherstinsky, Fundamentals of recurrent neural network (RNN) and long short-term memory (LSTM) network, in: March 2020: Special Issue on Machine Learning and Dynamical Systems, vol. 404, Elsevier, 2018, https://doi.org/10.1016/j.physd.2019.132306.

[19] Recurrent Neural Network Tutorial, Part 4, 2015, October 28. Retrieved December 20, 2019, from: http://www.wildml.com/2015/11/recurrent-neural-network-tutorial-part-4-implementing-a-grulstm-rnn-with-python-and-theano/.

[20] Autoencoders — Bits and Bytes of Deep Learning — Towards, 2017, August 4. Retrieved December 20, 2019, from: https://towardsdatascience.com/autoencoders-bits-and-bytes-of-deep-learning-eaba376f23ad.

[21] S. Chopra, R. Hadsell, Y. LeCun, Learning a similarity metric discriminatively, with application to face verification, in: Proceedings of the 2005 IEEE Computer Society Conference on Computer Vision and Pattern Recognition (CVPR'05) - Volume 1 — Volume 01 (CVPR'05), IEEE Computer Society, USA, 2005, pp. 539—546, https://doi.org/10.1109/CVPR.2005.202.

[22] C. Lin, A. Kumar, Multi-Siamese Networks to Accurately Match Contactless to Contact-Based Fingerprint Images, in: IEEE International Joint Conference on Biometrics (IJCB), Denver, CO, 2017, 2017, pp. 277—285, https://doi.org/10.1109/BTAS.2017.8272708.

[23] P. Viola, M.J. Jones, Robust real-time face detection, Int. J. Comput. Vis. 58 (2004) 137—154, https://doi.org/10.1023/B:VISI.0000013087.49260.fb.

[24] O. Deniz, G. Bueno, J. Salido, F. De la Torre, Face recognition using histograms of oriented gradients, Pattern Recogn. Lett. 33 (2011) 1598—1603, https://doi.org/10.1016/j.patrec.2011.01.004.

[25] Machine Learning Is Fun! Part 4: Modern Face Recognition, July 25, 2016. Retrieved December 21, 2019, from: https://medium.com/@ageitgey/machine-learning-is-fun-part-4-modern-face-recognition-with-deep-learning-c3cffc121d78.

[26] A.K. Jindal, S. Chalamala, S.K. Jami, Face Template Protection Using Deep Convolutional Neural Network. 2018 IEEE/CVF Conference on Computer Vision and Pattern Recognition Workshops (CVPRW). 2018 IEEE/CVF Conference on Computer Vision and Pattern Recognition Workshops (CVPRW), 2018, June.

[27] R. Kumar, B.D. Vikram, Fingerprint matching using multi-dimensional ann, Eng. Appl. Artif. Intell. 24 (2) (2010) 222—228.

[28] H. Jang, D. Kim, S. Mun, S. Choi, H. Lee, Deep Pore: fingerprint pore extraction using deep convolutional neural networks, IEEE Signal Process. Lett. 25 (13) (2017) 1808—1812.

[29] H. Wang, X. Yang, L. Ma, R. Liang, Fingerprint pore extraction using U-Net based fully convolutional network, in: J. Zhou, et al. (Eds.), CCBR 2017. LNCS, vol. 10568, Springer, Cham, 2017, pp. 279—287, https://doi.org/10.1007/978-3-319-69923-3_31.

[30] R. Labati, A. Genovese, E. Muñoz, V. Piuri, F. Scotti, A novel pore extraction method for heterogeneous fingerprint images using convolutional neural networks, Pattern Recogn. Lett. (2017), https://doi.org/10.1016/j.patrec.2017.04.001.

[31] Y. Zhao, F. Liu, L. Shen, Fingerprint pore extraction using convolutional neural networks and logical operation, in: Biometric Recognition, 2018, pp. 39—48.

[32] J. Bernsen, Dynamic thresholding of grey-level images, in: International Conference on Pattern Recognition, 1986.

[33] H. Lin, Y. Wan, A.K. Jain, Fingerprint image enhancement: algorithm and performance evaluation, IEEE Trans. Pattern Anal. Mach. Intell. 21 (8) (1998) 777—789.

[34] L.N. Darlow, B. Rosman, Fingerprint minutiae extraction using deep learning, in: IEEE International Joint Conference on Biometrics (IJCB), Denver, CO, 2017, 2017, pp. 23—31, https://doi.org/10.1109/BTAS.2017.8272678.

[35] Q. Sun, J. Zhang, A. Yang, Q. Zhang, Palmprint recognition with deep convolutional features, in: Chinese Conference on Image and Graphics Technologies, 2018, pp. 13—20, https://doi.org/10.1007/978-981-11-7389-2_2.

[36] D. Zhong, Y. Yang, X. Du, Palmprint recognition using siamese network, in: Biometric Recognition, Springer International Publishing, 2018, pp. 49—56.

[37] Iris Recognition Immigration System — Wikipedia. Retrieved March 26, 2020, from: https://en.wikipedia.org/wiki/Iris_Recognition_Immigration_System.

[38] N. Liu, H. Li, M. Zhang, J. Liu, Z. Sun, T. Tan, Accurate iris segmentation in noncooperative environments using fully convolutional networks. 2016, in: International Conference on Biometrics (ICB), 2016, pp. 1—8.

[39] A. Rattani, R. Derakhshani, Ocular biometrics in the visible spectrum: a survey, Image Vis Comput. 60 (2017) 1—17.

[40] A. Gangwar, A. Joshi, DeepIrisNet: Deep Iris Representation with Applications in Iris Recognition and Cross-Sensor Iris Recognition, 2016, https://doi.org/10.1109/ICIP.2016.7532769.

[41] H. Li, Y. Wang, X. Jiang, Dorsal Hand Vein Recognition Method Based on Multi-Bit Planes Optimization: 13th Chinese Conference, CCBR 2018, Urumqi, China, August 12—13, 2018, Proceedings, 2018, https://doi.org/10.1007/978-3-319-97909-0_1.

[42] A. Boles, P. Rad, Voice Biometrics: Deep Learning-Based Voiceprint Authentication System, 2017, pp. 1—6, https://doi.org/10.1109/SYSOSE.2017.7994971.

[43] Building a Speaker Identification System from Scratch with Deep, 2018, October 2. Retrieved December 21, 2019, from: https://medium.com/analytics-vidhya/building-a-speaker-identification-system-from-scratch-with-deep-learning-f4c4aa558a56.

[44] M.Z. Uddin, W. Khaksar, J. Torresen, A Robust Gait Recognition System Using Spatiotemporal Features and Deep Learning, 2017, pp. 156—161, https://doi.org/10.1109/MFI.2017.8170422.

[45] Q. Zou, Y. Wang, Y. Zhao, Q. Wang, C. Shen, Q. Li, Deep Learning Based Gait Recognition Using Smartphones in the Wild, 2018. ArXiv, abs/1811.00338.

[46] R. Tolosana, R. Vera-Rodriguez, J. Fierrez, J. Ortega-Garcia, Biometric Signature Verification Using Recurrent Neural Networks, 2017, https://doi.org/10.1109/ICDAR.2017.112.

[47] Database - PolyU COMP - Hong Kong Polytechnic. Retrieved March 26, 2020, from: https://www.comp.polyu.edu.hk/~csajaykr/database.php.

[48] T. Sim, S. Baker, M. Bsat, The CMU pose, illumination, and expression (PIE) database, in: Proceedings of the 5th IEEE International Conference, 2002, pp. 47—52, https://doi.org/10.1109/AFGR.2002.1004130.

[49] C. Thomaz, G. Giraldi, A new ranking method for Principal Components Analysis and its application to face image analysis, Image Vis. Comput. 29 (2010) 902—913, https://doi.org/10.1016/j.imavis.2009.12.005.

[50] C. Rallings, M. Thrasher, C. Gunter, P.J. Phillips, H. Wechsler, J. Huang, P.J. Rauss, The FERET database and evaluation procedure for face-recognition algorithms, Image Vis. Comput. 17 (1998) 295—306, https://doi.org/10.1016/S0262-8856(97)00070-X.

[51] H. Proenca, S. Filipe, R. Santos, J. Oliveira, L.A. Alexandre, The UBIRIS.v2: a database of visible wavelength Iris images captured on-the-move and at-a-distance, IEEE Trans. Pattern Anal. Mach. Intell. 33 (8) (2010) 1529—1535.

[52] CASIA Iris Image Database Version 4.0 — Biometrics Ideal Test. Retrieved March 26, 2020, from: http://biometrics.idealtest.org/dbDetailForUser.do?id=4.

[53] V. Panayotov, G. Chen, D. Povey, S. Khudanpur, Librispeech: An ASR Corpus Based on Public Domain Audio Books, 2015, pp. 5206—5210, https://doi.org/10.1109/ICASSP.2015.7178964.

[54] A.M. Martinez, R. Benavente, The AR Face Database. Technical Report 25, Computer Vision Center(CVC) Technical Report, 1998. Barcelona.

[55] D. Maio, D. Maltoni, R. Cappelli, J. Wayman, A. Jain, FVC2002: second fingerprint verification competition, in: Proceedings — International Conference on Pattern Recognition 3, 2002, pp. 811—814, https://doi.org/10.1109/ICPR.2002.1048144.

[56] R. Cappelli, D. Maio, D. Maltoni, J.L. Wayman, A.K. Jain, Performance evaluation of fingerprint verification systems, IEEE Trans. Pattern Anal. Mach. Intell. 29 (1) (2006) 3—19, https://doi.org/10.1109/tpami.2006.21.

[57] R. Cappelli, M. Ferrara, A. Franco, D. Maltoni, Fingerprint verification competition 2006, Biom. Technol. Today 16 (2007) 7—9, https://doi.org/10.1016/S0969-4765(8) 70140-6.

[58] Gait Dataset. Retrieved March 26, 2020, from: http://www.cbsr.ia.ac.cn/users/szheng/?page_id=71.

[59] Common Voice. Retrieved March 26, 2020, from: https://voice.mozilla.org/.

[60] U. Sinha, A. Singh, D.K. Sharma, Machine learning in the medical industry, in: A. Solanki, S. Kumar, A. Nayyar (Eds.), Handbook of Research on Emerging Trends and Applications of Machine Learning, IGI Global, 2020, pp. 403—424.

[61] Google Dataset Search. Retrieved March 26, 2020, from: https://datasetsearch.research.google.com/.

[62] Find Open Datasets and Machine Learning Projects | Kaggle. Retrieved March 26, 2020, from: https://www.kaggle.com/dataset.

[63] H.Y. Jung, Y.S. Heo, S. Lee, Fingerprint liveness detection by a template-probe convolutional neural network, IEEE Access 7 (2019) 118986—118993.

[64] V. Vashishth, A. Chhabra, D. K. Sharma,"A Machine Learning Approach Using Classifier Cascades for Optimal Routing in Opportunistic Internet of Things Networks", 16th IEEE International Conference on Sensing, Communication, and Networking (SECON), 11—14 June 2019, Boston, MA, USA.

[65] Z. Xia, C. Yuan, R. Lv, S. Xingming, N. Xiong, Y.Q. Shi, A novel weber local binary descriptor for fingerprint liveness detection, IEEE Trans. Syst. Man Cybern. Syst. (2018) 1—12, https://doi.org/10.1109/TSMC.2018.2874281.

[66] C. Yuan, X. Sun, Q.M. Jonathan Wu, Difference co-occurrence matrix using BP neural network for fingerprint liveness detection, Soft Comput. 24 (2018), https://doi.org/10.1007/s00500-19-3182-1.

[67] R. Koshy, A. Mahmood, Optimizing deep CNN architectures for face liveness detection, Entropy 22 (2019) 423, https://doi.org/10.3390/e21040423.

[68] E. Abdellatef, N.A. Ismail, S.E.S.E. Abd Elrahman, et al., Cancelable Multi-Biometric Recognition System Based on Deep Learning, Vis Comput, 2019.

[69] S. Kumar, A. Yadav, D.K. Sharma, Deep learning and computer vision in smart agriculture, in: Modern Techniques for Agricultural Disease Management and Crop Yield Prediction, IGI Global, 2020, pp. 67—88.

[70] V. Talreja, M.C. Valenti, Multibiometric Secure System Based on Deep Learning, 2017 arXiv:1708.02314.

[71] X. Li, Y. Jiang, M. Chen, et al., Research on iris image encryption based on deep learning, J. Image Video Proc. 126 (2018).

[72] D.K. Sharma, S.K. Dhurandher, I. Woungang, R.K. Srivastava, A. Mohananey, J.J.P.C. Rodrigues, A machine learning-based protocol for efficient routing in opportunistic networks, IEEE Syst. J. (December 2016) 1—7, https://doi.org/10.1109/JSYST.2016.2630923. ISSN (Print): 1932-8184, ISSN (Online): 1937-9234.

[73] A. Albakri, C. Mokbel, Convolutional neural network biometric cryptosystem for the protection of the Blockchain's private key, Procedia Comp. Sci. 160 (2019) 235—240, https://doi.org/10.1016/j.procs.2019.10.462.

CHAPTER 2

Deep learning in big data and data mining

Deepak Kumar Sharma[1], Bhanu Tokas[2], Leo Adlakha[2]
[1]Department of Information Technology, Netaji Subhas University of Technology, New Delhi, India;
[2]Department of Computer Engineering, Netaji Subhas University of Technology, New Delhi, India

1. Introduction

Data analytics is a method of applying quantitative and qualitative techniques to analyze data, aiming for valuable insights. With the help of data analytics, we can explore data (exploratory data analysis) and we can even draw conclusions about our data (confirmatory data analysis). In this chapter, we will study big data, starting from the very basics and slowly getting into the details of some of the common technologies used to analyze our data. This chapter helps the reader to examine large datasets and recognize patterns in data, hence generating reports. We will focus on the seven Vs of big data analysis and will also study the challenges that big data gives and how they are dealt with. We also look into the most common technologies used while handling big data, i.e., Hive, Tableau, etc.

Now, as we know, exploratory data analysis (EDA) and confirmatory data analysis (CDA) are the fundamental concepts of data analysis, hence it is crucial to know the difference between the two. EDA involves the methodologies, tools, and techniques used to explore data, aiming at finding various patterns in our data and the relation between various elements of data. CDA involves the methodologies, tools, and techniques used to provide an answer to a specific question in brief based on the observation of the data. Once the data is ready, it is analyzed by data scientists using various statistical methods. Data governance also becomes a key factor for ensuring the proper collection and security of data. Now, there is the less well-known role of a data steward who specializes in knowing our data, where it comes from, all the changes that occur, and what the company or organization really needs from the column or field of that data. Data quality is a must to ensure so that the data being collected is correct and will match the needs of data scientists. One of the main goals is

Trends in Deep Learning Methodologies
ISBN 978-0-12-822226-3
https://doi.org/10.1016/B978-0-12-822226-3.00002-7

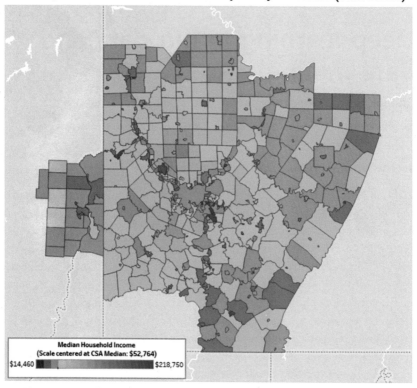

Pittsburgh CSA: Median Household Income by County Subdivision (2012-16 ACS)

Figure 2.1 Median household income by county subdivision (2012—16) [1].

to fix the data quality problems that affect the accuracy of our analysis. Common techniques include profiling the data, cleansing the data to ensure the consistency of our datasets, and removing redundant records from the data. Data visualization is an important piece of big data analysis as its quite hard to understand a set of numbers. However, large-scale visualization may require more custom applications but there is an increasing dependence on tools like Tableau, QlikView, etc. It is definitely better to look at the data in a graphic space rather than a bunch of x, y coordinates (Fig. 2.1).

2. Overview of big data analysis

Twitter, Facebook, Google, Amazon, and so on are the companies that run their businesses using data analytics and many decisions for the company are taken on the basis of analytics. You may wonder how much data they are collecting and how they are using that data to make certain decisions. There is a lot of data out there such as tweets, comments, reviews, customer complaints, survey activities, competition among various stores, demographics or economy of the local area, and so on. All this information might help to better understand customer behavior and various revenue models. For example, if we see increasing negative reviews against a store's parking facility, then we could analyze it and take corrective measures such as negotiating with the city's public transportation department to provide more public transport for better reach. As there is an increasing amount of data, it isn't uncommon to see terabytes of data. Every day, we create about 2—3 quintillion bytes of data (2 exabytes) and it has been estimated that 90% of this data alone was stored in the last few years. Such large amounts of data accumulating since the 1990s and the need to understand the data gave rise to the term big data. The following are the seven Vs of big data.

2.1 Variety of data

Data can be obtained from various sources such as tweets, Facebook comments, weather sensors, censuses, updates, transactions, sales, and marketing. The data format itself may be structured or unstructured. Data types can also be different such as text, csv, binary, JSON, or XML.

2.2 Velocity of data

Data may be from a data warehouse, batch mode file archives, or instantaneous real-time updates from the Uber ride you just booked. Velocity refers to the increasing speed at which the data is being created, and the increasing speed at which the data can be examined, stored, and analyzed by relational databases (Fig. 2.2).

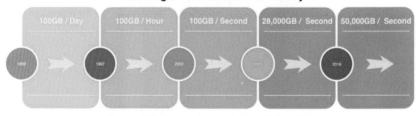

Figure 2.2 Increasing velocity of data [2].

2.3 Volume of data

Data may be collected and stored for an hour, a day, a month, a year, or 10 years. The size of data is growing to hundreds of terabytes for many companies such as Google, Facebook, Twitter, etc. Volume refers to the scale of the data, which is why big data is big.

2.4 Veracity of data

With various data sources gathered from all around the world, it is quite tough to provide the proof of accuracy of the data. With these four Vs of big data, we are no longer able to cover the capabilities and needs of big data analytics, hence nowadays we generally hear of seven Vs rather than just four Vs (Fig. 2.3).

To make some sense out of the data and to apply big data analytics, we need to expand the concept of big data analytics to work for a large extent of data that deals with all the seven Vs of big data. This shifts not only the technologies used for analyzing our data, but it also modifies the way we approach a particular problem. If an SQL database was being used for a business, now we need to change it a little bit and use a distributed SQL database for better scalability and adaptability of the nuances of big data space.

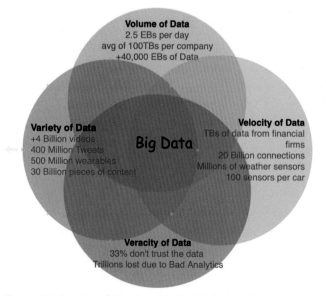

Figure 2.3 Four Vs of big data [2]. *EBs*, Exabytes; *TBs*, terabytes.

2.5 Variability of data

Variability basically refers to dynamic data whose meaning is changing constantly. Most times, organizations need to build complex programs to understand their exact meaning.

2.6 Visualization of data

Visualization of data is used when you have analyzed or processed your dataset and you now need to present your data in a readable or presentable manner.

2.7 Value of data

Big data is large and is increasing day by day, with data being noisy and constantly changing. It is available for all in a variety of formats and is in no position to be used without any analytical preprocessing.

2.8 Distributed computing

We are surrounded by various devices such as smart watches, smartphones, tablets, laptops, ATM machines, and many more because we are able to perform those tasks that were nearly impossible or unimaginable just a few years ago. Instagram, Snapchat, Facebook, and YouTube are some applications that 60% of the world uses every day. Today, cloud computing has made us familiar with the following services:

- Infrastructure
- Platform
- Software

Behind the scenes is a world full of highly scalable distributed computing, which makes it possible to process and store several petabytes of data (1 petabyte is equivalent to 1 billion gigabytes). Massively parallel processing is a paradigm that was used years ago for monitoring earthquakes, oceanography, etc. Eventually, big tech giants such as Google and Amazon pushed the niche region of scalable distributed computing to a new evolution. This led to the creation of Apache Spark by Berkeley University. Google even published a paper describing the MapReduce Framework and Google File System (GFS) that defined the principles of distributed computing.

Eventually, Doug Cutting implemented these ideas and introduced us to the world of Apache Hadoop. Apache Hadoop is an open-source framework written and implemented in Java. The key areas that are focused on by this framework are storage and processing. For storage, Hadoop uses the Hadoop Distributed File System (HDFS), which is based on GFS. For processing, the framework depends on MapReduce. MapReduce evolved from V1 (Job Tracker and Task Tracker) to V2 (YARN).

2.8.1 MapReduce Framework

This is a framework used for computing large amounts of data in a Hadoop cluster. It uses YARN to schedule the mappers and reducers as tasks, making use of containers. Fig. 2.4 is an example showcasing a MapReduce Framework in action on a simple count frequency of words.

MapReduce works in coordination with YARN to plan a job accurately and various tasks for the job. It also requests computing resources from the resource or cluster manager, schedules the execution of the tasks for the resources on the cluster, and then executes the plan. With the help of MapReduce, we can read and write various types of files of various formats and perform complex computations in a distributed manner.

2.8.2 Hive

Hive basically provides a layer of abstraction using SQL with several optimizations over the MapReduce Framework. Due to the complexity in writing code using MapReduce Framework, Hive was needed. For example, if we were to count records in a simple file using MapReduce Framework, it would easily take a few dozen lines, which is not at all productive. Hive basically abstracts the MapReduce code by encapsulating the logic from the SQL statements, which means that MapReduce is still working on the backend. This saves a huge amount of time for someone who needs to find something useful from the data, by not using the same

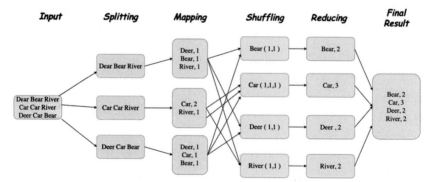

Figure 2.4 MapReduce Framework for a count frequency of words [2].

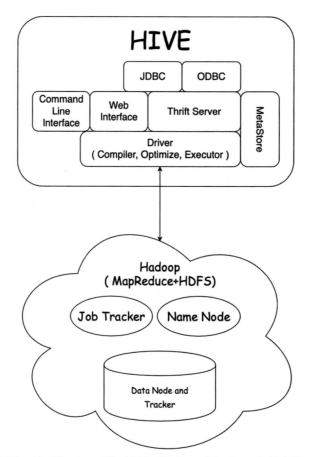

Figure 2.5 Hive Architecture [2]. *HDFS*, Hadoop Distributed File System; *JDBC*, Java Database Connectivity; *OBDC*, Open Database Connectivity.

code or the boiler plate coding for various tasks that need to be executed and every single computation that is desired as part of the job.

Fig. 2.5 depicts the Hive Architecture, which clearly shows the levels of abstraction. Hive is not made for online transactions and does not offer row–level updates and real-time queries. Hive query language can be used to implement basic SQL-like queries.

2.8.3 Apache Spark

This is a unified distributed computing engine for different platforms and workloads. Apache Spark can easily pair up with different platforms and process different data workloads using various paradigms, for example, Spark ML, Spark SQL, and Spark Graphx.

Apache Spark is very fast because of the in-memory data processing mechanism with suggestive application programming interfaces, which allow data handlers to accurately process machine learning or SQL workloads that need quick and interactive connection to the database.

Various other libraries are built on the core, which collectively allow loads for SQL, streaming, machine learning, and graph processing. For example, Spark ML has been devised for data scientists and its abstracted levels make data science very easy.

Spark provides machine learning, queries, real-time streaming, and graph processing. These tasks are quite difficult to perform without Apache Spark. We need to use various technologies for these different types of workloads, for example:

- One for batch analysis
- One for interactive queries
- One for real-time streaming processes
- One for machine learning algorithms

Apache Spark can do all of this, whereas multiple technologies are not always integrated. One more advantage of Apache Spark is that you can write client programs using various languages of your choice, i.e., Scala, Java, R, Python.

Apache Spark has some key advantages over the MapReduce paradigm:

- It it possible to use in-memory processing.
- It is a general-purpose machine that can be used for various workloads.
- It is compatible with YARN.
- It integrates well with various file systems and data sources such as Cassandra, AWS S3, MongoDB, HDFS, HBase, etc.

Hadoop and Spark are prominent big data frameworks, but they are not used for the same purpose. Hadoop provides shared storage, MapReduce distributes computing frameworks, and Spark is a data processing framework that operates with distributed data storage given by other technologies.

It should be noted that Spark is quicker than the MapReduce Framework due to the data processing rate. Spark engages with datasets much more efficiently than MapReduce because the performance improvement of Apache Spark is efficient for off-heap-in-memory processing rather than solely relying on disk-based computations.

When your reporting requirements and data methods are not changing, then MapReduce's style of processing data may be sufficient, and it is

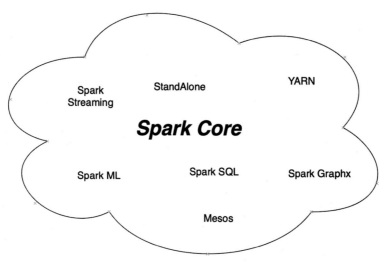

Figure 2.6 Apache Spark [2].

definitely acceptable to use batch processing for your purposes. But if you would like to operate with data analytics on cascaded data or processing requirements for multistage processing logic, then you need to use Spark (Fig. 2.6).

2.8.3.1 Visualizations using tableau

When we perform distributed computing on big data, it is quite hard to comprehend the meaning of the datasets without tools like Tableau, which provides a graphic interface to the data in the dataset for better understanding and visualization of the data. There are other tools for the same purpose, such as Python's matplotlib, JavaScript, Cognos, KineticaDB, R+ Shiny, etc. Figs. 2.7 and 2.8 are screenshots of geospatial views of data using various tools for visualization.

2.9 Data warehouse versus data lake

Data structure:

Data lakes (Fig. 2.9) generally have unprocessed or raw data, while data warehouses store refined and processed data. Due to this, data lakes usually occupy more space than data warehouses (Fig. 2.10).

Moreover, data lakes are quite flexible, hence they can be analyzed swiftly and are ideal for machine learning.

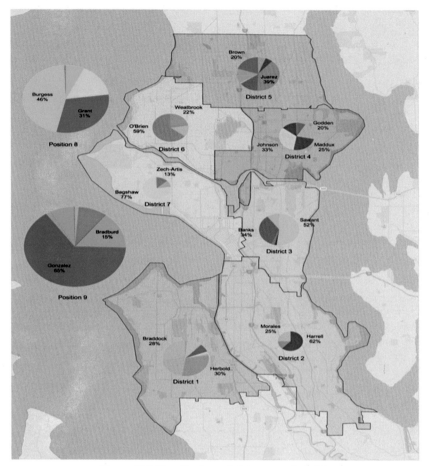

Figure 2.7 Visualization of data example 1 [3].

Because of this, some risks also arise, one being the conversion of data lakes into data swamps without appropriate quality measures and data governance.

Purpose of data:

The use of various data chunks in data lakes is not static. Raw data combines with or forms a data lake just to have it handy or for some future purpose. This also means that a data lake has less filtration and less organization than a data warehouse. Data warehouses store processed and organized data, hence storage space is not wasted.

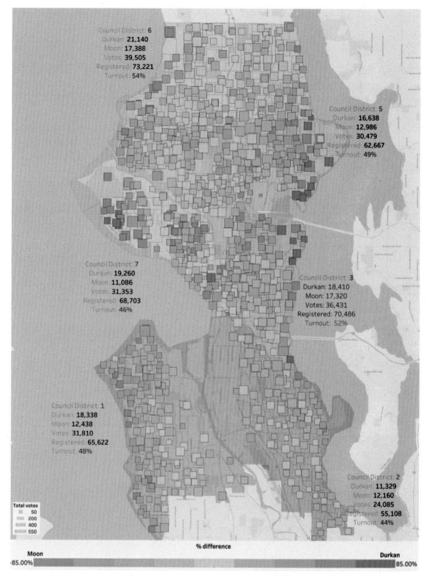

Figure 2.8 Visualization of data example 2 [4].

Users:

Raw, unstructured data cannot be easily understood by business professionals, but can be easily transformed, which is easily understood by anyone. Processed data is usually represented in charts, e.g., pie charts, etc., which can be easily understood.

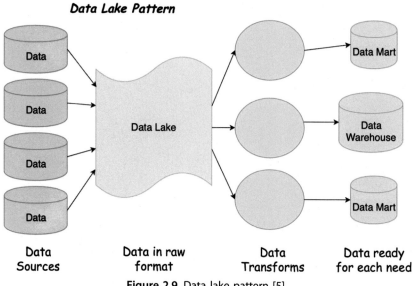

Figure 2.9 Data lake pattern [5].

	Data Warehouse	Data Lake
Data Structure	Processed	Raw
Purpose of Data	Currently in use	Undetermined
Users	Business Professionals	Data Scientists
Accessibility	More complex and costly to make changes	Highly Accessible and quick to update

Figure 2.10 Data warehouse versus data lake [6].

Accessibility:

Accessibility refers to the database collectively. Data lakes do not have a definite pattern and hence are quite easy to control, use, and alter. Any modifications may be done easily and quickly because data lakes have fewer limitations.

Data warehouses are well ordered and hence are difficult to modify.

One major advantage is that the order and operation of data in a warehouse make the data itself very easy to decipher. It is very difficult and costly to manipulate data warehouses due to their limitations.

3. Introduction

3.1 What is data mining?

Databases today can be as large as several terabytes in size. In these vast clusters of data there remains concealed information, which can be of strategic importance. But how does one find a needle in these heaps of haystacks?

Data mining is a multidisciplinary field that responds to the task of analyzing large databases in research, commerce, and industry. The aim is to extract new knowledge from databases where complexity, dimensionality, or the sheer amount of data is so exorbitantly large for human analysis to be viable. It is not confined to the creation of models that can find particular trends in data either; it also deals with why those trends impact our business and how to exploit it. Data mining can be viewed as an interactive process that requires the computational efficiency of modern computer technology coupled with the background knowledge and intuition of application experts.

Now that we know what data mining is, the reader may still wonder what are the individual steps involved in this process.

The data mining process can be represented as a cyclic process that can be broadly divided into six stages as shown in Fig. 2.11.

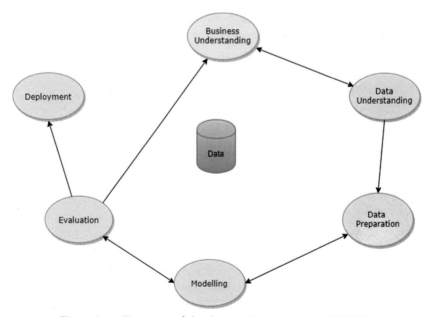

Figure 2.11 Six stages of the data mining process in CRISP-DM.

This cycle is referred to as CRISP-DM (CRoss Industry Standard Process for Data Mining) [7].

The six stages of the CRISP-DM cycle are:

1. Business understanding: This stage deals with analysis of the task objectives and requirements from a commercial sense, and then this knowledge is used to create a data mining problem definition and a preliminary plan of action.

2. Data understanding: This stage begins with preliminary data gathering and proceeds with experimentation to become familiar with the data, to identify major problems with the data, to learn the first insights in the data, or to detect useful subsets that may help in forming useful hypotheses for the unknown data.

3. Data preparation: This stage involves all activities that lead to the transformation of the original raw data to obtain the final dataset.

4. Modeling: In this stage, various modeling methods are chosen and tested. But some methods like decision trees and neural networks have specific conditions concerning the form of the input data. Thus one may have to cycle back to the data preparation stage to obtain the required data in a suitable format.

5. Evaluation: Also called "validation," this stage deals with testing model performance. After single or even multiple models have been constructed that perform satisfactorily based on the chosen loss functions, these models need to be tested to ensure that they maintain a satisfactory performance even against unseen data and that all crucial commercial concerns have been adequately resolved. The result is the selection of those model(s) that are able to give optimum results.

6. Deployment: Normally, this stage includes deploying a code equivalent of the selected model to estimate or classify the new data as it comes and to define the machinery that will use this new information in the solution for the initial business task.

The models used in data mining can be broadly divided into the following two categories: descriptive models and predictive models. Descriptive models are used to describe trends in existing data, and are usually used to generate meaningful subgroups such as demographic clusters, i.e., a model that can show regions where sales have been more frequent or of higher value. These types of models are based on unsupervised learning. Predictive models are often utilized to estimate particular values, based on patterns deduced from previously known data, i.e., supervised learning. For example, using a database containing records of previous sales, a model could be constructed that estimates an increase/decrease in sales of a particular group of products.

Now that we have understood what data mining is, let us have a look at what role machine learning plays in it.

3.2 Why use deep learning in data mining?

As you may have guessed after looking at the CRISP-DM cycle, machine learning has an important application in the modeling stage of the cycle. As previously stated, data mining usually deals with databases that are exorbitantly large for manual analysis. Hence, machine learning provides the set of tools required for an extensive analysis of such databases.

Even then, one may ask, why should one prefer deep learning algorithms over other machine learning algorithms for data mining? Let us take a look at the argument in favor of deep learning.

Traditional machine learning algorithms face what Richard Bellman had coined the "curse of dimensionality." This states that with a linear increase in dimensionality of the data, the learning complexity grows exponentially, i.e., a small increase in dimensionality of data results in a large increase in learning complexity. Considering that real-world databases usually consist of high-dimensional data, the learning complexity is exceedingly large such that it is not practical to apply these algorithms directly to unprocessed data.

To combat this hurdle, feature extraction is often applied to the data. Feature extraction refers to a process used for dimensionality reduction in which the original set of raw data is reduced to a smaller, more compact subset that is easier to process, i.e., it refers to the methods that select and/or combine variables into features, thus reducing the total data that needs to be processed, while still accurately and completely describing the original dataset. But, since these are human-engineered processes, they can often be challenging and application dependent. Furthermore, if features extracted from the data are inaccurate or incomplete, the classification model is innately limited in its performance. Thus it becomes quite challenging to automate the process for application in data mining.

On the other hand, deep learning algorithms do not require explicit feature extraction on data before training. In fact, several deep learning algorithms, such as autoencoders, self-organizing maps (SOMs), and convolutional neural networks (CNNs), are implicitly able to select the key features to improve model performance. This makes them more suitable for use in data mining.

4. Applications of deep learning in data mining

4.1 Multimedia data mining

With the gaining popularity of the usage of multimedia data over the internet, multimedia mining has developed as an active region for research. Multimedia mining is a form of data mining wherein information is obtained from multimedia files such as still images, video, and audio to perform entity resolution, identify associations, execute similarity searches, and for classification-based tasks. It has applications in various fields, including record disambiguation, audio–visual speech recognition, facial recognition, and entity resolution. Deep learning has been essential in the progress of various subject areas, including natural language processing and visual data mining.

A task often faced in multimedia data mining is image captioning. Image caption generation is the process of generating a descriptive sentence for an image, a task that is undeniably mundane for us humans, but remains a problematic task for machines. The caption generation model deals with two major branches of machine learning. First, it must solve the computer vision problem of identifying the various objects present in the given image. Second, it also has to solve the natural language processing problem of expressing the relation between the visual components in natural language.

A novel approach for tackling this problem has been discussed in [8]. The model consists of a CNN network, which is responsible for encoding the visual embeddings present in the image, followed by two separate long short-term memory (LSTM) networks, which generate the sentence embeddings from the encodings given by the CNN. What makes this approach unique is the usage of bidirectional long short-term memory (Bi-LSTM) units for sentence generation.

Fig. 2.12 is a diagram showing the internal components of an LSTM cell. It constitutes the following components: a memory cell C_t, an input gate I_t, an output gate O_t, and a forget gate F_t. The input gate is responsible for deciding if the incoming signal will go through to a memory cell or if it will be blocked. The output gate is responsible for deciding if a new output is allowed or should be blocked. The forget gate is responsible for deciding whether to retain or forget the earlier state of the memory cell. Cell states are updated by feeding previous cell output to itself by recurrent connections in the two consecutive time steps.

On analyzing the model one may ask the following questions. First, why do we use recurrent neural networks (RNNs) instead of other mainstream methods for sentence generation? Second, what benefit does the use of Bi-LSTM provide for this application? Let us try to answer these questions.

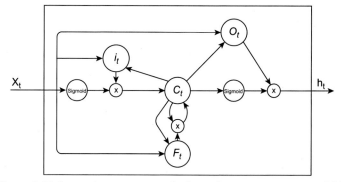

Figure 2.12 Internal components of a long short-term memory cell [2].

Mainstream methods used to solve the task of image captioning mainly compromise either the usage of sentence templates, or treating it as a retrieval task by finding the best matching sentences present in the database and using them to create the new caption. The problem with these approaches is that they face a constant hurdle in the creation of original and/or variable length sentences. Thus they may not be suitable for use on data sufficiently different from the training data, limiting their application in real-world scenarios. On the other hand, even relatively shallow RNNs have shown considerable success in the creation of original and variable length sentences.

Let us now look at how Bi-LSTM networks are better than unidirectional LSTM networks. In unidirectional sentence generation, the common method of forecasting the subsequent word W_t with visual context V and prior textual context $W_{1:t-1}$ is to choose the parameters such that the value of $\log P\ (W_t|V,\ W_{1:t-1})$ is maximized. While a unidirectional model is able to account for past context, it is still unable to retain the future context $W_{t+1}:T$, which should be considered for evaluation of the previous word W_t by maximizing the value of $\log P\ (W_t|V,\ W_{t+1}:T)$. The bidirectional model overcomes this shortcoming that plagues both unidirectional (backward and forward direction) models by exploiting the past and future dependencies to generate the new caption. Thus making them more suitable for tasks of language generation.

4.2 Aspect extraction

Aspect extraction can be defined as a subfield of sentiment analysis wherein the aim is identification of opinion targets in opinionated text. For example, where a company has a database of reviews given for its various products, aspect extraction would be used to identify all those reviews where a user either liked a product or disliked a product.

Before we look at the deep learning-based approach, let us look at why the existing mainstream methods for aspect extraction are not sufficient. These include:

Linear discriminant analysis: While this is ideal for datasets with high dimensionality, it is not optimal for text sentiment analysis because it treats each word as an independent entity, thus failing to extract coherent aspects from the given text.

Supervised techniques: Herein, the task is treated as a sequence labeling problem. While there exist several algorithms capable of achieving high accuracy for such problems, the fact that they heavily rely on quality data annotation to give good results makes them nonviable for real-life application in data mining.

Rule-based methods: These rely on extracting noun phrases and use of modifiers to deduce the aspects being referred to. But, a major issue with this approach is limited scalability, i.e., this approach is more suited to small datasets as compared to large datasets. Thus it is not suitable for data mining.

A suitable approach mentioned in [9] talks about using an autoencoder setup that reconstructs the input text. But the latent encoding thus generated would itself be able to represent the aspects mentioned in the text. This proposed model has been termed attention-based aspect extraction (Fig. 2.13). Let us have a closer look at the model.

An example of the attention-based aspect extraction structure [9] starts with mapping the words that usually co-occur within the same context. These words are assigned to nearby points in the embedding space. This process is known as neural word embedding. Then, the word embeddings present in a sentence are filtered by an attention-based mechanism and the filtered words are used to construct aspect embeddings. The training process for aspect embeddings is quite similar to that observed in autoencoders, i.e., dimension reduction is used to extract the common features in embedded sentences and recreate each sentence as a linear combination of the aspect embeddings. The attention-based mechanism deemphasizes words that did not belong to any aspect, thus the model is able to concentrate on aspect words.

The architecture of the model can be divided into the following components:
- Input sentence representation: word embeddings.
- Encoded sentence representation: attention-transformed embedding.

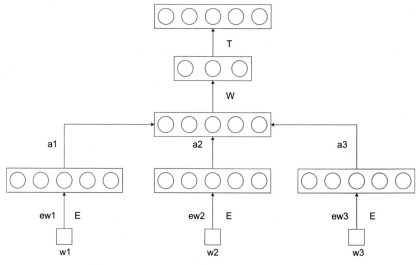

Figure 2.13 Attention-based aspect extraction [5].

$$z_s = \sum_{i=1}^{n} a_i e_{wi} \qquad (2.1)$$

- Attention of a token is calculated using two pieces of information: embedding of the token itself (word embedding) and global context (average of all word embeddings in the sentence).

  (Note: (a)' represents transpose of a)

$$a_i = \frac{e^{d_i}}{\sum_{j=1}^{n} e^{d_i}} \qquad (2.2)$$

$$d_i = (e_{wi})' \cdot M \cdot \gamma_s \qquad (2.3)$$

$$Y_s = \frac{1}{n} \sum_{i=1}^{n} e_{wi} \qquad (2.4)$$

- Reconstruction of sentence: dimension reduction of encoded representation → softmax to determine the weights for aspects → linear combination of aspect embeddings where weights come from the computed softmax.

4.3 Loss function

- We can use hinge loss to maximize the inner product of encoded representation and reconstructed representation of positive samples and minimize the same for negative samples.
- Regularization terms encourage uniqueness for aspect embeddings.

$$U(\theta) = \left\| T_n \cdot (T_n)' - I \right\| \tag{2.5}$$

The dot product of any two different aspect embeddings should be zero.

4.4 Customer relationship management

Customer relationship management (CRM) can be described as the process of managing a company's interactions with its present and potential clients. It improves business relationships with customers, specifically focusing on ultimately driving sales growth and customer retention by applying data analysis to recorded data from previous interaction of the businesses with their clients. The aim of CRM is to integrate marketing, sales, and customer care service such that value is added to both the business and its clients.

For a company to grow and increase its revenue, it needs to compete for the more profitable customers. Businesses are using CRM to add value to their products and services, which will allow them to attract the more profitable customers. One vital subset of CRM is customer segmentation, which refers to the process of assigning customers into sets based on certain shared features or needs. Customer segmentation gives businesses the opportunity to better adapt their advertising attempts to different audience subsets. This can help boost both product development and communication. Customer segmentation allows businesses to:

- Select the communication channels that are most suitable to reach their target audience.
- Test different pricing decisions.
- Create and broadcast targeted advertisements that can have maximum impact on specific sections of customers.
- Identify areas of improvement for existing products and services.
- Identify the more profitable groups of customers.

Clustering algorithms have been extensively used to tackle the task of customer segmentation. Meanwhile, visualization techniques have also become a vital tool for helping to understand and assess the clustering results. Visual clustering can be considered an amalgamation of these two processes. It consists of techniques that are simultaneously able not only to carry out the clustering tasks but also to create a visual representation that is able to summarize the clustering outcomes, therefore helping in the search for useful trends in the data.

But when we analyze the data available, we realize that it is usually heterogeneous, spatially associated, and multidimensional. Due to these properties, the basic assumptions of conventional machine learning algorithms become invalid, making them usually highly unsuitable for this category of data. Thus we use deep learning-based algorithms to overcome these hurdles.

One of these algorithms includes the SOMs, which allow the emergence of structure in data and support labeling, clustering, and visualization. As humans are typically not apt at visualizing or detecting patterns in data belonging to high-dimensional space, it is necessary to project this higher-dimensional data into a two-dimensional map such that the input records that are more similar to each other are located closer to each other. When this projection is represented in a form of a mesh of neurons it is called an SOM. This allows the clustering results to be presented in an easy-to-understand way and to interpret the format for the user.

There are two different usages of SOM. The first type refers to the traditional SOM, which was introduced by Kohonen [10] in 1982. In this category of SOMs, each cluster in the data is matched to a limited set of neurons. These are known as K-means SOMs.

The second form of SOMs, which were introduced by Ultsch [11] in 1999, uses the mapping space as an instrument to convert the high-dimensional data space into a two-dimensional vector space, thus enabling visualization. These SOMs contain a huge number of neurons, growing as big as thousands or tens of thousands of neurons. These SOMs are able to represent the intrinsic structural features present in the data space, i.e., they allow these features to emerge, and hence are referred to as emergent SOMs. The emergent SOM utilizes its map to visualize the spatial correlations present in the high-dimensional data space and the weight vectors of the neurons are used to represent a sampling point of the data.

Fig. 2.14 is a helpful visualization of the training process of an SOM.

The blue (dark grey in printed version) spot represents the training data's distribution, and the white grid-like structure represents the current map state, which contains the SOM nodes. Initially, the nodes are placed randomly in space. The distances of these nodes are calculated. The node that is nearest to the training datum (highlighted in yellow [light grey in printed version]) is chosen and shifted toward the training datum, as are its

Figure 2.14 Training process of a self-organizing map [12].

neighboring nodes on the map. But the displacement of these neighboring nodes is relatively smaller. This changes the shape of the map as the nodes on the map continue to be pulled toward the training datum. As the grid gradually changes, it is able to closely replicate the data distribution (right) after numerous iterations.

Functioning in an SOM can be divided into two parts:
1. Mapping data items with their best-matching units.
2. Updating each unit such that it moves closer toward the corresponding data item, including those units that are in adjacent positions.

The following formula is used to obtain the mappings:

$$||x_j - m_b|| = \min||x_j - m_i|| \tag{2.6}$$

where $j, i \in I, i \in [1, M]$, and $j \in [1, N]$ m_i refers to the network's reference vectors, x_j refers to the input data vectors, and m_b refers to the best-matching unit.

The reference vectors are updated using the following formula:

$$m_i(t+1) = \frac{\sum_{j=1}^{N} h_{ib(j)}(t)x_j}{\sum_{j=1}^{N} h_{ib(j)}(t)} \tag{2.7}$$

where t represents the time coordinate with discrete intervals and $h_{ib(j)}$ is a reducing function of time and neighborhood radius.

Each unique unit formed in an SOM can be viewed as an individual cluster. When visualizing, it is preferable to have a large number of neurons as it leads to increased projection granularity (i.e., detail). But, increasing the number of neurons incessantly can lead to the processing of the SOM resembling the process of data compression into a characteristic set of units rather than standard cluster analysis, thus hindering the interpretability of the data presented by the clusters. Thus these SOM units are collected into clusters by applying a second-level clustering. In a two-level SOM, the SOM is used to project the initial dataset onto a two-dimensional display. This is followed by clustering the SOM units.

Previous research has proved the effectivity of the two-level SOM technique; among these, Li H [13] has shown the higher effectiveness of the combined approach of both the SOM and Ward's hierarchical clustering, compared to several conventional clustering algorithms.

We can describe Ward's clustering [14] in the following manner. It starts by treating each unit as a separate cluster on its own. Then, we proceed by selecting the two clusters that have the minimum distance and merging them. This step is repeated until there is a single cluster left. Ward's clustering can be restricted such that only the neighboring units are merged to conserve the spatial ordering of SOM. The Ward distance can be modified in the following manner to reflect the new clustering scheme [14]:

$$d_{kl} = \frac{n_k n_l}{n_k + n_l} \cdot \left\| c_k - c_l \right\|^2; \text{ if } k \text{ and } l \text{ are adjacent else } \infty \qquad (2.8)$$

where l and k represent clusters, D_{kl} represents modified Ward distance between the two clusters, $\left\| c_k - c_l \right\|^2$ represents the squared Euclidean distance between the cluster centers of clusters l and k, and n_l and n_k represent the cardinality of clusters l and k, respectively. Also, we consider the distance between two nonadjacent clusters to be infinity. Thus when clusters l and k are merged to form a new cluster z, the cardinality of z can be defined as the sum of the cardinalities of l and k and the centroid of z is the mean of c_l and c_k weighted by their cardinalities.

5. Conclusion

In this chapter, we focused on two major topics: big data and data mining. We learnt about the two fundamentals of data analytics, i.e., EDA and CDA. Then, we focused on the seven Vs of big data, which are equivalent to the basic definition of big data. Then, we took a deep dive into distributed computing and why it is important for big data analytics and various frameworks for big data analytics such as MapReduce Framework and Hive. Then, we studied Apache Spark and why is it better to analyze data using it. After this we covered visualizations of the processed data and why it is important, and various technologies used for data visualizations. Then, we learnt about the difference between data lake and data warehouse and which is better for a particular group of people. We talked about some of the limitations of both data lakes and data warehouses. We also tried to answer questions like "What is data mining? Why is deep learning used in data mining? What are some real-world applications of deep learning in data mining?" We now understand why deep learning algorithms are more suitable than other mainstream machine learning algorithms for application in data mining and to that effect we studied their application in real-world problems in the form of Bi-LSTM for multimedia data mining, ABAE for aspect extraction, and SOM for CRM.

We have tried to give a brief introduction to the various applications and the mathematics involved in them; however, this is by no means a complete guide. The author would recommend the reader to see the references for sources to enable further in-depth study of the techniques discussed in this chapter.

References

[1] Wikimedia Commons, Retrieved February 20th, 2020. https://commons.wikimedia.org/wiki/File:Pittsburgh_CSA_-_Median_Household_Income_by_County_Subdivision_(2012-16_ACS).svg.

[2] JGraph (https://github.com/jgraph); Draw.io, https://app.diagrams.net.

[3] Wikimedia Commons, Retrieved February 20th, 2020. https://commons.wikimedia.org/wiki/File:2015_Seattle_City_Council_final_results.gif.

[4] Wikimedia Commons, 2020. Retrieved February 20th, https://commons.wikimedia.org/wiki/File:Seattle_mayoral_election_2017,_final_result_by_precinct,_square_marks_with_percent_difference.png.

[5] Shana Pearlman, (last updated October 10th, 2019), Talend, Retrieved January 20, 2020. https://www.talend.com/resources/what-is-data-lake/.

[6] Shana Pearlman, (last updated October 10th, 2019), Talend, Retrieved January 20, 2020. https://www.talend.com/resources/data-lake-vs-data-warehouse/.

[7] R. Wirth, J. Hipp, CRISP-DM: Towards a Standard Process Model for Data Mining, 2000.

[8] C. Wang, H. Yang, C. Bartz, C. Meinel, Image Captioning with Deep Bidirectional LSTMs, University of Potsdam, 2016.

[9] R. He, W. Sun Lee, H.T. Ng, D. Dahlmeier, An Unsupervised Neural Attention Model for Aspect Extraction, National University of Singapore, 2017.

[10] T. Kohonen, Self-Organizing Maps, Springer Series in Information Sciences, Springer-Verlag, Berlin Heidelberg, 1997.

[11] A. Ultsch, Maps for the visualization of high dimensional data spaces, in: T. Yamakawa (Ed.), Proceedings of the 4th Workshop on Self-Organizing Maps, 2003, pp. 225—230.

[12] https://commons.wikimedia.org/wiki/File:Somtraining.svg.

[13] H. Li, Data Visualization of Asymmetric Data Using Sammon Mapping and Applications of Self-Organizing Maps, University of Maryland, College Park, Md, 2005.

[14] J.H. Ward Jr., Hierarchical grouping to optimize an objective function, J. Am. Stat. Assoc. 58 (1963).

Further readings

[1] "Semantic Tagging with Deep Residual Networks", J. Bjerva, B. Plank, J. Bos.
[2] "Predictive and Prescriptive Maintenance of Machine Industry with Machine Learning"; P. Deka, Medium.
[3] "by C.D. Manning, P. Raghavan, H. Schutze, An Introduction to Information Retrieval" Cambridge University Press, England.
[4] J. Bjerva, Semantic Tagging, Github. https://github.com/bjerva/semantic-tagging.
[5] A. Deshpande, M. Kumar, Artificial Intelligence for Big Data, Packt Publishing Ltd, May 2018.
[6] EMC Education Services, Data Science and Big Data Analytics, John Wiley & Sons, Inc, 2015.
[7] Big Data Analytics with Hadoop 3, Sridhar Alla, Packt Publishing Ltd, May 2018.
[8] D. Fisher, R. DeLine, M. Czerwinski, S. Drucker, Interactions with big data analytics, Interactions 19 (3) (2012) 50−59.
[9] D. Laney, META Group, 3D data management: controlling data volume, velocity, and variety, Tech. Rep. (2001).
[10] (Online). Available: http://blogs.gartner.com/doug-laney/files/2012/01/ad949-3D-Data-Management-Controlling-Data-Volume-Velocity-and-Variety.pdf.
[11] G. Press, $16.1 billion big data market: 2014 predictions from IDC and IIA, Forbes Tech. (2013) (Online). Available: http://www.forbes.com/sites/gilpress/2013/12/12/16-1-billion-big-data-market-2014-predictions-from-idc-and-iia/.
[12] Y. Huai, R. Lee, S. Zhang, C.H. Xia, X. Zhang, DOT: a matrix model for analyzing, optimizing and deploying software for big data analytics in distributed systems, in: Proceedings of the ACM Symposium on Cloud Computing, 2011. pp 4:1−4:14, 2011.
[13] X. Wu, X. Zhu, G. Wu, W. Ding, Data mining with big data, in: IEEE Transactions on Knowledge and Data Engineering 26, Jan. 2014, pp. 97−107.
[14] D. Gillick, A. Faria, J. DeNero, MapReduce: Distributed Computing for Machine Learning, Dec. 2006.

CHAPTER 3

An overview of deep learning in big data, image, and signal processing in the modern digital age

Reinaldo Padilha França[1], Ana Carolina Borges Monteiro[1], Rangel Arthur[2], Yuzo Iano[1]
[1]School of Electrical Engineering and Computing (FEEC) — State University of Campinas (UNICAMP), Campinas, São Paulo, Brazil; [2]Faculty of Technology (FT) — State University of Campinas (UNICAMP), Limeira, São Paulo, Brazil

1. Introduction

Data in its raw and natural state does not present much value, but due to big data techniques, it can provide valuable information that helps in many perspectives of people's daily lives such as business decision making, political campaigning, and advancing medical science. The unprecedented expansion in the availability of valuable information, connected with advances in technology, makes this analysis more attractive to use, build, and execute [1–3].

Machine learning is at the heart of what makes this possible, where machine learning algorithms learn iteratively from this volume of data, which allows computers to discover hidden or abstract ideas without being explicitly designed to observe for them. Machine learning is fundamentally about giving the computer the ability to clarify problems by developing algorithms that are able to learn by looking at lots of data, and then employing that experience to solve equivalent or similar problems in new contexts [4,5].

Unlike deep learning, which is a class-specific of machine learning, which involves a deeper degree and competence of automation, working with a major learning challenge is attribute extraction, where the algorithm needs to look for certain types of features to make a decision. Feature extraction is the potential of deep learning, which is applied in particular in the matter of object recognition for complex problems. Deep learning attempts to simulate the way our brains assimilate and process information

Trends in Deep Learning Methodologies
ISBN 978-0-12-822226-3
https://doi.org/10.1016/B978-0-12-822226-3.00003-9

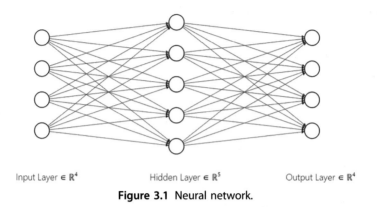

Input Layer ∈ $\mathbf{R}^4$ Hidden Layer ∈ $\mathbf{R}^5$ Output Layer ∈ $\mathbf{R}^4$

Figure 3.1 Neural network.

by creating artificial "neural networks" as illustrated in Fig. 3.1, that can extract complex relationships and concepts from data, which iteratively improves by recognizing complex patterns in text, sounds, photos, and other data to produce more accurate information and forecasts [4–7].

In recent times, the world has witnessed the union of big data and deep learning tools to enable the increased strategic performance of companies through investment in technology, where in practice this combination, which together machine learning and the processing of large amounts of data, can bring a number of benefits to organizations. Companies generate a very large volume of data every day (more than n petabytes per day), as is the case with modern technology giants, especially considering that this volume grows rapidly every day and there is a need to analyze this big mass of data [7,8].

Big data is a term used in information technology that refers to the broad set of data (unstructured and structured) that is present in business, and is further used to describe the process of analysis, processing, and strategic use of existing data. More important than the amount of data therefore is what companies do with this complex information, which can be used to generate insights and for strategic decisions for organizations. Basically, the better the processing of data, the more accurate corporate decision making becomes. Added to this, big data allows you to increase operational efficiency, reduce costs, and avoid risks, among many other advantages [9,10].

Deep learning establishes advances in special classes of neural network learning from complicated patterns in vast amounts of data and computational power; this technology is based on its "enabling the computer to learn from data observation" paradigm. Deep learning techniques are the

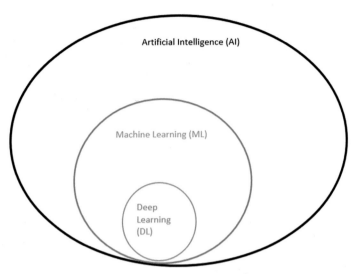

Figure 3.2 Deep learning paradigm.

most advanced today for identifying words in sounds as well as objects in images, as machine learning is nothing more than a method that uses algorithms that can interactively learn from data analysis, i.e., machine learning technology makes the development of analytical models automatic for computers to assimilate information and learn on their own. It is a data analysis mechanism that through strategy construction of analytical models performs automation. It is a subdivision of artificial intelligence, as illustrated in Fig. 3.2, that is based on a design that enables systems to learn from data, make decisions, and identify patterns with minimal human intervention [11—13].

Using machine learning enables companies to be able, for example, from historical sales data, to define future forecasts of their sales with a relevant level of accuracy, as long as these applications already exist in leading companies demonstrating proven returns with significant gains generated through cross-selling and upselling and also reduced operating costs, reduced losses, and lack of goods. Thus the result of this process is that, today, computers are already able to discover hidden insights without having been previously projected to consider any specific data [13—15].

In this context, using big data and machine learning, it is possible through so-called predictive analytics, one of the most common uses of combining big data and machine learning, to use data and machine learning methods to determine the likelihood of future data results based on information obtained in the past. Precisely for this reason, the combination of machine learning and big data is extremely useful in bringing confidence and clarity to business decisions. Based on data processing, a company can anticipate demands by considering various financial, economic, and marketing factors [16—18].

Therefore whereas digital image processing techniques have been the subject of recent research [19—26] this chapter aims to provide an updated review and overview of deep learning and machine learning in big data, image processing, audio/speech, and signal processing by addressing its evolution and fundamental concepts, and showing its relationship as well as its success, with a concise bibliographic background, categorizing and synthesizing the potential of technology.

1.1 Deep learning concepts

The world has been undergoing a revolution in the field of artificial intelligence in recent years, having as its main engine deep learning-based technologies, since this technique comes from the field of study of artificial intelligence, which is the study and design of intelligent agents [27,28].

Within artificial intelligence, there are several different techniques that model this "intelligence." Some techniques can be classified in the machine learning area that generally "learn" to make a decision based on examples of a problem rather than specific programming. Machine learning algorithms require data to extract features and learning that can be used to make future decisions. Deep learning is the emerging term that is included in the science of artificial intelligence and machine learning, and represents intelligent computers and devices that are connected and capable of performing their functions without the need for human interaction. In addition, this technology can "learn" according to the context in which it is used. A specific subset of machine learning techniques is called deep learning, often using deep neural networks, as illustrated in Fig. 3.3, and relying on a lot of data for training. There are many factors that differentiate these techniques from classical machine learning techniques, and some of these factors favor the use of these techniques in areas such as natural language processing (NLP) and computer vision [29—31].

It uses neural networks to make things better, such as computer vision, speech recognition, and NLP, as illustrated in Figs. 3.4—3.6. The learning that this technology represents has become a central theme of discussions in companies due to the impressive results they have presented and can be

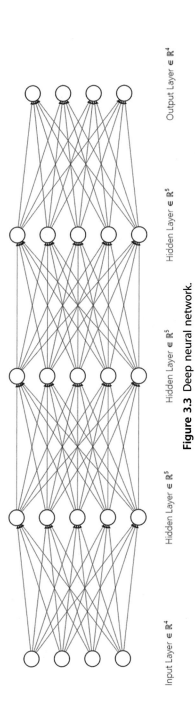

Figure 3.3 Deep neural network.

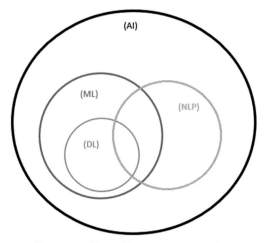

Figure 3.4 Natural language processing.

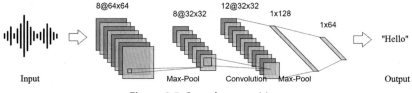

Figure 3.5 Speech recognition.

applied to businesses with different purposes. It is already used mainly in the healthcare, education, and e-commerce industries [32,33].

Deep learning runs so that it can learn on its own and is powered by the multiples of data generated at all times, so it can decipher natural language and relate terms, generating meaning. There are different, important points between classical machine learning techniques from deep learning methods, the main ones being the need and effect of a lot of data, computational power, and flexibility in problem modeling. This approach uses algorithms that do not preprocess and automatically generate properties that do not vary in their hierarchical layers of representation [34].

These layers are nonlinear data, which allow a complex and abstract representation of the data to form an ordered classification. The number of algorithms keeps increasing and makes deep learning generate as many natural languages as possible so that more subjects can be understood more deeply. Too much data is the absolute truth about machine learning, since technology does not exist if there is no data. Without data, there is nothing to learn or to discover patterns about. While data is the "fuel" of machine learning techniques, there are two problems that plague classic data

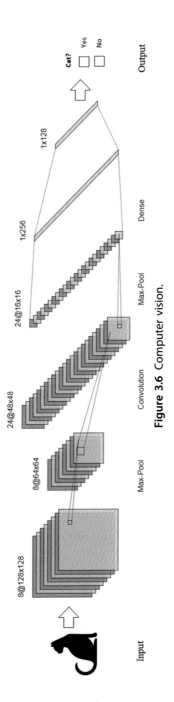

Figure 3.6 Computer vision.

techniques"dimensionality" and performance stagnation by adding more data after a certain threshold [35,36].

Making an analysis, as buying a product based on price, brand, model, year, color, or size, among others, there are so many characteristics, that is, so much information about a given problem that a person sticks to the details and loses the main focus. This is what happens with most classical techniques related to the dimensionality of a problem. And so, through research already focused on dimensionality reduction, machine learning methods already use certain techniques to minimize this problem. More than being able to scale is to understand today's avalanche of information, since it is fundamental to use intelligent technologies to decode and perform an analysis of this data, from which it is possible to extract insights and understand behaviors and trends, identify opportunities, and, especially, define market strategies [35].

Another point is that classical techniques reach a saturation point concerning the amount of data, that is, they cannot extract more information from that data volume. This is one reason why the technique of deep learning is prepared to work with a larger amount of data, because it has the philosophy of "the more data the better" More specifically, it deals with artificial neural networks, an area that seeks to computationally simulate the brain as a learning machine, and deep learning architectures are often complex and need a lot of data for their training. Thus reliance on too much computational power to apply these techniques is inevitable. Although there are several classic techniques that are general purpose, the structure of deep learning and its most basic unit, the neuron, can be as generic and flexible as possible [37,38].

In short, a neuron is composed of inputs (the dendrites), a processing nucleus (the nucleus), and outputs (the axon). This way, a signal goes in, is processed, and comes out differently. While only one neuron is not useful, the flexibility of interconnecting multiple neurons into more complex problem-solving structures is a major differentiator of deep learning architectures. Over the years, computers have become more powerful in processing, which has allowed a neural network, which is a weight-weighted connectionist paradigm, to be able to create intelligent models in the connections of a significant number of artificial neurons while still relying on arithmetic operations growing exponentially with respect to deep networks [39,40].

A simplified structure of a convolutional neural network (CNN) is a widely used category for image object detection, face recognition, feature extraction, and other applications, which works directly with the complexity of the problem over time and power computing available to solve them. Still evaluating that for this, these networks are usually multilayered, which depending on the problem the number of layers varies as a VGG16 that has 16 layers or even hundreds of deep layers, like a Microsoft ResNet of 152 layers. And so, there are countless different architectures for different purposes, and with their structure and context-dependent operation applied, however, the freedom of architecture allows deep learning techniques to solve numerous problems, and actually be like a Lego box of parts, just waiting to be assembled and disassembled to build new things [41].

Ultimately, deep learning by nature is a machine learning technique that provides deep neural networks for information processing and learning. Unlike other existing techniques, it is capable of working with raw data analysis, which enables a broader field of action than other techniques, and can classify information contained in different formats, such as text, images, audios, sensors, and, most essentially, a database. In deep learning practice, when an intelligent system is fed with new data, each artificial neuron that performs this task is responsible for assigning a weight to that information and transmitting this assessment to the next level of the neural network [42].

1.2 Machine learning

Machine learning is a topic of artificial intelligence where it is possible to elaborate algorithms to teach a particular machine to perform a task. It is necessary to have a dataset, and from that data, explore the correlation between them, discovering patterns and applying algorithms, which makes it possible to take a sum of input data and based on certain patterns to produce the outputs. Each entry in this dataset has its own features, and generates models that can be generalized for a specific task [43].

The idea of machines learning on their own from a vast volume of data may be the simplified definition of machine learning. In general, machine learning is a field of artificial intelligence that is intended to explore constructs of algorithms that make it possible to understand autonomously, where it creates the possibility to recognize and extract patterns from a large volume of data, thus building a model of learning [43,44].

Basically, it is a way of doing better in the future based on past experiences, since this learning is based on observing data as direct experience or instruction, or even examples. Once the algorithm has learned, it is capable of performing complex and dynamic tasks, predicting more accurately, reacting in different situations, and behaving intelligently. Therefore machine learning can be defined as a kind of research area that allows computers the competence to learn without them necessarily being programmed for it [43–45].

This learning process is called model training, where after having trained the model, it is able to generalize to new data, which is not presented in the training stage, where it is provided with correlations and predictions generation to accomplish the specified task. The interest in machine learning in recent times comes from the analog factors that have been made for data mining, which is one of the most popular and essential tasks of the modern era, since the increasing volume and variety of data available and computer processing have become cheaper and more powerful, and data storage has become more affordable leading to the growth of this type of process. Additionally, the results are high-value forecasts that are much more accurate and lead to a much more qualified and assertive investment, meaning they can lead to smart actions in real time and better decisions without any kind of human intervention [43,44].

Machine learning is generally divided into supervised learning, as illustrated in Fig. 3.7. This consists of labeled data, where the algorithm receives a set of labeled data, that is, a set of inputs together with the respective correct outputs, causing the algorithm to learn by making comparisons with the expected output, readjusting its parameters until it reaches an acceptable and predetermined a priori threshold. Unsupervised

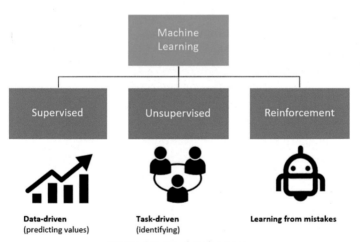

Figure 3.7 Big data learning.

learning, as illustrated in Fig. 3.7, operates well in transactional data where the data is unlabeled, as opposed to data that has no historical labels. In this case, the algorithm receives an unlabeled dataset and seeks to find similarities between data groups, generating clusters, or data groups, that is, the system does not know the "right answer" in this case, and the algorithm must find out what is being shown for the purpose of exploring the data and thus finding some structure in it [46,47].

Semisupervised learning is generally used for equivalent applications as a supervised learning technique; however, both labeled and unlabeled data can be used for training, and in practice the relationship is a small portion of labeled data with a large volume of unlabeled data. This form of learning can be employed with tools such as prediction, classification, and regression. In this type of learning it is very useful to relate the cost associated with labeling as being very high, which allows for a completely labeled training process, since simple examples may include the identification of a face on a webcam [48,49].

Reinforcement learning, as illustrated in Fig. 3.7, is regularly used for games, robotics, and navigation, since the algorithm can discover through trial and error which actions can produce the best rewards [50].

Machine learning in the most elementary way to apply algorithms to collect data, to be able to learn from it, and then to be able to point or predict something in the world. It is a data analysis strategy that automates the development of analytical models through algorithms that interactively learn from data. Instead of implementing software routines by hand, with a specific set of rules to complete an exclusive task, the machine goes through "training" using a broad volume of data and algorithms that grants it the competence to learn how to do the task. This allows computers to gain hidden insights without explicitly being programmed to perceive something specific [43].

So, machine learning has come straight from artificial intelligence, and the algorithm approach through the years has included learning trees, reinforced learning, Bayesian networks, inductive logic programming, and clustering, among others. With machine learning, human inference is practically zero, since the machine manages itself, where everything happens through algorithms and big data, which together identify data patterns and create connections between each other. This provides the ability to execute, based on statistical analysis, any tasks without human interference and predict answers more accurately. In this context, big data at its core stores tons of data from social networks and search engines, and then increasingly intelligent machine learning algorithms perform a real scan of this gigantic amount of information, and from the moment patterns are discovered, systems are able to make predictions based on these patterns [51].

The distinction between deep learning and machine learning is that the first is one of the techniques used by the second, which consists of training computers to perform activities that humans usually do, such as speech recognition, prediction, and image identification. Thus it enhances the opportunities that algorithms have to learn through the use of neural networks [52].

1.3 Big data

Big data can be outlined as a set of techniques that can perform analyses on a vast amount of data to generate important results that would be difficult to achieve in smaller volumes. The concept is related to an extremely large dataset, and for this reason it needs special tools to handle the large amount of data that must be found, organized, extracted, and transformed into information to enable broad and timely analysis skills, as illustrated in Fig. 3.8 [9].

Big data is also considered an information technology for the treatment of large datasets that need to be processed and stored. Such a concept started basically with velocity, since this is related to the premise that in modern times, 1 min can be considered a long time for the analysis of medical data, fraud detection, payment releases, or any other time-sensitive information. So, because for some analyzes, the closer they are to real-time, the more

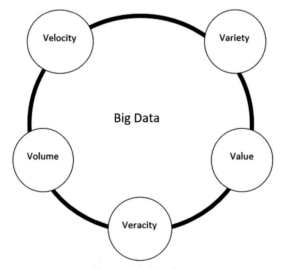

Figure 3.8 Big data.

critical competitive advantage is to business. Thus velocity is related to the fastest rate at which data is received and administered [53–55].

Volume looks at the scale of gigabytes to terabytes and petabytes, which has now declined. It is inversely proportional to the reality of data generation and storage today, since it averages n terabytes of data on social networks, and all that volume is gold to be mined and insights extracted. The philosophy is that the amount of data is important, and with big data technology it is possible to process huge volumes of low-density unstructured data. **Variety** is considered as any data, since today the ability to capture and analyze structured and unstructured data, web browsing, audio, text, sensors, videos, log files, and access control turnstiles in subway, among others is practically routine. So, referring to the various data types available, traditional data types have been structured to fit perfectly into a database just like the new unstructured data types [53–55].

Structured information is information that has some pattern or format that can be used for reading and extracting data, which can be text files (such as txt, csv, or XML), database data, or legacy systems. And unstructured information is information that does not have a standardized format for reading, which can be web pages, Word files, videos, audios, tweets, social network posts, photos, and geolocations, among others. This means that they have no relationship to each other or a definite structure [56].

Simply put, big data is a more complex and larger dataset, mainly from new data sources that have datasets so immense that conventional data processing software cannot manage them. However, these large datasets can be used to clarify business problems with the use of technology. Data has intrinsic value; however, it is useless until this value is found. Of equal importance is how reliable the data is, and how much this data can be trusted. This relationship has become essential with big data; a large part of the value that modern technology companies dispose of comes from data, which they continuously analyze to produce and develop new products with more efficiency, and where **value** and **veracity** have emerged in recent years as pillars of big data. The benefits of big data and advanced data analysis are that more absolute answers are obtained because more information is created, and more absolute answers mean greater confidence in the data, which is an entirely different approach to dealing with problems and finding solutions [9,53–55].

Machine learning is one of the best-suited technologies for working with high data, since data (exclusively big data) is one of the reasons why it is possible to teach machines without programming them, and makes the

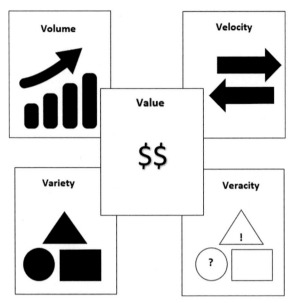

Figure 3.9 Vs of big data.

availability of big data to perform training on machine learning models a reality [57–59].

Big data is a conception that depicts the vast volume of unstructured and structured data that is generated every second. And its differential is properly linked to the opportunity and possibility to cross-check this data through several sources for valuable and quick insights. Since it is possible to obtain market information through consumers, desires, dissatisfactions, satisfactions, and needs, among many others, it is still feasible to capture and cross-check social media data with internal company data to create insights [9,52,60,61].

The pillars of this technology are in the **Vs**, as illustrated in Fig. 3.9, but all intelligence is in the analysis of data, which without correct and careful analysis it is impossible to generate insights and direct the right path. Thus the foundation of this technology is business value generation, since the more data there is, the higher will be the processing effort to generate information, and the speed to obtain that information that has value is an essential piece of the success big data can deliver [56,62,63].

1.4 Scientific review

In 2015, a study has shown that Deep Learning shifted a new wave of technology to machine learning and advanced human/computer interaction with artificial intelligence. Deep learning was applied to the recognition of handwritten characters and two main algorithms were explored: deep belief network (DBN) and CNN. Then an evaluation for both networks for a real-world handwritten character database in association with the Modified National Institute of Standards and Technology (MNIST) database was performed. An accuracy rating rate of 99.28% was obtained for CNN and 98.12% for DBN in the MNIST database, and 92.91% for CNN and 91.66% for DBN in the real-world handwritten character database, showing that deep learning has excellent resource learning capabilities and can obtain increased learning from the nature of the data [64].

In 2016, it was revealed that precision medicine was dependent on an increasing volume of heterogeneous data, where advances in cancer radiation using computed tomography, imaging, and dosimetry employed before each portion can generate data streams that need to be incorporated. In this scenario, electronic health records of phenotypic profiles of a broad patient group could be correlated. Thus the research described the techniques that can be employed in the creation of integrative predictive models aimed at radiation oncology, discussing the ability of the use of machine learning strategies such as deep learning and artificial neural networks [65].

In 2017 a huge volume of industrial data, called big data, gathered from the Internet of Things (IoT), was studied. Big data is characteristically heterogeneous, making any object in a multimodal dataset create challenges in a CNN, which is one of the most significant models in deep learning. In this context a deep convolutional computation model was proposed that learns from big data hierarchical resources making use of the tensor representation model, which is achieved by finely using numerous fundamental representation tensor products, thus extending the CNN to the vector space. The approach uses topologies contained in big data and local resources by defining a convolution operation that improves training efficiency and avoids excessive tuning. Thus the high-order backpropagation algorithm, which performs training of the parameters of the deep convolutional computational model technique regarding high-order space, was shown. The results showed that the deep convolutional computation model provided increased classification accuracy compared to the multimodal model or even the IoT big data deep computation model [66].

In 2018 it was shown that the characteristics of current modern life were changing by machine learning and big data, as digital streaming platforms learned particular preferences related to what people watched and search engines learned what people were looking for based on their browsing histories. Because these digital platforms were replacing their existing machine technology with lower learning technology using machine learning algorithms, these techniques provided improved insights from data. As well as addressing the applicability of machine learning to healthcare issues, it was expressed that machine learning and big data have the ability to create algorithms with similar performance to human doctors; however, in the early stages they demonstrated that they were totally related to the conventional statistical models that were recognized by most doctors, and, just like these methods, could enable a reasonable set of perspectives for the role of big data and machine learning in healthcare [67].

BigDL was introduced in 2019, consisting of a distributed deep learning framework for Apache Spark, which has been employed by many industry clients to build production big data platforms with deep learning applications. It enables deep learning software to be executed on the Apache Hadoop/Spark cluster by relocating processing exactly to data production and analyzing regarding end-to-end data to management and deployment. BigDL, different from existing deep learning frameworks, considers the parallel training of distributed data properly over the Spark operational computing model. Also presented was the experience of users who have opted for BigDL to create complete and efficient end-to-end data analysis, and advanced learning channels regarding production data [68].

Also in 2019, progress and the achievement of deep, high-level, knowledge based on low-level sensors that perform the reading and recognition of human activities were seen through conventional pattern recognition approaches. In this context, a summary was carried out from the perspective of the literature considering aspects related to sensor modality, deep modeling, and application of the technique, presenting detailed information under each perspective in relation to deep learning [69].

Also in the same year, the relationship between deep learning techniques and mobile and wireless networks was studied, discussing the ease and efficient implementation of deep learning in mobile systems. What was categorized by different domains was reflected in how to adapt deep learning to mobile environments [70]. Additionally, deep learning methods were able to identify complex patterns in large datasets. And from this perspective, general guidelines were studied and provided, as a practical guide to tools and resources, on the effective use of these methods for genome analysis, evaluating applications in the areas of regulatory genomics, pathogenicity scores, and variant calling [71].

In 2020, it was shown that the prediction of a protein structure is of fundamental importance in determining the three-dimensional shape of a protein from its amino acid sequence. However, these protein structures are difficult to determine experimentally, but their determination results in extensive knowledge of their function. In this context, deep learning was used to train a neural network to generate accurate predictions of the gap between pairs of residues, which convey more information about the structure than the contact forecasts. And so, a medium-strength potential was built to accurately describe the shape of a protein [72].

Also in 2020, a hybrid deep learning approach was developed for cooperative and privacy-preserving analyses. An IoT device was used to execute the initial layers of this neural network and then send the outputs to a cloud structure feeding the remaining layers, generating the final result. And based on the information exposed to the cloud service, the privacy benefits of this approach were assessed in the same way that the cost of local inference of different layers in a modern handset was assessed [73].

2. Discussion

Although deep learning is a general-purpose technique, the most advanced areas are computational vision with semantic segmentation, object recognition, scenario description, and having a more direct application in autonomous cars. With NLP and speech recognition, improvement in personal assistants in recent years has become clear. Deep learning can also be found in healthcare, specifically in imaging diagnosis.

Because deep learning is a parcel of a group of general-purpose techniques, any classic machine learning problem can be solved, such as virtual recommendation systems with behavior-based movies, books, and music found on digital streaming platforms. And social networking has its applications in sentiment analysis in text, videos, or images for brand monitoring.

Deep learning has helped to advance many areas and is still conducive to being a great tool for businesses that have embraced digital transformation, since technology corporations have come to use more efficient data analysis techniques that automate their systems, enabling the development of rules and techniques capable of analyzing data and extracting high-speed learning.

The implementation of machine learning has been made easier with deep learning techniques, as long as technologies are fully connected. With this union, online campaigns and ads are optimized, user experience is improved, new ways are found to offer products through the analysis of connected consumer behavior, and detecting network problems, frauds, and intrusions has become easier, as well as filtering spam in emails.

With improved analytics through big data, creating an approach that combines special classes of neural networks, it is possible to establish learning patterns that can handle large volumes of complex data, while considering the high performance possible with deep learning and also enabling rapid problem identification. This can provide the solution that optimizes decision making and reporting to reduce the need for manual rework and operational activities.

The self-learning capability of this technology brings more accurate results and faster processing, generating a competitive advantage for companies while still providing new skills and adjustments that can further improve business performance, which is crucial for businesses not to become obsolete.

Deep learning can be used in various applications such as image recognition medicine for breast cancer, Alzheimer's disease, cardiovascular diagnosis, stroke, skin cancer, as well as genomics. Other possibilities are the development of systems that perform automatic recognition of documents; understand customer behavior and the propensity to buy a particular product or service; fight against fraud in a financial system by detecting anomalies; elaborate the accurate diagnosis of diseases; recommend information, products, and services to customers; and perform voice, face, and vehicle recognition functions.

Many of today's simple daily actions are fueled by machine learning methods like real-time ads on both mobile devices and web pages, web search results, credit scores and best offers, sentiment analysis, text-based, pattern, and image recognition, email spam filtering, as illustrated in Fig. 3.10, and network intrusion detection.

An example of supervised learning in machine learning is when technology detects when a transaction with a particular bank account is suspected of fraud, or when there is a complaint from customers. These events require prior experience before a pattern can be identified and this becomes a machine's source of learning. An unsupervised learning application in machine learning is the recommendation of items in a store, for example, and though a person's search order has never been made before, the technology looks for similar attributes to perform this item recommendation action.

An example of the application in semisupervised learning is in identifying people's faces, serving to create classifications, categories, as well as predictions. With regard to reinforcement, it is commonly used in navigation, robotics, and games with the simple objective of finding the best strategy to use. In this way, machine learning is also present in Industry 4.0 and has already been employed in factories around the world for some time.

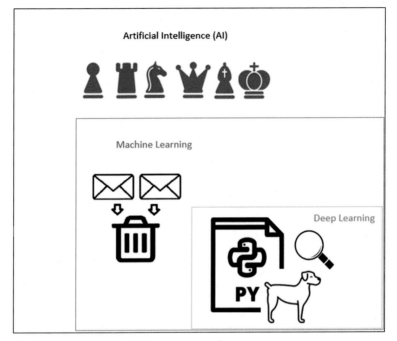

Figure 3.10 Applications.

Machine learning has been present in people's lives since the reading of an online article, which was found by a search engine, performing this search with almost complete accuracy that the user was looking for. Or when writing an email and, before completing the sentence, the tool suggested exactly the intended phrase.

When driving or using a transportation app, the fastest routes are offered by apps with virtual maps from tech giants that have various patterns and points to analyze the ideal route. Interest in a type of movie, documentary, style of music, or TV series can be observed by digital streaming platforms that can recommend specific content to a user. E-commerce has long been using machine learning as a shopping recommendation that has digital "stalking" sensations, providing on every site visited an offer for a particular product searched for.

Big data is the analysis and interpretation of huge volumes of data, where specific solutions are needed to work with unstructured information at high speed and are of great importance in defining strategies, providing marketing solutions, increasing productivity, reducing costs, and making smarter business decisions.

Big data analysis can also be employed to support government actions during flu epidemics by getting people to move safely during the outbreak or to leave infected places, validating government actions to combat the crisis.

In industry, big data tracking allows you to set up alerts in case of machine failures in real time, for example, helping to understand processes and optimize them. By monitoring social networks, big data can analyze company keyword references, analyzing what people are saying about their actions or products, whether positive or negative, and categorizing and structuring data from social media.

On websites and e-commerce through big data, by analyzing customer buying habits and data it is possible to create more assertive promotions, based on trends and customizations. In a bank, big data can minimize business risk by detecting fraudulent behavior, and while in hospital, patient records are used to generate insights to improve care and service.

3. Conclusions

In short, machine learning is the science that empowers computers to have the ability to perform actions without having to be coded with programming, and deep learning is a kind of more sophisticated machine learning algorithm built on the principle of neural networks. Machine learning techniques can be loaded with data and then learn on their own to make predictions and guide decisions from models. What unlike deep learning algorithms are able to support and work with big data and even act as processing by overlapping nonlinear data processing layers.

Machine learning algorithms when they are exposed to new data can adapt from previous calculations, and patterns are shaped to provide reliable answers. This means that instead of programming rules on a computer and waiting for the result, the machine will learn these rules on its own. Deep learning algorithms are complex, built from a stack of several layers of "neurons" Their main applications are classification tasks, fed by immense amounts of data, which are able to process natural language, recognize images, and speak and learn to perform extremely advanced tasks without human interference.

The main purpose of big data is to leverage analytics and make smarter decisions. This technology is twice as likely to achieve superior performance, meaning that in business it has twice the ability to win in a modern competitive market. Regardless of the environment, industry, or business model, deepening analytics means better control of the situation and knowing exactly how to act to maximize results because information is power, and big data represents an empire of knowledge.

Using technology intelligently can make a company secure its market space by standing out from competitors and even becoming an industry leader. In addition, the combination of technologies such as machine learning, big data, and deep learning in applications can make the dreams of business success in the modern world come true. These technologies together can act as a compass to make the right decision about the direction an organization should take, increasing efficiency, and speeding the development of entities of any size and business.

4. Future trends

Voice interfaces through voice recognition technology have greatly evolved over the last few years with advances in machine and deep learning, enabling increasingly fluid communications between humans and machines due to NLP, which boosted smartphone voice assistants and expanded into other industries such as home automation. It is hoped that in the future, through machine and deep learning, highly intelligent solutions capable of differentiating contexts to perform actions will be even more common and natural to perform different activities such as audio transcription, translations, and executing commands in smart houses, such as switching on a light using only the voice [68,74,75].

With the coming of the IoT, there is a clear increase in the number of connected devices, which is estimated to increase surprisingly over the next few years; however, the latency challenges of cloud solutions lead organizations to lean toward solutions that use edge intelligence. Edge intelligence changes the way data is captured, stored, and extracted, which shifts the process from cloud storage devices to the edge, making peripheral devices more independent, moving decision making closer to the data source. By reducing communication delays and improving near-real-time results, machine learning and deep learning technologies will make it possible to design intelligent devices that work independently [76].

Transfer learning is the quick and easy way for organizations to take their first steps toward digital transformation, since this technology relies on pretrained open-source networking models used as a starting point in the machining process. The use of learning transfer enables rapid solutions by facilitating the adoption of artificial intelligence in the digital transformation journey of those companies that have difficulty training and developing models that require access to computational power and a huge volume of data [77–79].

References

[1] P. Zikopoulos, C. Eaton, Understanding Big Data: Analytics for Enterprise Class Hadoop and Streaming Data, McGraw-Hill Osborne Media, 2011.

[2] A. McAfee, et al., Big data: the management revolution, Harv. Bus. Rev. 90 (10) (2012) 60−68.

[3] T.H. Davenport, P. Barth, R. Bean, How 'big data' is different, MIT Sloan Manag. Rev. (2012).

[4] P. Harrington, Machine Learning in Action, Manning Publications Co., 2012.

[5] P.M. Domingos, A few useful things to know about machine learning, Commun. ACM 55 (10) (2012) 78−87.

[6] Y. LeCun, Y. Bengio, G. Hinton, Deep learning, Nature 521 (7553) (2015) 436−444.

[7] I. Goodfellow, Y. Bengio, A. Courville, Deep Learning, MIT Press, 2016.

[8] L. Deng, D. Yu, Deep learning: methods and applications, Found. Trends Signal Process. 7 (3−4) (2014) 197−387.

[9] A.Y. Zomaya, S. Sakr (Eds.), Handbook of Big Data Technologies, Springer, Berlin, 2017.

[10] G. Manogaran, C. Thota, D. Lopez, V. Vijayakumar, K.M. Abbas, R. Sundarsekar, Big data knowledge system in healthcare, in: Internet of Things and Big Data Technologies for Next Generation Healthcare, Springer, Cham, 2017, pp. 133−157.

[11] Y. Bengio, I. Goodfellow, A. Courville, Deep Learning, vol. 1, MIT press, 2017.

[12] G. Litjens, T. Kooi, B.E. Bejnordi, A.A.A. Setio, F. Ciompi, M. Ghafoorian, C.I. Sánchez, A survey on deep learning in medical image analysis, Med. Image Anal. 42 (2017) 60−88.

[13] S. Min, B. Lee, S. Yoon, Deep learning in bioinformatics, Briefings Bioinf. 18 (5) (2017) 851−869.

[14] S. Raschka, V. Mirjalili, Python Machine Learning, Packt Publishing Ltd, 2017.

[15] F. Hutter, L. Kotthoff, J. Vanschoren, in: Automated machine learning: methods, systems, challenges, Springer Nature, 2019, p. 219.

[16] Z. Obermeyer, E.J. Emanuel, Predicting the future—big data, machine learning, and clinical medicine, N. Engl. J. Med. 375 (13) (2016) 1216.

[17] M. Chen, Y. Hao, K. Hwang, L. Wang, L. Wang, Disease prediction by machine learning over big data from healthcare communities, IEEE Access 5 (2017) 8869−8879.

[18] L. Zhou, S. Pan, J. Wang, A.V. Vasilakos, Machine learning on big data: opportunities and challenges, Neurocomputing 237 (2017) 350−361.

[19] A.C.B. Monteiro, Y. Iano, R.P. França, Detecting and counting of blood cells using watershed transform: an improved methodology, in: Brazilian Technology Sympo-sium, Springer, Cham, 2017, December, pp. 301−310.

[20] A.C.B. Monteiro, Y. Iano, R.P. França, An improved and fast methodology for automatic detecting and counting of red and white blood cells using watershed transform. VIII Simpósio de Instrumentação e Imagens Médicas (SIIM)/VII Simpósio de Processamento de Sinais da UNICAMP, 2017.

[21] Monteiro, A. C. B., Iano, Y., França, R. P., and Arthur, R. Applied Medical Infor-matics in the Detection and Counting of Erythrocytes and Leukocytes through an Image Segmentation Algorithm.

[22] A.C.B. Monteiro, Y. Iano, R.P. França, R. Arthur, V.V. Estrela, A.D. Rodriguez, S.L.D.L. Assumpção, Development of Digital Image Processing Methodology WT-MO: An Algorithm of High Accuracy in Detection and Counting of Erythrocytes, Leucocytes, Blasts, 2019.

[23] A.C.B. Monteiro, Y. Iano, R.P. França, R. Arthur, Methodology of high accuracy, sensitivity and specificity in the counts of erythrocytes and leukocytes in blood smear

images, in: Brazilian Technology Symposium, Springer, Cham, 2018, October, pp. 79—90.

[24] A.C.B. Monteiro, Y. Iano, R.P. França, R. Arthur, V.V. Estrela, A comparative study between methodologies based on the hough transform and watershed transform on the blood cell count, in: Brazilian Technology Symposium, Springer, Cham, 2018, October, pp. 65—78.

[25] A.C. Borges Monteiro, Y. Iano, R.P. França, R. Arthur, Medical-laboratory algorithm WTH-MO for segmentation of digital images of blood cells: a new methodology for making hemograms, Int. J. Simulat. Syst. Sci. Technol. 20 (2019).

[26] A.C.B. Monteiro, Y. Iano, R.P. França, N. Razmjooy, WT-MO algorithm: automated hematological software based on the watershed transform for blood cell count, in: Applications of Image Processing and Soft Computing Systems in Agriculture, IGI Global, 2019, pp. 39—79.

[27] P.S. Grewal, F. Oloumi, U. Rubin, M.T. Tennant, Deep learning in ophthalmology: a review, Can. J. Ophthalmol. 53 (4) (2018) 309—313.

[28] X.X. Zhu, D. Tuia, L. Mou, G.S. Xia, L. Zhang, F. Xu, F. Fraundorfer, Deep learning in remote sensing: a comprehensive review and list of resources, IEEE Geosci. Remote Sens. Mag. 5 (4) (2017) 8—36.

[29] S.J. Russell, P. Norvig, Artificial Intelligence: A Modern Approach, Pearson Education Limited, Malaysia, 2016.

[30] D. Gunning, Explainable artificial intelligence (xai), Def. Adv. Res. Proj. Agency (DARPA) 2 (2017) nd Web.

[31] R. Miikkulainen, J. Liang, E. Meyerson, A. Rawal, D. Fink, O. Francon, B. Hodjat, Evolving deep neural networks, in: Artificial Intelligence in the Age of Neural Networks and Brain Computing, Academic Press, 2019, pp. 293—312.

[32] S. Walczak, Artificial neural networks, in: Advanced Methodologies and Technologies in Artificial Intelligence, Computer Simulation, and Human-Computer Interaction, IGI Global, 2019, pp. 40—53.

[33] S. Samarasinghe, Neural Networks for Applied Sciences and Engineering: From Fundamentals to Complex Pattern Recognition, Auerbach publications, 2016.

[34] E. Nachmani, E. Marciano, L. Lugosch, W.J. Gross, D. Burshtein, Y. Be'ery, Deep learning methods for improved decoding of linear codes, IEEE J. Sel. Top. Signal Process. 12 (1) (2018) 119—131.

[35] J. Wang, Y. Ma, L. Zhang, R.X. Gao, D. Wu, Deep learning for smart manufacturing: methods and applications, J. Manuf. Syst. 48 (2018) 144—156.

[36] L. Zhang, L. Zhang, B. Du, Deep learning for remote sensing data: a technical tutorial on the state of the art, IEEE Geosci. Remote Sens. Mag. 4 (2) (2016) 22—40.

[37] M. Van Gerven, S. Bohte, Artificial neural networks as models of neural information processing, Front. Comput. Neurosci. 11 (2017) 114.

[38] I.N. Da Silva, D.H. Spatti, R.A. Flauzino, L.H.B. Liboni, S.F. dos Reis Alves, Artificial Neural Networks, Springer International Publishing, Cham, 2017.

[39] N. Garg, P. Nikhitha, B.K. Tripathy, An insight into deep learning architectures, in: Encyclopedia of Information Science and Technology, fourth ed., IGI Global, 2018, pp. 4528—4534.

[40] G. Huang, Y. Sun, Z. Liu, D. Sedra, K.Q. Weinberger, Deep networks with stochastic depth, in: European Conference on Computer Vision, Springer, Cham, 2016, October, pp. 646—661.

[41] L. Lu, Y. Zheng, G. Carneiro, L. Yang, Deep learning and convolutional neural networks for medical image computing, in: Advances in Computer Vision and Pattern Recognition, Springer, New York, NY, USA, 2017.

[42] P. Mamoshina, A. Vieira, E. Putin, A. Zhavoronkov, Applications of deep learning in biomedicine, Mol. Pharm. 13 (5) (2016) 1445—1454.

[43] M. Kubat, An Introduction to Machine Learning, vol. 2, Springer International Publishing, Cham, Switzerland, 2017.

[44] Y. Bengio, Machines who learn, Sci. Am. 314 (6) (2016) 46–51.

[45] A.C. Müller, S. Guido, Introduction to Machine Learning with Python: A Guide for Data Scientists, O'Reilly Media, Inc., 2016.

[46] A. Voulodimos, N. Doulamis, A. Doulamis, E. Protopapadakis, Deep learning for computer vision: a brief review, Comput. Intell. Neurosci. (2018).

[47] L. Wang, Discovering phase transitions with unsupervised learning, Phys. Rev. B 94 (19) (2016) 195105.

[48] E. Tu, J. Yang, A Review of Semi Supervised Learning Theories and Recent Advances, 2019 arXiv preprint arXiv:1905.11590.

[49] J. Liu, P. Timsina, O. El-Gayar, A comparative analysis of semi-supervised learning: the case of article selection for medical systematic reviews, Inf. Syst. Front 20 (2) (2018) 195–207.

[50] P. Goyal, H. Malik, R. Sharma, Application of evolutionary reinforcement learning (ERL) approach in control domain: a review, in: Smart Innovations in Communication and Computational Sciences, Springer, Singapore, 2019, pp. 273–288.

[51] R. Bhatnagar, Machine learning and big data processing: a technological perspective and review, in: In International Conference on Advanced Machine Learning Technologies and Applications, Springer, Cham, 2018, February, pp. 468–478.

[52] E. Charniak, Introduction to Deep Learning, The MIT Press, 2019.

[53] E. Hofmann, Big data and supply chain decisions: the impact of volume, variety and velocity properties on the bullwhip effect, Int. J. Prod. Res. 55 (17) (2017) 5108–5126.

[54] I. Lee, Big data: dimensions, evolution, impacts, and challenges, Bus. Horiz. 60 (3) (2017) 293–303.

[55] N. Khan, M. Alsaqer, H. Shah, G. Badsha, A.A. Abbasi, S. Salehian, The 10 Vs, issues and challenges of big data, in: Proceedings of the 2018 International Conference on Big Data and Education, ACM, 2018, March, pp. 52–56.

[56] C.S. Kruse, R. Goswamy, Y.J. Raval, S. Marawi, Challenges and opportunities of big data in health care: a systematic review, JMIR Med. Inform. 4 (4) (2016) e38.

[57] W. Van Der Aalst, Data science in action, in: Process Mining, Springer, Berlin, Heidelberg, 2016, pp. 3–23.

[58] M. Wu, L. Chen, Image recognition based on deep learning, in: 2015 Chinese Automation Congress (CAC), IEEE, 2015, pp. 542–546.

[59] F.R. Padilha, et al., Potential proposal to improve data transmission in healthcare systems, in: Deep Learning Techniques for Biomedical and Health Informatics, Academic Press, 2020, pp. 267–283.

[60] F.R. Padilha, et al., A proposal of improvement for transmission channels in cloud environments using the CBEDE methodology, in: Modern Principles, Practices, and Algorithms for Cloud Security, IGI Global, 2020, pp. 184–202.

[61] F.R. Padilha, et al., Improvement for channels with multipath fading (MF) through the methodology CBEDE, in: Fundamental and Supportive Technologies for 5G Mobile Networks, IGI Global, 2020, pp. 25–43.

[62] F.R. Padilha, et al., Lower memory consumption for data transmission in smart cloud environments with CBEDE methodology, in: Smart Systems Design, Applications, and Challenges, IGI Global, 2020, pp. 216–237.

[63] F.R. Padilha, et al., Improvement of the transmission of information for ICT techniques through CBEDE methodology, in: Utilizing Educational Data Mining Techniques for Improved Learning: Emerging Research and Opportunities, IGI Global, 2020, pp. 13–34.

[64] J.-E. Bibault, P. Giraud, A. Burgun, Big data and machine learning in radiation oncology: state of the art and future prospects, Cancer Lett. 382 (1) (2016) 110–117.

[65] P. Li, et al., Deep convolutional computation model for feature learning on big data in Internet of Things, IEEE Trans. Ind. Inf. 14 (2) (2017) 790—798.

[66] A.L. Beam, I.S. Kohane, Big data and machine learning in health care, Jama 319 (13) (2018) 1317—1318.

[67] J.J. Dai, Y. Wang, X. Qiu, D. Ding, Y. Zhang, et al., Bigdl: A distributed deep learning framework for big data, Proc. ACM Sym. Cloud Comp. (2019) 50—60.

[68] J.L.J. Marquez, I.G. Carrasco, J.L.L. Cuadrado, Challenges and opportunities in analytic-predictive environments of big data and natural language processing for social network rating systems, IEEE Latin Am. Trans. 16 (2) (2018) 592—597.

[69] J. Wang, Y. Chen, S. Hao, X. Peng, L. Hu, Deep learning for sensor-based activity recognition: a survey, Pattern Recogn. Lett. 119 (2019) 3—11.

[70] C. Zhang, P. Patras, H. Haddadi, Deep learning in mobile and wireless networking: a survey, IEEE Commun. Surv. Tutor. 21 (3) (2019) 2224—2287.

[71] J. Zou, M. Huss, A. Abid, P. Mohammadi, A. Torkamani, A. Telenti, A primer on deep learning in genomics, Nat. Genet. 51 (1) (2019) 12—18.

[72] A.W. Senior, R. Evans, J. Jumper, J. Kirkpatrick, L. Sifre, T. Green, et al., Improved protein structure prediction using potentials from deep learning, Nature (2020) 1—5.

[73] S.A. Osia, A.S. Shamsabadi, S. Sajadmanesh, A. Taheri, K. Katevas, H.R. Rabiee, et al., A hybrid deep learning architecture for privacy-preserving mobile analytics, IEEE Internet Things J. 7 (5) (2020) 4505—4518.

[74] N. Hartmann, E. Fonseca, C. Shulby, M. Treviso, J. Rodrigues, S. Aluisio, Portuguese Word Embeddings: Evaluating on Word Analogies and Natural Language Tasks, 2017 arXiv preprint arXiv:1708.06025.

[75] L. Espinosa-Anke, Knowledge Acquisition in the Information Age: The Interplay between Lexicography and Natural Language Processing, Doctoral dissertation, Universitat Pompeu Fabra, 2017.

[76] J. Park, S. Samarakoon, M. Bennis, M. Debbah, Wireless network intelligence at the edge, Proc. IEEE 107 (11) (2019) 2204—2239.

[77] R.R. Parente, R.B. Prudencio, Transfer learning for synthetic examples selection in meta-learning, in: Anais do XV Encontro Nacional de Inteligência Artificial e Computacional, SBC, 2018, October, pp. 811—822.

[78] M. Long, H. Zhu, J. Wang, M.I. Jordan, Deep transfer learning with joint adaptation networks, in: Proceedings of the 34th International Conference on Machine Learning-Volume 70, 2017, August, pp. 2208—2217. JMLR. org.

[79] K. Weiss, T.M. Khoshgoftaar, D. Wang, A survey of transfer learning, J. Big Data 3 (1) (2016) 9.

CHAPTER 4

Predicting retweet class using deep learning

Amit Kumar Kushwaha, Arpan Kumar Kar, P. Vigneswara Ilavarasan
Information Systems Area, Department of Management Studies, Indian Institute of Technology, Delhi, India

1. Introduction

Social media platforms, including Facebook and Twitter, which have users on all platforms such as mobile, tablet, laptop, and desktop, have started giving users the flexibility of not only connecting with friends but also following opinion leaders in various domains. Every single hour, several thousands of messages are generated with or without embedded media, floated, and consumed on the platform. Twitter is one such microblogging website that has attracted the attention of users, opinion leaders, and, more interestingly, researchers to test various sociotechnical theories. Twitter provides every user with an unparalleled option to interact with other users. These options support the spread and exchange of information, and while doing so sometimes the real meaning of the original data is lost or distorted. A user posts a message using a tweet. With an upper capping of 140 characters for each tweet, the user must be calculative, specific, and factual with the information he/she is posting in every tweet. This upper limit of the characters in every tweet is to enable a higher rate of information or tweet propagation, defined as a retweet in the paradigm of Twitter. At the same time, a retweet is defined as the critical metric to measure the diffusion of information or a tweet on Twitter; it has also been a topic for researchers to test and augment various theories. If they are able to predict the possibility of diffusion or rate of retweet ability in the paradigm of Twitter, users, consumers, and organizations managing the information can benefit from this. However, since most of these social media platforms are arbitrary connections, it is least affected by major exogenous and external factors, and becomes a challenge to calculate the probability of the event of a retweet [1] of these tweets with a limited set of features. Several researchers and experimenters have tested the hypothesis that a retweet is a predictable pattern and can be established as a function of various factors [2–5].

Trends in Deep Learning Methodologies
ISBN 978-0-12-822226-3
https://doi.org/10.1016/B978-0-12-822226-3.00004-0

89

Most of the existing work on retweet prediction uses content-based features resulting in sentiment features having values such as positive, negative, and neutral. However, in more recent works [6—11], researchers and experimenters have focused on extracting other content-based features describing aspects different from sentiment using the quick feature-engineering process and these features are further used in a supervised learning framework to test the hypothesis around retweeting behavior. The classification power of the supervised learning framework using these features is a function of how robust the feature engineering framework is, how generalizable the features are irrespective of the topic under discussion, and how well these features have captured the information and trend of the tweets posted by users. This gap is more evident in the case of handcrafted features where feature extraction is mostly dependent on the individual researcher's or experimenter's knowledge of the domain and subject matter. There is a degree of subjectivity in the feature-engineering process. This poses a challenge to the design of manual feature extraction methods. Some of these challenges are captured as questions about the feature-engineering framework: Are the features able to capture the systematic trend? Are the features easily generalizable? Are the features scalable? Are the features reproducible in an unseen (test) dataset? Is the topic of the features independent? Are the features geographically separate? Are the features able to capture the nonsystematic trend or the nonlinear trend with limited dimensions?

In the case of labeled or unlabeled data, when the data points in the sample are not separable given the current set of feature sets, we explore machine learning techniques that separate the data points with the same features, possibly in a higher dimension. The tradeoff of projecting the sample points using the features in the lower dimensions to a higher dimension is the complexity of feature definition, maintenance, and computation response. Creating these handcrafted features for higher dimensions can further lead to the complexity of dimensionality [12]. Deep learning is the go-to technique when it comes to addressing the complexity of creating handcrafting features and learning features, which are, in other traditional machine learning techniques, not learnable. The only tradeoff for a researcher to pursue a deep learning framework like a convolutional neural network for learning features is the generalization of feature definitions for other domains. A few authors have studied generative methods in a similar field [13—15]. Hence, with the gap identified, apart from the automatic feature extraction technique, we also propose a more generalizable feature extraction framework, which we define as word expletives, which can be generalized and reproduced in any scenario and domain. Throughout this chapter, we propose a novel approach of using an amalgamation of feature extraction through deep learning and also an algorithmically driven extracted feature.

Most of the classifier frameworks tested and researched in the landscape of the information or tweet diffusion paradigm fall into two major categories. First is the majority of earlier work using generalized machine learning frameworks built on human-defined features within the guide rails of content, time-stamp, structural characteristics [16], and temporal [17,18] and demographics aspects of the text. Furthermore, in these machine learning frameworks, researchers have derived a formula as a function of these frameworks as illustrated in Fig. 4.1. These frameworks become challenging to learn and store the features when the sentences/texts/tweets are long and the features extracted are not in sequence. These frameworks do not have any memory of their own to store any learnings from a series of words. When we have large sentences/texts/tweets, it is vital that the classifier should be able to learn the features, store the trend in a sequence of the words in a sentence, and pass on only those learnings that are helpful in further classification. The second type of framework tries to answer this exact issue. The second set of models, defined as a class of deep learning

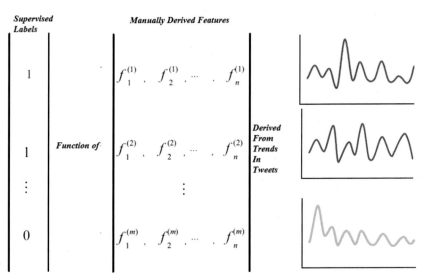

Figure 4.1 First set of the machine learning framework.

frameworks, has the capability of storing the learned trend from the sentence/text/tweet and passing only the consistent pattern, which helps to predict a particular behavior; in our case this behavior is the retweeting behavior. An illustration of this discussed framework is shown in Fig. 4.2.

A critical set of aspects describing the user content posted through a tweet on Twitter is lexical understanding. The field of any language learning defined as linguistics has a set of rules and sequences not only to learn but also to write sentences that carry a specific meaning. Linguistics has several branches. One such branch is lexical semantics, which defines the structure of the sentence, choice of words, and form of a verb or noun used to convey a particular meaning. Several works [19–22] have proposed and defined the selection of words and forms of words as an intentional exercise to convey a particular meaning. This motivates us to pursue research on a word expletive feature derived from lexical semantics theory with a hypothesis that using this feature in the classification framework will improve the accuracy.

Having established the uses and applications of machine learning, there are a number of limitations too. The first limitation is the enormous number of features in the data produced through social media platforms like Twitter. So, with an overwhelming quantity and variety of features, traditional machine learning algorithms cannot deal with the high dimensionality of the input feature matrix. Another limitation with conventional machine learning is that it is unable to solve some of the crucial artificial intelligence problems, which can be natural language processing or image recognition. One of the biggest challenges with the traditional machine learning models is feature extraction. We consider features like variables;

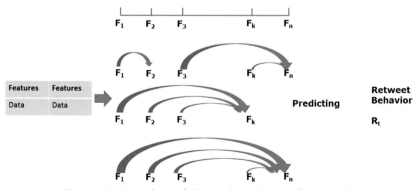

Figure 4.2 Second set of the machine learning framework.

however, in the case of complex problems like image or text application, these features must be created automatically with minimal human intervention. For a simple question like predicting whether there will be a match on a specific day or not is dependent on various features, e.g., weather conditions—sunny or windy. If all the features in our dataset are present, then the machine learning models are likely to make correct predictions. However, if the researcher does not add a feature like humidity conditions, then machine learning models are not that efficient in automatically generating this feature and learning on their own.

With advancements in the processing power of computing resources, researchers are at liberty to use more sophisticated techniques to save time defining and extracting the features. Initially, mathematicians began understanding the behavior of humans when learning and replicating. For instance, a person can recollect the classification of an image seen during childhood at a much later age to the same class or group. Biologically, this is referred to as memory, which is stored as information in the multiple neurons in the human brain. Researchers began borrowing and replicating the working principles of a biological neuron through an artificial neuron, which in its most basic form was referred to as a single perceptron. With improved support from hardware processing power, scientists began adding more artificial neurons and in multiple layers, and the resulting framework was thus defined as a deep neural network, also referred to as a deep learning framework. Deep learning can also resolve the complication of dimensionality by learning only the right feature set. Before proceeding further on designing a deep neural network and experimenting on the collected dataset, it is crucial to understand the core working of any neural network.

We use the demonstration of the single biological neuron as shown in Fig. 4.3. The human brain consists of multiple neurons that are connected through terminal axons. A single neuron receives signals through the eyes, touch through the hands, or smell through the nose through dendrites. Hence, dendrites act as input sockets for a neuron. These signals through dendrites can flow in parallel, and therefore there are multiple dendrites. It can be interpreted that a single neuron has the capability of processing multiple signals. Once the dendrites process the signals, the nucleus cell body inside neuron stores or, if required, performs further processing on the processed signals through dendrites and passes the output signals through

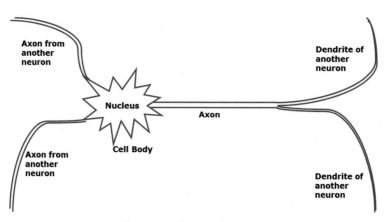

Figure 4.3 A natural neuron.

axons to the receipts. These receipts could be a body part like a hand that acts accordingly, or legs, or even another neuron for further processing connected through terminal axons.

By understanding how a biological neuron works inside a human brain, we now try to understand the theoretical concept of replicating an artificial neuron. In a real-world scenario, we capture multiple variables or features defined through business or domain logic, illustrating a single data sample. We further capture the data using the same features, which leads us to build a population for analysis. Hence, in the real world, too, we face problems that require the processing of collective inputs and replicating similar processing through different logics to understand the characteristics of a sample defining the population. With this objective in mind, we replace the dendrites with actual data inputs. These inputs would have to go through processing, which we define as a preactivation function. This preactivation function would weigh the data with randomly initialized weights and add biases to it. The data or the input signals passing through the preactivation function now reach the body of the neuron, where a second processing on these weighted inputs takes place called an activation function. The nature of this activation function could be linear or nonlinear, depending on the input data. Once the data or the processed signals pass through the activation function, too, it is ready to be used for classification or prediction of a numerical value. With this short set of steps, we have designed a single artificial neuron, also referred to as a perceptron.

A single neuron network or artificial neuron can classify the data samples into two classes. Hence, a perceptron will be the right choice when it comes to distinguishing the data points belonging to two linearly separable classes. A simple example would be using a perceptron to classify data points of an AND logical gate. However, in the real world, we do not have the leverage of working or analyzing linearly separable data. At the same time, we also have access to higher processing units like a graphical processing unit or tensor processing unit. These processing units can process data in considerably less time. Hence, we now take a single neuron and replicate the same structure by joining the neurons in parallel, which are called layers. We can replicate multiple layers of the same structure to process the nonlinearly separable data to make sure that the data becomes separable with highest accuracy. The new structure with multiple single artificial neurons placed in multiple layers will work as an independent unit while processing the data through preactivation and activation functions. Each neuron is activated when the output after processing data through the preactivation and activation function is beyond a threshold value. Hence, apart from the input and the output layers, we will have an architecture consisting of multiple intermediary layers called hidden layers. Researchers began defining these architectures of artificial neurons as deep neural networks because of the depth of the number of layers in the network. The process of learning the trend in data in this way is called deep learning.

A standard deep learning network output at time T is independent of output at time $T - 1$ as there is no relation between the new output and the previous output, so we can accurately say that the vanilla deep learning network's outputs are independent of each other. There might be a few scenarios where we need the new output to use the previous output. To demonstrate one such situation, let us discuss what happens when a person reads a book; he/she will understand that book only on the understanding of the previous words. If we use a feed-forward network and try to predict the next word in a sentence, we cannot do that for the logical reason that the new output will depend on the previous outputs, but in the normal feed-forward deep learning framework, the new output is independent of the previous output. Hence, we cannot use standard feed-forward deep learning networks for predicting the next word in a sentence.

Recurrent neural networks (RNNs) help to solve this issue by storing the learning from previous outputs. The most straightforward equation defining the working of an RNN is shown in Fig. 4.4. Through RNNs, we can process a sequence of vectors applying a recurrence formula at

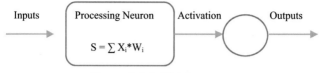

Figure 4.4 Artificial neuron.

every step. The new state h_t can be represented as some function f_w with parameters W established with old state h_{t-1} and input vector at time $t(x_t)$:

$$h_t = f_w(h_{t-1}, x_t)$$
$$h_t = \tanh(W_{hh}h_{t-1} + W_{xh}x_t) \qquad (4.1)$$
$$Y_t = W_{hy}h_t$$

However, as the length of a sentence on which an RNN is trained increases, the problem of vanishing gradient or exploding gradient does not let the model train itself. A vanishing gradient problem would mean that the new weights are close to weights from the previous iterations. An exploding gradient problem would mean that the old weights are way higher or way smaller than the scales of the weights of previous gradients. In either of these cases the neural network model does not learn any trend from the data. To solve this issue, researchers have proposed another version of a deep learning framework defined as long short-term memory (LSTM), which stores only selective information from the previous learning. LSTMs are designed to combat the vanishing gradients through a gating mechanism through which it gives better accuracy than RNNs. So, LSTM is made of three gates and one cell state. The first gate is defined as the forget gate, which takes the old state and the input and multiplies it by the respective weights and passes it through a sigmoid activation function. There are two more similar gates: input gate and output gate, and we apply the same operation on these gates as well, but with a different set of weights. A detailed explanation of LSTM can be found in Section 4.1.

For the classification model, we propose using a deep learning variant, also defined as the LSTM framework. LSTM [23], also known as LSTMIC, is designed to automatically learn sequential features from tweet diffusion (retweet), learning in fully feature-driven steps. Apart from word embedding, we also propose to use the handcrafted feature of word expletives.

2. Related work and proposed work

While sharing factual or nonfactual information on Twitter, the platform has started gaining momentum. Hence, a lot of researchers are taking on work to predict the probability or chances of this information being tweeted further and being cascaded or retweeted. For instance, Yokoyama and Ma [24] proposed a basic algorithm using the features to forecast future retweet probability associated with a tweet. However, there is a gap in this work in terms of clarity of the features used to predict the retweet. For the structured literature review, we have divided the prior research into three broad groups. First, handcrafted feature-driven basic machine learning classifiers, followed by generative models. We also diligently analyze the existing work done by researchers in the field of lexical semantics as the third section of the review. At the end of this section, we will submit our work as a novel approach, which considers all of the methods.

2.1 Handcrafted feature: basic machine learning classifiers

The creation of handcrafted features with due diligence and using the domain knowledge of the subject matter and field of the study can be further extended by using these features to predict the degree to which a tweet will be retweeted. This can be done by predicting the number of retweets associated with a piece of information posted on tweets either by regressing these features on retweet as a continuous variable [25—27] or by using these features for classification (retweet or no retweet) [8,9,28]. The researchers in these works have extracted features that are often restricted within the guide rails of the dataset explicitly created to the platform, e.g., Twitter [6,7,25,28,29]. These features can be further classified as temporal features [6,7], structural features [14,28,30], content features [27,31—33], and features derived with the idea of early adoption [25,34,35]. Tatar et al. [6] in their work observed that the future popularity or retweet ability of a tweet can be established as a linear function of the initial popularity a tweet has received during the very early stages of a retweet.

Furthermore, other researchers [7] have extended the previous research by introducing numerous gradual popularities placed in equal intervals of time within the time period of analysis, that has shown promises of improvement in the accuracy. Reviewing the literature, we observed that the most significant feature in this kind of research is the temporal or time-stamp feature capturing the time when early users have started participating in the retweeting behavior, which further cascades to a broader set of users. Zhang et al. [30] proved in their research that future retweet ability of a particular tweet can be established as a function of initial retweet trend in the communities formed on Twitter.

Liu et al. [27] further increased the accuracy power by combining classification and regression on features from the content of tweets posted with time-stamp and structure features. Wang et al. [25] in their research found and proved that features defining various aspects of a particular user on Twitter like how many retweets his/her tweet has received in the past, how many users he/she is connected to, or how many users follow him/her can predict the degree of retweet his/her tweet will receive in the future. The work tries to establish every user as an influencer. In another related work, Can et al. [26] explored the possibility of using social networks to judge the past success of receiving retweets on a particular tweet combined with some of the content-based variables that capture less than 50% of the variability of the actual number of retweets every tweet is receiving. To summarize and interpret the review of past work done in this domain, we can see that most of the handcrafted features created are based on domain/topic, content, historical trends, and time-stamp aspects of a tweet. Also, the machine learning frameworks using these features are not able to predict the degree of retweet beyond 60% accuracy. This highlights a gap in the research area of developing a classifier that can extract, learn, and store the features on its own and increase the prediction power. This motivates us to take this as the first aspect of our research question in this chapter.

2.2 Generative models

This principle of research usually marks the popularity or diffusion of information using a tweet on Twitter as a means of entry of retweet behavior and models this retweet function in the initial stages for each tweet independently [14,15,36—39]. A number of authors, e.g., [40], used reinforced Poisson processes to establish a relationship between trends of social network structure formed on various platforms. Other researchers, e.g., [37], attempted to further improve the model by introducing time-based features capturing the activity on timelines to find the chances of a tweet receiving a retweet. Furthermore, the same authors improved their model by introducing a self-exciting point process to estimate the retweets on Twitter. At this juncture, we also surveyed that researchers [41,42] have now started using deep learning frameworks to use the features they have extracted in the scope of research to predict the tweeting behavior. However, these rules are commonly not instantly optimized for predicting future diffusion or retweet and determine parameters for each tweet individually. These features, though, might fail to capture the hidden trends in the tweet data, which are currently not visible in lower dimensions and could be evident if we project the data onto higher dimensions with some transformation. Hence, there is still a considerable gap in using deep learning frameworks to extract the features. This motivates us to take this as the second aspect of our research question in this chapter.

2.3 Lexical semantics

There is a minimal and unknown area of work using lexical aspects to extract features that can potentially help to estimate if a tweet will be retweeted or not. Semantics is defined as the branch of linguistics that outlines the rules and logic concerned with the meaning of communicating in a language. There are two main areas in linguistics: logical semantics and lexical semantics. Lexical semantics defines the set of rules to learn the usage and placement of a word in the presence of other words in the same sentence. Writing a sentence or phrase in a language is considered to be the art of expressing emotions with a selection of right words and placing these words in an order so that the targeted reader or group of readers interpret the meaning in the same context and order. There have been enhancements in this domain [43,44], and researchers have started considering lexical semantics to extract the features in language processing. This domain has still not been entirely explored for research in the paradigm of tweet diffusion on Twitter. Hence, we take this as the third and last aspect of our research question in the scope of this chapter.

2.4 Proposed framework

With clearly identified gaps in all three previous sections, we intend to use word embedding and a custom input to an LSTM layer. The primary input to the LSTM model will be the tweet text with a well-written sequence of words and phrases. This model is further improved by introducing a handcrafted feature proposed in the current research as word expletives and is defined in Section 3.4. This deep learning framework will be optimized using two separate loss functions. The framework for the deep learning model is described in Fig. 4.5.

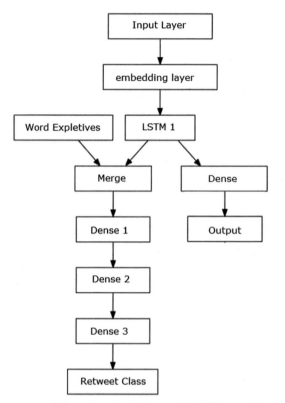

Figure 4.5 The proposed deep learning framework. *LSTM*, Long short-term memory.

3. Data collection and preparation

With the hypothesis of better predicting the retweeting behavior on Twitter, we started scrapping the tweets. This phase can be further divided into three steps as follows:

3.1 Tweet corpus creation

We created custom Python scripts to access the tweets using the open-source application programming interface (API) provided by Twitter. Microblogging site Twitter is a developer-friendly platform that lets researchers and developers scrap or download 1% of the total tweets posted on a topic using Twitter Streaming API. This API has to be rested for a minute after downloading the tweets continuously. Twitter relies on letting the developers and researchers download the tweets using a specific keyword usually prefixed with a "#" sign. Hence, the developers and users on Twitter collectively identify the trending or successfully diffused topic with more retweets attached to a specific "#" sign. The topic that we chose for our analysis was "Game of Thrones," which is an online media series watched in many countries. We targeted and restricted our research to the most recent season aired, "Game of Thrones Season 8." There were general reactions and opinions formed and expressed that the latest season was not up to the expectations of viewers of "Game of Thrones." Hence, we pursued this as our topic of the tweet on Twitter. Some of the keywords that we used to extract and download the tweets were ["#GOT8," "Game of Thrones S08," "Game of Thrones Season 8," "Thrones S08," "Game of Thrones"]. The art of scrapping quality tweets on Twitter is mainly driven by the type and right selection of keywords used. Hence, we diligently read tweets daily to create a list of "#" keywords that users were using to express their opinion about the latest season of the series. After downloading the tweets for 3 months, at the end of this step of data collection we were able to create a corpus of 270,000 tweets.

3.2 Tweet data cleaning

Tweets downloaded from Twitter contain a lot of noise in the data. The primary reason behind this is the causal usage of Twitter as a tool to communicate messages using mobile platforms as well as laptop platforms. While using a small handheld device like a mobile for writing a message on Twitter, users tend to use shorthand writing skills and images, also known as emoticons, to express emotions like sadness, happiness, or neutrality. There are links, URLs, and unique icons that if used as a structured feature do not add much to the learning process of the classifier algorithm. Hence, in an ideal case before using tweets for analysis, we should clean up the data from these unhelpful aspects of a tweet. We started looking at the tweet corpus by reading some of the tweets and interpreting that the data required a lot of cleaning up followed by a structured sequence of steps as follows:

First, there were a lot of unwanted URLs present in the tweets of the corpus. To train a text classification model to figure out the chances of a retweet in the tweets, the URLs would not add any meaning. Hence, we removed these.

Second, we removed the user ids and the "@" sign, because while twitter allows developers and researchers to download the tweet, it also masks the user id at the same time from which the tweet was generated prefixing with an "@" sign. This sign is not useful in classification or regression.

Third, we also removed all the alphanumeric characters used in the tweet. The idea behind this was that these words did not add any meaning to the language and would not be helpful in any analysis related to the tweet.

Fourth, we removed some of the frequently occurring words like "a," "an," and "the," which were used in nearly all the sentences as fillers or to point to a noun or a subject. Because these words were used very frequently and present in every tweet, when used as a feature to classify a tweet, they would not be able to add to the classification power. Hence, we removed these words. In the paradigm of tweet cleansing using Python as a tool, we have standard packages available to run this step, and the functionality is defined by removing the "stop words," wherein stop words are defined as a dictionary of some of these most frequently occurring words in the English language. After cleaning 270,000 tweets, removing unwanted tweets, and dropping the tweets from official accounts used for branding, the corpus size came down to 234,884. We also cleaned the tweets that did not have any meaningful words related to the keyword around which we downloaded the tweets.

3.3 Tweet data preparation

While downloading the tweets from Twitter, we also downloaded retweets that each tweet received, ranging from zero to any number. For classification, we converted the retweet variable to a class variable with the logic as:
1. High: Number of retweets > 10 on a tweet, and
2. Low: Number of retweets < 10 on a tweet.

With this labeling exercise, we now have a supervised classification problem with the research question and objective to classify a tweet to one of these two classes. We further tokenize the words from the tweet text. As per literature, tokenization is a process of splitting the text to a list of tokens. These tokens are individual words or combinations of words like 2-words, 3-words up to an n-combination of words. For dimension control, we restricted the number of words to be tokenized to 40,000. This means that from the corpus of 234,884 tweets, if we consider every word as a unique token, then for the entire corpus we can put an upper cap of 40,000 unique words to convert to tokens. This capping is necessary as the execution of deep learning frameworks is computationally costly, and the response time is much less if the number of features is extremely high. At the end of the data collection and preparation step, we have a matrix of size 234,484 × 40,001 with one column as the class label defining the high, medium, or low number of retweets for the corresponding tweet.

3.4 Word expletive, a proposed feature

We use the text-mining algorithm to identify some of the key terms in the associated context of a tweet. A brief representation of the words using a word cloud is represented in Fig. 4.6.

These terms can be used to improve our classifier of predicting the retweet probability of a particular tweet, for example, words such as ["spoilers," "don't watch"] appearing in the aired season of Games of Thrones under review for a particular episode. We define this feature as "word expletives." Details of the algorithm used to compute this feature are summarized in the following algorithm:

T = {Corpus of Tweets}

Representative words(rw) = ['gameofthronesseason8,' 'got8']

Group restriction words(grw) = ['episode,' 'season']

Figure 4.6 The word cloud of most frequent terms in the corpus.

Expletives(e) = ['spoilers,' 'not up to mark,' 'work well']

Intense expletives(ie) = ['bad']

Enormous expletives words(ee) = ['demthrones,' 'pathetic']

Finally, at the end of this step, we have one additional feature, which is handcrafted in nature along with the 40,000 token word features.

4. Research set-up and experimentation

4.1 The long short-term memory neural network

Predicting retweet class for the tweet as "high" or "low" is a classic case of supervised learning. Compared to regular machine learning classifiers, deep neural networks have exhibited more reliable performance in classification problems [45−48]. They have, in modern research, won various trials in pattern recognition and machine learning [49]. RNN is a variant of deep learning framework. RNN learns the sequence from a text and reserves the learnings from these semantics of all the previously seen words to a state also defined as the hidden state. The principal benefit of using RNN is its strength to rigorously learn and store the contextual learning, which is helpful to determine the semantics of any sentence. The vital aspect of RNN to save the previous learning from the semantics of a sequence of texts offers a significant classification problem. It is best suited for our research experimentation. Research has proved time and again that the sequence classification problems based on RNN architecture or versions of RNN architectures have been very accurate [50].

However, RNN is inadequate for taking learning from prior learning as the size of the corpus increases. In the paradigm of our research, this would mean that the RNN might not be able to remember the meaning, which is, for instance, five words far off from the present one. To overcome this problem, experimenters began using the LSTM model derived as an improved case of RNN, which introduces a logical forget gate to solve complicated, lengthy sentence issues [51] by storing only relevant information. The LSTM model can be practiced to text categorization or classification research questions with a thoughtful amalgamation of convolutional and LSTM neural networks [52,53].

We first divided the entire tweet corpus into two datasets as a training dataset, which is 75% of the whole corpus to train the model, and the other 25% of the corpus is kept aside for the model to be tested on the classification power on an unseen dataset. The training dataset was further broken down into the training and validation dataset to validate the results before the model was tested on the unseen test dataset. In our research question in this chapter, the problem of classifying the tweet to the class of retweet (high, low) with automatically extracted features and a manually created feature can be best answered accurately by an LSTM framework. The model is trained to learn from the annotated labels in the dataset (training set), following which the trained classifier is tested using an unseen tweet corpus (test dataset).

The broader design of the LSTM network under the current research is demonstrated in Fig. 4.7. Each tweet is transformed as a sequence of 50 tokens represented by vectors—the number 50 represents the highest number of tokens from a tweet. If in a tweet the number of words sequence is less than 50 tokens, then the index of "pad" will be affixed to the order of tokens. Furthermore, each word token is now expressed in a vector of a dimension 128 corresponding to the index of the same term in the tweet. To summarize, for each tweet, a sequence of 50 vectors of a size 128 is used as an input to the LSTM model. LSTM, at its core, does a further mathematical transformation to learn and store the trend from this input data and calculates the output.

Once the base LSTM model is thoroughly trained, we introduce the word expletive feature by concatenating the same with the low LSTM output. Now the overall framework has two inputs (embedding and word expletives) and two outputs (base output and final output). The model is further compiled by assigning a weight of 1 to the initial loss function of embedding input and base output and a further weight of 0.4 to the loss of

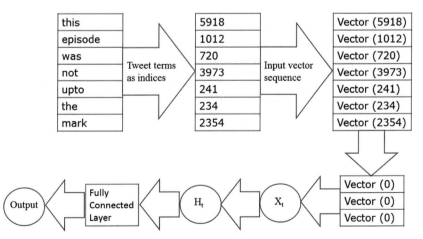

Figure 4.7 The long short-term memory (LSTM) architecture.

base output + word expletives as a whole input and final retweet class output. The last layer is a dense layer with sigmoid as the activation function.

For this research, we borrowed the LSTM application from Keras (https://keras.io/), a high-level deep learning API for high-level deep learning operations. For the low-level tensor operation, we used Tensor-Flow (https://www.tensorflow.org/) as the backend. The architecture of LSTM consists of four crucial layers: embedding, LSTM, concatenated input with word expletives, and fully connected or dense layer for the final prediction of results. We trained the model to parameters tuning on a training dataset with over 100 epochs, and all the model fit accuracies were recorded after every epoch. We noticed that the loss and accuracy stabilized after 15 epochs. Hence, based on this observation, we finally used 20 epochs to train the model. To avoid any overfitting while training the model, we also added a regularization term of L2. At the embedding layer, the units as output are a dense vector of a dimension of 128, and these are mainly 50 steps in the LSTM layer to learn the tweets with the highest number of words. From the initial data exploration, we also observed that the tweet corpus was imbalanced in the distribution in the retweet class, with a greater number of tweets in the low retweet class versus a lesser number of tweets in high retweet class. To accommodate this, while model training, we adjusted the class weights by deriving the weights of the smaller class by the ratio of instances among the class of retweets.

5. Results

To benchmark our findings from the proposed framework, we ran classifiers like decision tree, support vector machine, K-nearest neighbor, and logistic regression, as well as using the handcrafted features from some of the previous work that had a close resemblance to our work. A set of 35 handcrafted features used an input to the aforementioned classifiers, which were derived from mostly user-based, time-based, and content-based aspects of the tweet on Twitter. In comparison, the LSTM model in our research had a term vector of dimension 128 and an extra word expletive feature. We also included the results of an iteration with bag-of-words with the logistic regression model. By doing so, we ruled out the possibility of handcrafted feature engineering (Table 4.1). Table 4.2 shows the parameters set for each classifier model, followed by Table 4.3 showcasing the results at the end of fivefold cross-validation (CV). Finally, we also plot the receiver operating characteristic curve as shown in Fig. 4.8.

Table 4.1 A feature set: tweet expletives.

Algorithm to compute the degree of tweet expletives

For each tweet t in T

1 Count number of instances in t for the occurrences of any of the rw from RW
2 If rw > 1 → we are confident that t is relevant to the analysis; go to step 4
3 If rw = 1 → perform an additional check
4   A. Check if t contains any grw from GRW
5   B. If grw >= 1 then t can be used for analysis; go to step 7
6   C. If grw < 1, then ignore t; mark as "0"
7 Check if t has an occurrence from expletives; mark as "1"
8 Check if t has an occurrence from intense expletives along with expletives; mark as "2"
9 Check if t has an occurrence from enormous expletives words along with intense expletives and with expletives; mark as "3"

Table 4.2 Model parameters.

Classifier	
LR	Maximum iterations = 200, penalty: "l2"
SVM	kernel = "poly," degree = "2," tolerance = 1e − 3
DT	Minimum samples per split = 3, criterion = "entropy," maximum depth of the tree = 10
KNN	Number of neighbors = 2, tolerance = 1e − 3
BoW + LR	Random state = 0, C = 100
LSTM using embedding layer and word expletives	Regularization: L2 = 0.01, input and output dimension: 128, 20% of the training dataset used for validation

BoW, Bag-of-words; *DT*, decision tree; *KNN*, K-nearest neighbor; *LR*, logistic regression; *LSTM*, long short-term memory; *SVM*, support vector machine.

Table 4.3 Model performance.

Classifier	Accuracy	Precision	Recall	F1	ROC
LR	0.537	0.256	0.371	0.305	0.498
SVM	0.502	0.229	0.342	0.257	0.447
DT	0.569	0.283	0.381	0.311	0.504
KNN	0.535	0.239	0.378	0.293	0.48
BoW + LR	0.657	0.398	0.467	0.43	0.598
LSTM using embedding layer	0.765	0.548	0.652	0.595	0.726

BoW, Bag-of-words; *DT*, decision tree; *KNN*, K-nearest neighbor; *LR*, logistic regression; *LSTM*, long short-term memory; *ROC*, receiver operating characteristic; *SVM*, support vector machine.

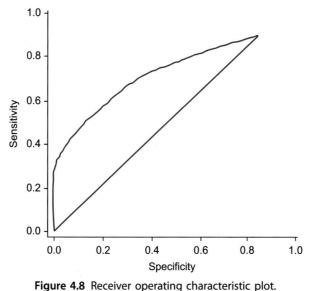

Figure 4.8 Receiver operating characteristic plot.

6. Discussion

From the observation of the results in Table 4.2, we see that the LSTM approach with the embedding layer and word expletive as features for classifying to tweet to the retweet class has the highest accuracy across all the metrics with a fivefold CV approach. Results show that the precision of predicting the "high" retweet class has increased when compared to the rest of the classifiers. Higher precision translates to higher true positives and lower false positives, which is a desirable state. Furthermore, we also notice that the sensitivity (recall) is even higher, which in terms of classification translates as the model correctly classifying more true positives and fewer false negatives, which is a desirable state. We can confidently interpret that the LSTM framework with the word embedding layer and a handcrafted feature of word expletive has proven to capture more precise information related to semantics from the tweet text, which further helps to classify and predict retweet ability. Inclusion of the adjustment of the weights for the class imbalance has also improved the accuracy.

7. Conclusion

In the current research, we studied and tested a proposition of blending neural network-based deep learning, a handcrafted feature of word expletive, and adding an embedding layer of words to predict tweets that diffuse concerning the experiences of watching Game of Thrones Season 8 among the audience and users of Twitter. The result of the current proposed framework in the research proved that the recommended method exceeded the rest state of the art classifier algorithms in predicting the retweet ability of a tweet. In the domain of online media content consumption, using social media data with less dependency on non-algorithmic feature engineering can improve overall accuracy remarkably and automate the analyses of Twitter text.

References

[1] P. Kaladevi, K. Thyagarajah, Integrated CNN- and LSTM-DNN-based sentiment analysis over big social data for opinion mining, Behav. Inf. Technol. (2019), https://doi.org/10.1080/0144929X.2019.1699960.

[2] X. Gao, Z. Zheng, Q. Chu, S. Tang, G. Chen, Q. Deng, Popularity prediction for single tweet based on heterogeneous bass model, IEEE Trans. Knowl. Data Eng. 2 (5) (2019).

[3] B.S.P. Prasad, R.S. Punith, R. Aravindhan, R. Kulkarni, A.R. Choudhury, Survey on prediction of smartphone virality using twitter analytics, in: IEEE International Conference on System, Computation, Automation, and Networking (ICSCAN), Pondicherry, India, 2019, pp. 1–5, https://doi.org/10.1109/ICSCAN.2019.8878839.

[4] B. Jiang, Z. Lu, N. Li, J. Wu, F. Yi, D. Han, Retweeting prediction using matrix factorization with binomial distribution and contextual information, in: International Conference on Database Systems for Advanced Applications, DASFAA, 2019.

[5] N. Vanetik, M. Litvak, E. Levi, A. Vashchenko, Twitter Event Detection, Analysis, and Summarization, Multilingual Text Analysis, World Scientific. https://www.worldscientific.com/doi/10.1142/9789813274884_0011.

[6] A. Tatar, J. Leguay, P. Antoniadis, A. Limbourg, M.D. Amorim, S. Fdida, Predicting the popularity of online articles based on user comments, in: Proceedings of the International Conference on Web Intelligence, Mining and Semantics 2011. Article No. 67. Pages 1–8, 2011, https://doi.org/10.1145/1988688.1988766.

[7] J. Beck, R. Huang, D. Lindner, T. Guo, Z.C.D. Helbing, N.A. Fantulin, Sensing Social Media Signals for Cryptocurrency News, 2019. www.researchgate.net/.

[8] A.H. Suarez, G.S. Perez, K.T. Medina, H.P. Meana, J.P. Portillo, V. Sanchez, L.J.G. Villalba, Using Twitter Data to Monitor Natural Disaster Social Dynamics: A Recurrent Neural Network Approach with Word Embeddings and Kernel Density Estimation, 2019. www.researchgate.net/.

[9] R. Aswani, A.K. Kar, P.V. Ilavarasan, Experience: managing misinformation in social media—insights for policymakers from twitter analytics, J. Data Inf. Qual. 12 (1) (2019).

[10] G. Stamatelatos, S. Gyftopoulos, G. Drosatos, P.S. Efraimidis, Revealing the political affinity of online entities through their Twitter followers, Inf. Process. Manag. 57 (2) (2020).

[11] R.P. Schumakera, A.T. Jarmoszko, C.S. LabedzJr, Predicting wins and spread in the Premier League using a sentiment analysis of twitter, Decis. Support Syst. 88 (2016).

[12] P. Gainza, F. Sverrisson, F. Monti, et al., Deciphering interaction fingerprints from protein molecular surfaces using geometric deep learning, Nat. Methods 17 (2020) 184–192, https://doi.org/10.1038/s41592-019-0666-6.

[13] Q. Hou, M. Han, Incorporating content beyond text: a high reliable twitter-based disaster information system, in: A. Tagarelli, H. Tong (Eds.), Computational Data and Social Networks. CSoNet, Lecture Notes in Computer Science, vol. 11917, Springer, Cham, 2019.

[14] R. Kobayashi, R. Lambiotte, TiDeH: Time-dependent Hawkes Process for Predicting Retweet Dynamics, AAAI Publications, 2016.

[15] Z. Chen, X. Ye, Modelling Spatial Information Diffusion, Complex Networks, and Their Applications VIII, 2019, pp. 337–348.

[16] X. Wang, B. Fanga, H. Zhang, X. Wang, Predicting the security threats on the spreading of rumor, false information of Facebook content based on the principle of sociology, Comput. Commun. 150 (2020) 455–462.

[17] F.J.J. Joseph, Twitter based outcome predictions of 2019 Indian general elections using decision tree, in: 2019 4th International Conference on Information Technology (InCIT), Bangkok, Thailand, 2019, pp. 50–53.

[18] S. Mishra, Bridging models for popularity prediction on social media, in: WSDM '19: Proceedings of the Twelfth ACM International Conference on Web Search and Data Mining, 2019, pp. 810–811, https://doi.org/10.1145/3289600.3291598.

[19] M. Sharples, How We Write: Writing as Creative Design, Routledge, London, 2016.

[20] I. Maun, D. Myhill, Text as design, writers as designers, Engl. Educ. 39 (2) (2005).

[21] G. Brown, G. Yule, Discourse Analysis, Cambridge University Press, Cambridge, 1983.

[22] G.N. Leech, J. Svartvik, A Communicative Grammar of English, 1975. London.

[23] Y. Bengio, P. Simard, P. Frasconi, Learning long-term dependencies with gradient descent is difficult, IEEE Trans. Neural Network. 5 (2) (1994) 157–166, https://doi.org/10.1109/72.279181.

[24] M. Yokoyama, Q. Ma, Topic model-based freshness estimation towards diverse tweet recommendation, in: IEEE International Conference on Big Data and Smart Computing, 2019.

[25] B. Wang, A. Zubiaga, M. Liakata, R. Procter, Making the Most of Tweet-Inherent Features for Social Spam Detection on Twitter, 2015 arXiv:1503.07405.

[26] E.F. Can, H. Oktay, R. Manmatha, Predicting Re-tweet Count using Visual cues, ACM, 2013, pp. 1481–1484.

[27] G. Liu, C. Shi, Q. Chen, B. Wu, J. Qi, A two-phase model for retweet number prediction, in: International Conference on Web-Age Information Management. WAIM 2014, Web-Age Information Management, 2014, pp. 781–792.

[28] F.R. Gallo, G.I. Simari, M.V. Martinez, M.A. Falappa, Predicting user reactions to Twitter feed content based on personality type and social cues, Future Generat. Comput. Syst. 110 (2020) 918–930.

[29] K. Lerman, User participation in social media: digg study, in: 2007 IEEE/WIC/ACM International Conferences on Web Intelligence and Intelligent Agent Technology — Workshops, 2007, pp. 255–258.

[30] Q. Zhang, Y. Gong, Y. Guo, X. Huang, Retweet Behavior Prediction Using Hierarchical Dirichlet Process. AAAI Publications, Twenty-Ninth AAAI Conference on Artificial Intelligence, 2015.

[31] I. Engelmann, K. Andrea, N. Christoph, B. Tobias, Visibility through information sharing: the role of tweet authors and communication styles in retweeting political information on twitter, Int. J. Commun. 13 (2019). Retrieved from, https://ijoc.org/index.php/ijoc/article/view/9099.

[32] N. Oliveira, J. Costa, C. Silva, B. Ribeiro, Retweet predictive model for predicting the popularity of tweets, in: Proceedings of the Tenth International Conference on Soft Computing and Pattern Recognition (SoCPaR), Advances in Intelligent Systems and Computing, vol 942, 2018 (Springer, Cham).

[33] Y. Xiao, X. Xie, Q. Li, T. Li, Nonlinear dynamics model for social popularity prediction based on multivariate chaotic time series, Phys. Stat. Mech. Appl. 525 (2019) 1259−1275.

[34] S. Yardi, D. Boyd, Dynamic debates: an analysis of group polarization over time on twitter, Bull. Sci. Technol. Soc. 30 (5) (2010) 316−327, https://doi.org/10.1177/0270467610380011.

[35] A. Khatua, A. Khatua, E. Cambria, A tale of two epidemics: contextual Word2Vec for classifying twitter streams during outbreaks, Inf. Process. Manag. 56 (1) (2019) 247−257.

[36] T. Niederkrotenthalera, B. Tilla, D. Garciabc, Celebrity suicide on Twitter: activity, content, and network analysis related to the death of Swedish DJ Tim Bergling alias Avicii, J. Affect. Disord. 245 (2019) 848−855.

[37] Z. Bao, Y. Liu, Z. Zhang, H. Liu, J. Cheng, Predicting popularity via a generative model with adaptive peeking window, Phys. Stat. Mech. Appl. 522 (2019) 54−68.

[38] P.K. Srijith, M. Lukasik, K. Bontcheva, T. Cohn, Longitudinal modeling of social media with hawkes process based on users and networks, Proc. ASONAM (2017) 195−202.

[39] A.H. Zadeh, R. Sharda, Hawkes point Processes for social media analytics, in: L. Iyer, D. Power (Eds.), Reshaping Society through Analytics, Collaboration, and Decision Support. Annals of Information Systems, vol. 18, Springer, 2015.

[40] Z. Zhang, C. Li, Z. Wu, A. Sun, D. Ye, X. Luo, NEXT: a neural network framework for next POI recommendation, Front. Comput. Sci. 14 (2) (2020) 314−333.

[41] F. Martin, J. Hutchinson, Deep data: analyzing power and influence in social media networks, in: J. Hunsinger, M. Allen, L. Klastrup (Eds.), Second International Handbook of Internet Research, Springer, Dordrecht, 2019.

[42] W. Lim, C. Ho, C. Ting, Tweet sentiment analysis using deep learning with nearby locations as features, in: R. Alfred, Y. Lim, H. Haviluddin, C. On (Eds.), Computational Science and Technology. Lecture Notes in Electrical Engineering, vol. 603, Springer, Singapore, 2020.

[43] Z. Zhang, A.L. Gentile, F. Ciravegna, Recent advances in methods of lexical semantic relatedness − a survey, Nat. Lang. Eng. 19 (4) (2013) 411−479. https://doi.org/10.1017/S1351324912000125.

[44] W.H. Gomaa, A.A. Fahmy, A survey of text similarity approaches, Int. J. Comput. Appl. 68 (13) (2013) 0975−8887.

[45] D.L.K. Yamins, J.J. DiCarlo, Using goal-driven deep learning models to understand sensory cortex, Nat. Neurosci. 19 (2016) 356−365.

[46] W. Ying, L. Zhang, Sichuan dialect speech recognition with deep LSTM network, Front. Comput. Sci. 14 (2) (2020) 378−387.

[47] P. Baldi, P. Sadowski, D. Whiteson, Searching for exotic particles in high-energy physics with deep learning, Nat. Commun. 5 (2014). Article number: 4308.

[48] X. Han, Z. Wang, E. Tu, G. Suryanarayana, J. Yang, Semi-supervised deep learning using improved unsupervised discriminant projection, Neural Inf. Process. 11955 (2019) 597–607. ICONIP.

[49] S. Paszkiel, Using neural networks for classification of the changes in the EEG signal based on facial expressions, in: Analysis and Classification of EEG Signals for Brain– Computer Interfaces. Studies in Computational Intelligence vol. 852, Springer, Cham, 2019.

[50] W. Zhang, Q. Wang, X. Li, T. Yoshida, J. Li, DCWord: a novel deep learning approach to deceptive review identification by word vectors, J. Syst. Sci. Syst. Eng. 28 (6) (2018) 731–746.

[51] M. Sundermeyer, R. Schlüter, H. Ney, LSTM neural networks for language modeling, in: INTERSPEECH-2012, 13th Annual Conference of the International Speech Communication Association, 2012, pp. 194–197.

[52] R. Kadari, Y. Zhang, W. Zhang, T. Liu, CCG super tagging via Bidirectional LSTM-CRF neural architecture, Neurocomputing 283 (2018) 31–37.

[53] W. Dalmet, A. Das, V. Dhuri, M. Khaja, S.H. Karamchandani, Siamese manhattan LSTM implementation for predicting text similarity and grading of student test papers, in: H. Vasudevan, Z. Gajic, A. Deshmukh (Eds.), Proceedings of International Conference on Wireless Communication. Lecture Notes on Data Engineering and Communications Technologies, vol. 36, Springer, Singapore, 2019.

CHAPTER 5

Role of the Internet of Things and deep learning for the growth of healthcare technology

Dinesh Bhatia[1], S. Bagyaraj[2], S. Arun Karthick[2], Animesh Mishra[3], Amit Malviya[3]
[1]Department of Biomedical Engineering, North Eastern Hill University, Shillong, Meghalaya, India;
[2]Department of Biomedical Engineering, SSN College of Engineering, Chennai, Tamil Nadu, India;
[3]Department of Cardiology, North Eastern Indira Gandhi Regional Institute of Health and Medical Sciences, Shillong, Meghalaya, India

1. Introduction to the Internet of Things

The Internet of Things (IoT) has tremendously transformed and revolutionized the way present healthcare services are being provided to patients. It is also referred to as the Internet of Medical Things in the healthcare field, which allows continuous and safe remote monitoring of the patient's health condition to empower physicians to deliver quality healthcare at reasonable costs. This could lead to a state of healthcare services being out of the reach of ordinary people, making them unproductive and prone to chronic diseases. The level of patient/doctor interaction has increased tremendously leading to widespread satisfaction with improved healthcare efficiency among patients due to the ease of interaction with healthcare providers [1]. It has also helped in reducing the duration and length of hospital stay for patients and their families, thereby reducing healthcare costs significantly and improving treatment outcomes. Several healthcare applications employing IoT are presently available to benefit healthcare providers, hospitals, insurance companies, and patients at large. IoT has largely benefited critically ill patients and the elderly population living alone who require continuous monitoring due to their diseased condition by tracking their health conditions on a regular basis and allowing any disturbances or changes in routine daily living activities to trigger an alarm to a family member or concerned healthcare providers for immediate check on their condition and provide instant care and treatment to avoid any fatalities or long-term damage.

Trends in Deep Learning Methodologies
ISBN 978-0-12-822226-3
https://doi.org/10.1016/B978-0-12-822226-3.00005-2

With the help of advanced technological tools, it is possible to continuously monitor the different health aspects of an individual and predict the advent of any diseased condition. This would help to reduce patient load and burden on existing healthcare infrastructure facilities while maintaining the quality and standard of healthcare services provided. With the help of IoT, artificial intelligence, big data, and machine learning tools it is possible to accurately predict the diseased condition of a patient that even experienced and expert clinicians fail to understand and diagnose. These techniques employ test data to train and develop learning algorithms that can help to accurately predict any patient abnormality with the help of different statistical techniques and scientific analysis employing data accumulated in cloud servers from IoT devices. The IoT technique has gained much significance in the present-day scenario as it drastically reduces the load on existing healthcare infrastructure, continuously monitoring patients with chronic diseases and their rehabilitation.

The healthcare industry is in a state of great despair with rising healthcare costs, an aging global population, and an increase in new and chronic diseases. One of the major challenges of this industry is the availability and distribution of precise and real-time patient information for continuous health monitoring. This can be facilitated by the use of IoT as it enhances a professional culture at home, at work, or in any social setting by allowing individuals to monitor their health and assist service providers to deliver better treatment opportunities to their clients. However, several potential challenges exist while designing any IoT-based healthcare system such as security and privacy, user identification and authentication, and regular communication and exchange of healthcare data [2]. IoT has evolved rapidly from the field of information and communication technology (ICT) by connecting different small devices consuming less power through a communication network for the transmission of information. It has applications in several fields related to healthcare and technology. The advancements in medical technology and availability of smarter healthcare devices to support and improve available processes can produce a higher amount of data that can enable the exchange of information over a network within the hospital and global environment. IoT is being employed in healthcare for automatic patient identification and real-time patient physiological parameter monitoring with correct patient drug dosage, thereby improving the efficacy and performance of existing healthcare systems [3].

2. Role of IoT in the healthcare sector

The healthcare industry is considered to be among the fastest-growing revenue generators worldwide, giving employment to millions. It is witnessing major changes due to its association of individual entrepreneurs, start-up ventures, and small and medium-sized enterprises. This is due to high demand in the sector that cannot be fulfilled by traditional solutions, and advanced digital services are required to meet this future objective. IoT is expected to have a major impact on the development of healthcare services globally in the near future. The IoT infrastructure uniquely identifies and links physical objects to their virtual representations on the internet. This creates virtual representation of any physical object in the technology space. It allows operations on their virtual reflections, thereby replacing actions on their physical counterparts making the process much faster, cheaper, and more comfortable for people. This flexibility allows scope for developing and applying new business models in the industry [4].

The goal of IoT technology is to enable easy, secure, and efficient use of technology for the transmission and sharing of data globally. It offers several potential benefits in the dynamic digital world leading to personalized healthcare benefits for patients and care providers, which is no longer a challenging technological problem. With the help of IoT technology for healthcare systems, it is possible to track and monitor anything within the system at any convenient time and place on demand. With present-day advancements in sensor technology, communication networks, and the availability of high-performance computing systems, IoT is taking rapid strides and developing as a new potential technology that can be explored to provide numerous healthcare benefits at reduced cost and time. With the help of IoT, any device can be used to sense its surroundings and perform computations by employing a wireless network and address. This allows the development of real-time mapping of virtual objects to establish communication channels between them using different communication technologies for information on the status of the connected entity as and when required [3,4].

The deployment of an IoT structure in the healthcare industry is an ambitious approach as it connects different body sensor networks (BSNs) with available communication networks. The main challenge lies in selecting the proper sensors and seamless established network technologies to send accurate and error-free patient data to healthcare service providers and caregivers over the available wireless networks. The use of IoT technology allows the utilization of different networking tools to collect patient data from scattered sensor nodes, data analytics postacquisition, and automation to deliver a complete solution for continuous healthcare monitoring. The higher flexibility and rigidity of the IoT infrastructure can help in its deployment in any sector or industry for large-scale automation of factory outputs. It is pertinent that each device in the sensor network acquires accurate information with the capability of continuous monitoring and sensing and the ability to communicate, display, and transmit the acquired information as and when required [2,3].

Present-day smartphone devices can act as personalized healthcare monitoring set-ups for continuous monitoring, which can be connected to a range of sensors to measure different body parameters and vital indicators such as blood pressure, heart rate, oxygen saturation, glucose levels, etc. Having several advanced features, these devices can track regular fitness routines and exercise schedules forpatients. The major issue with these devices is widespread concerns regarding the data security, confidentiality, and reliability of the information being collected despite the costs and benefits being provided. Wearable devices procure patient data that can be transmitted through a communication network using gateways or base stations. With the advent of future technology, the design and complexity of the available architecture is evolving rapidly to enable early detection of diseases and efficient patient diagnoses [3,4].

In hospitals, IoT-based healthcare systems are designed to help physicians monitor patients' critical health parameters using available sensor nodes with fast communication channels to transmit the acquired information. Different patient parameters such as blood pressure, pulse rate, partial pressure of oxygen, etc. can be accurately measured by clinicians as well as at home by the patient's relatives with the help of communication technology. This helps to eliminate distance as a factor where data needs to be collected from rural areas that are located in remote locations, much like a telemedicine system; however, the set-up costs are much less and make the system economically viable. With the advent of 4G and 5G network technologies in the near future and network data availability at reduced costs, it is possible to accommodate more users and devices, which can deliver data and information at a faster pace employing sensor networks [4,5].

IoT-based healthcare systems are presently playing a significant role in the growth and development of medical information systems and ICTs as shown in Fig. 5.1. They are helping to improve the productivity and quality of healthcare services being provided to the patient. However, to

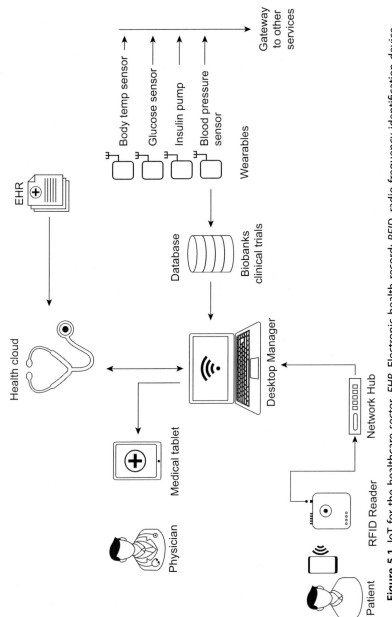

Figure 5.1 IoT for the healthcare sector. *EHR*, Electronic health record; *RFID*, radio frequency identification device.

take complete advantage of IoT, healthcare organizations must have unending trust in the abilities of this technology, which depends on its performance, security, and reliability of information acquired and transferred, privacy for the patient, and higher return on investments. Due to the increased burden on healthcare resources caused by the growing aging population in several countries, it is essential that continuous monitoring and tracking of such patients is conducted regularly. This is a real challenge to achieve due to scattered medical resources and available technological tools that could acquire patient data safely and accurately on a long-term basis at reduced costs [4].

3. IoT architecture

IoT framework systems are designed for optimal performance and control by employing different technologies using sensors, artificial intelligence, machine learning, network communication, and big data, etc. to provide real-time solutions to everyday problems. The basic set-up of the IoT consists of different medical devices with sensors to record data, patient monitoring tools, and wearables that could be connected to other devices through the internet. Since a huge amount of data is generated employing these tools, the acquired data must be classified, analyzed, and stored in proper files to generate new knowledge and actionable insights for the management of chronic diseases and acute patient care needs [5].

The advent of internet technology along with ICT has helped to shape the future of IoT and its applications across several fields. IoT systems consist of three basic components, namely a radio frequency identification device (RFID) tag, middleware system, and internet systems. The most crucial component of the IoT architecture is the RFID tag, which allows transmission of patient data using a portable device that can be processed when required. The RFID tag helps in patient identification, and provides patient-specific information related to blood pressure, heart and pulse rate, glucose levels, etc., as well as their current location. This information can help monitor patient information in real time without being in the vicinity of the patient continuously. Hence, it allows the mapping of real-world information to a virtual system. The middleware system software acts as a conduit between the RFID hardware and different healthcare applications, which links to the medical data server for transmission and storage of information for future use. The internet systems comprise computer systems and secure network servers that can help transmit accurate and error-free patient information over long distances. The IoT network system must comply with different healthcare guidelines and safety mechanisms to avoid misuse of healthcare information, loss of data, and protect patients' privacy and the confidentiality of their medical records [6].

Modern-day technology is playing a vital role in collecting sensory data from the patient, analyzing and processing it, communicating it over long distances, storing it, and displaying it when required. It is crucial to regularly monitor patients' conditions, hence the role of IoT and machine learning techniques is gaining prominence. The machine learning technique has evolved from artificial intelligence, which can help to develop smart and sophisticated devices as it is based on experience and precedents from data fed into a developed algorithm using established logic. Machine learning can be combined with cloud computing and big data to analyze large data chunks and help in simplifying tasks to develop automated processes [6,7].

If these goals are achieved it is possible to use IoT for easy patient identification at remote locations, automated data collection, safety of patient information, improvement in the efficiency of healthcare systems and hospital working environments at lower costs, avoidance of errors, and better quality of healthcare services. This way, IoT technology is effectively shaping up to play a crucial role in the healthcare environment [7].

4. Role of deep learning in IoT

Deep learning plays a pivotal role in IoT technology, which became a prominent area in the machine learning field in 2006 thanks to Yoshua Bengio, and covers applications in different areas such as image web search, image retrieval, and natural language processing. Conventional rule-based models are unable to understand the dynamics of human brain functioning, its hidden complexities, and assessment of available knowledge that severely affects the decision-making ability and outcome assessment by employing computer-aided technology in a healthcare delivery system. This can be overcome by applying deep learning tools with IoT, which can help in decision making and combining learning with pattern recognition in a unified model. A deep learning technique helps effective training of huge patient datasets, which can be utilized from a hospital information system (HIS) or a conventional manual converted to an electronic medical record. It helps in medical diagnosis and reveals new knowledge, which is much better than conventional models and analysis techniques. Hence, it helps in effective decision-making processes, cost—benefit analyses, and improved performance efficiencies in the healthcare sector. The deep learning technique employs models with longer processing paths as compared to conventional models by employing a support vector machine (SVM) and decision tree (DT). The SVM encompasses a three-layer input-to-output approach by combining sets of linear values. DT is also a three-layered structure where each path is considered as a processing node with the final path rendering coding for each path [8].

The multiple-layer deep learning models can help in simulating the complex decision-making process followed by the human brain. It stores the features as weights with interconnections between the nodes. They also help in revealing new knowledge and underlying features that are not clearly expressed by conventional models. The deep learning technique has shown promising applications in the healthcare area such as histopathological image analysis for disease diagnosis, analysis of data retrieved from HIS, study of hypertension and overall functioning of the human heart, and learning and decision-making capabilities of the human brain. These models automatically disclose abstract feature representations from limited data inputs and help to improve the ability of the machine learning models to learn abstract concepts. Since huge costs are involved in developing a knowledge base or expert system, deep learning models can be designed and implemented for several medical requirements and help in discovering new knowledge and concepts that improve patient diagnosis and overall healthcare services [7,8].

5. Design of IoT for a hospital

The advent of internet technology has shown widespread applications in the medical field leading to the arrival of an e-health subfield. This allows better quality of healthcare services, improving efficiency and access to patients in remote locations or to those who are not in a position to visit their nearest healthcare facility. It is widely used to schedule online appointments with clinicians and online interaction between them, and provides quick access to online patient healthcare records. The IoT-based healthcare system allows identification and tracking of the location of clinicians and patients, access to the patient's medical records, auto alarm status in case of medical emergencies, and the availability of hospital infrastructure and equipment by the clinician and hospital staff when required. This protects patient's safety and the confidentiality of medical records, provides easy location tracking of the patient, clinician, and hospital infrastructure, improves healthcare systems, and enhances efficiency and competitiveness with other healthcare service providers in the region. Hence, the appropriate use of information and communication technology with secure IoT technology has become an immense challenge for the software developer with the potential benefits of making them efficient and competitive [9].

When designing an effective IoT system for the hospital environment it is important to allow quick and safe transmission of healthcare information, as well as a more personalized service with strict storage conditions. This is possible with advancements in technology and communication networks to provide an efficient and stable healthcare system with easy patient traceability. To achieve this, all nodes in the healthcare system must be integrated and work harmoniously with Electronic Product Code (EPC) technology and RFID tags as shown in Fig. 5.2. The EPC tag can adapt to frequent changes in a healthcare information system, has good penetration to acquire timely clinical data, and has widespread applications in warehouse management, transportation management of hospital goods, and medical production management. This allows secure databases that would integrate different medical objects and continuously track their movements with effective availability of quality information and data protection. The main objective of an IoT system in healthcare is to manage and streamline medical administration, identify processes, reduce harmful incidents, and improve patient safety with quality of service. This has been further possible with advancements in microelectromechanical systems to develop smart hospital environments with integration of different sensors for vital signs monitoring of patients anywhere and at any time, thereby allowing innovative services to be available to people at reduced costs [10].

Several RFID applications are presently available for easy tracking of patients; these monitor the state of the elderly and disabled population at odd hours with help of the NIGHT-care RFID system. This system works on an intelligent technology platform to monitor sleep parameters, classify them, and report any abnormality detection immediately to the connected healthcare system for immediate care and patient assistance. RFID technology has also been employed for localization of hospital equipment and their availability on demand. However, RFID technology has limitations as it can be employed in smaller environments and is limited to the monitoring of patients and equipment in hospitals. Hence, the development of wireless sensor networks (WSNs) allows patient tracking in indoor environments and continuous monitoring in a pervasive healthcare environment provided the received signal strength is good.

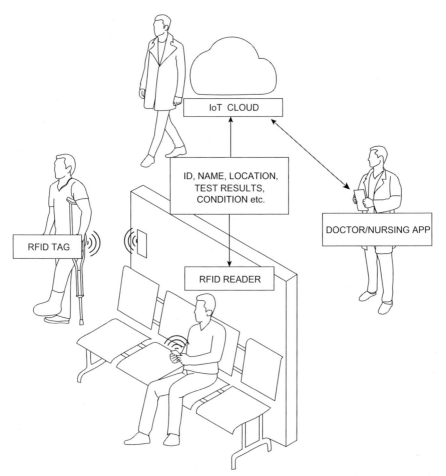

Figure 5.2 Design of an Internet-of-Things-(IoT) based system for a hospital environment employing radio frequency identification device (RFID) technology.

Hence, it can be concluded that a smart innovative healthcare system employing RFID, WSN, and a Global System for Mobile communication together can be developed to help in quick and safe monitoring of physiological parameters and automatic tracking of patients in hospitals. The system can collect vital patient information and promptly inform nursing staff through software applications designed for smartphones and tablets. For effective seamless framework integration, it is advised to develop WSN based on Constrained Application Protocol to connect and monitor a large number of patient sensors through resource observation in a real-time dynamic environment and automatic detection and configuration of available resources in the network. This allows mobile monitoring of a patient's healthcare condition and provides beneficial healthcare services [11].

IoT is evolving as an artificial intelligence tool that can assist older adults through the automatization of technologies to assist home-based care providers. The caregivers, when supported by technology, can deliver better assistance if an evidence-based artificial intelligence tool is available. It is quite beneficial in cases of multimorbidity conditions in aging adults. The assisted living environment comprises a body area network, local area network, and wide area network, which can trigger alarms in case of medical emergencies and allow evidence-based decision making through the supercomputing framework with the help of an Internet Cache Protocol [12].

6. Security features considered while designing and implementing IoT for healthcare

With the advent of IoT technology, data privacy and protection has gained prominence to avoid data leakage or abuse of information. However, several issues still need to be addressed with regard to the gathering of private patient information, its storage, and overall responsibility and management. Security is a major issue in the smooth implementation of IoT technology to avoid intrusion attacks, denial of services, malware attacks, network jamming, etc. Although the IoT utilizes effective resources and bandwidth to transmit medical records, it has fewer security features to avoid loss of medical information. As such, different homomorphic data encryption and cryptography techniques during confidential transportation of collected information had several issues when data was transferred over WSNs such as fast encryption and decryption techniques, fewer memory costs, and easy implementation in hardware and software. To overcome these problems, a homomorphic strategy based on the scrambling matrix and encryption algorithm can provide enhanced data security and privacy [7].

To overcome the security risk factors, different machine learning techniques and communication protocols are employed to eliminate the attacks on IoT devices during the exchange of medical information, thereby enhancing user privacy, security, and reliability of healthcare information employing IoT technology. It also allows for user authentication, malware detection, and access control by detecting affected nodes from source nodes using learning concepts. The different machine learning techniques can be classified as supervised, unsupervised, and reinforcement learning methodologies [11]. The different communication protocols used are User Datagram Protocol, Transmission Control Protocol, Hypertext Transfer Protocol, Simple Service Discovery Protocol, etc.

For the safe transmission of medical data employing IoT, user authentication can be initiated before the transaction. Postrequest, different signal features such as signal strength, channel impulse response, and channel state information are analyzed and extracted employing deep learning networks. This eliminates the risk of intermediate attacks in the IoT network and prevents unauthorized access to sensitive medical data. Deep learning also helps to reduce data leakage as it effectively learns device features and behavior. Hence, deep learning in combination with IoT allows safe transmission of medical data, keeping user privacy and confidentiality in the process [10].

7. Advantages and limitations of IoT for healthcare technology

Although IoT along with deep learning is an upcoming field in the area of healthcare technology, several challenges need to be addressed before its smooth implementation. The most crucial of these challenges is the enormous amount of patient data generated through the sensors. Hence, identifying relevant information and capturing it by employing smart BSNs is crucial. This allows the development of other fields such as artificial intelligence and machine learning. Furthermore, it is crucial to identify and optimize the amount of real-time data that needs to be transferred for diagnosis and patient care. If several devices are connected at one time in the IoT network, it would create a severe bottleneck and occupy available network resources. Therefore better computation algorithms and distribution of available resources are major areas of interest in the field, which can be developed quickly [12].

The next crucial challenge lies in the security and confidentiality of the medical data as it may be prone to misuse and manipulation. Hence, user authentication and identification is a crucial task in the field. The power consumption of devices may also lead to the rapid depletion of battery life and the availability of power at all times to recharge these devices. Hence, it is important to off-load certain tasks to a back-end server and save battery life and power required for in-house computing. This would help to expand the research domain by improving the computing abilities of present devices through decentralization.

Despite the challenges, IoT is playing a crucial role in the health sector by improving the efficiency and quality of healthcare service being provided. RFID tags record data anywhere and anytime from patients, clinical staff, hospital wards, and other locations conveniently. RFID tags interact with the hospital information system and allow automation of routine tasks such as patient admissions, discharges, transfer, etc., thereby assisting the hospital staff to provide safe, reliable, and good quality service to the patients and their care providers [12,13].

8. Discussions, conclusions, and future scope of IoT

IoT technology is revolutionizing every industry in the present era due to better information sharing and the use of appropriate communication technologies. These are being revolutionized from the interconnection of embedded computing devices to the interconnection of smart sensing devices. Employing technology to identify and improve the visibility of connected objects in a network allows continuous real-time monitoring, which has widespread applications in different industries, one of them being the healthcare sector. This has a large-scale impact on the health sector by way of useful research as well as realistic applications. However, the technology still requires further development with regard to fast processing, improving storage capabilities, and computational abilities to provide better services in the healthcare domain. With the help of artificial intelligence and deep learning techniques, IoT technology can be further enhanced by introducing human-like intelligence to smart healthcare frameworks [13,14]. This can help to improve decision making and the cognitive behavior of the devices in the network.

IoT technology and its associated infrastructure is evolving rapidly in the healthcare sector with the development of smart wearable devices and advanced communication technologies with cloud-based data analytics. Since a massive amount of medical data is generated in healthcare centers, it is crucial to follow appropriate mapping techniques for different applications of the IoT, which is the future of advancement in healthcare technologies and has potential challenges. Furthermore, it is important to understand that existence and reliance on these new technologies in complex, real-time, and heterogeneous situations could delay and slow communication networks that could severely compromise a patient's condition. Hence, the need for the development of advanced communication protocols, with improved architecture designs and very low data rate latency, is the need of the hour [13,14].

This chapter will help the reader to develop insights into the recent advancements in the field of healthcare technology by employing IoT technology and deep learning tools. It is a crucial service sector that is rapidly growing and cannot survive on traditional methods. Hence, it is undergoing modernization and digitization rapidly by employing IoT, deep learning, machine learning, artificial intelligence, and related technological tools to improve its working performance and provide benefits to its users (patients and clinicians) as well as associated service providers. However, these technologies have certain associated problems that need to be addressed to make them work better and provide the desired service quality levels [15]. The chapter focused on such technologies and their adoption and applicability in the healthcare sector.

IoT has largely benefited critically ill patients and the elderly population living alone who require continuous monitoring due to their diseased condition by tracking their health on a regular basis. This will allow any disturbances or changes in routine daily living activities to trigger an alarm to a family member or concerned healthcare provider for an immediate check on their condition and provide instant care and treatment to avoid any fatalities or long-term damage. The focus would be on the emergent healthcare technologies and their relevance for those who plan to visit various places for the treatment of specific diseases. Wellness tourism, which is an upcoming and developing concept, is being correlated with technologies and IoT and can be beneficial for the swift recovery of those who require healthcare services at affordable costs without comprising on quality [16,17]. Moreover, the advent of this area will provide a blueprint for practitioners and patients to offer or have the best possible remedial options around the world.

References

[1] P.M. Kumar, S. Lokesh, R. Varatharajan, G.C. Babu, P. Parthasarathy, Cloud and IoT based disease prediction and diagnosis system for healthcare using Fuzzy neural classifier, Future Gener. Comput. Syst. 86 (2018) 527–534. Elsevier.

[2] S. Qamar, A.M. Abdelrehman, H.E.A. Elshafie, K. Mohiuddin, Sensor-based IoT industrial healthcare systems, Int. J. Sci. Eng. Sci. 11 (2) (2018) 29–34.

[3] S.M. Kumar, D. Majumder, Healthcare solution based on machine learning applications in IoT and edge computing, Int. J. Pure Appl. Math. 119 (16) (2018) 1473–1484.

[4] M.S.H. Talpur, The appliance pervasive of Internet of Things in healthcare systems, Int. J. Comput. Sci. Issues (IJCSI) 10 (1) (2013) 1–6.

[5] Z. Liang, G. Zhang, J.X. Huang, Q.V. Hu, Deep learning for healthcare decision making with EMRs, in: IEEE International Conference on Bioinformatics and Biomedicine, 2014, pp. 556–559.

[6] L. Catarinucci, D. de Donno, L. Mainetti, L. Palano, L. Patrono, M.L. Stefanizzi, L. Tarricone, An IoT-aware architecture for smart healthcare systems, IEEE Int. Things 2 (6) (2015) 515–526.

[7] E. Balandina, S. Balandin, E. Balandina, Y. Koucheryavy, S. Balandin, D. Mouromtsev, IoT use cases in healthcare and tourism, in: IEEE 17th Conference on Business Informatics, 2015, pp. 37–44.

[8] T. Gong, H. Huang, P. Li, K. Zhang, H. Jiang, A medical healthcare system for privacy protection based on IoT, in: Seventh International Symposium on Parallel Architectures, Algorithms and Programming, 2015, pp. 217–222.

[9] M.M. Alam, H. Malik, M.I. Khan, T. Pardy, A. Kuusik, Y.L. Moullec, A survey on the roles of communication technologies in IoT-based personalized healthcare applications, IEEE Access 6 (1) (2018) 36611–36631.

[10] S.U. Amin, M.S. Hossain, G. Muhammad, M. Alhussein, Md.A. Rahman, Cognitive smart healthcare for pathology detection and monitoring, IEEE Access 7 (1) (2019) 10745–10753.

[11] M. Alhussein, G. Muhammad, M.S. Hossain, S.U. Amin, Cognitive IoT-cloud integration: case study for smart healthcare: case study for epileptic seizure detection and monitoring, Mobile Netw. Appl. 23 (2018) 1624–1635.

[12] C. Fonseca, D. Mendes, M. Lopes, A. Romão, P. Parreira, Deep learning and IoT to assist multimorbidity home based healthcare, J. Health Med. Inf. 8 (3) (2017) 1–4.

[13] D.M.J. Priyadharsan, K.K. Sanjay, S. Kathiresan, K.K. Karthik, K.S. Prasath, Patient health monitoring using IoT with machine learning", Int. Res. J. Eng. Technol. 6 (3) (2019) 7514–7520.

[14] P.M. Shakeel, S. Baskar, V.R.S. Dhulipala, S. Mishra, M.M. Jaber, Maintaining security and privacy in health care system using learning-based deep-Q-networks, J. Med. Syst. 42 (186) (2018) 1–10.

[15] D.J.M. Mendes, I.P. Rodrigues, C.F. Baeta, C. Solano-Rodriguez, Extended clinical discourse representation structure for controlled natural language clinical decision support systems, Int. J. Reliab. Qual. E-Healthc. 4 (2015) 1–11.

[16] M. Cocosila, N. Archer, Adoption of mobile ICT for health promotion: an empirical investigation, Electron. Mark. 20 (2010) 241–250.

[17] D. Bhatia, A. Mishra, A novel artificial intelligence technique for analysis of real-time electro-cardiogram signal for the prediction of early cardiac ailment onset, in: Handbook of research on advancements of artificial intelligence in healthcare engineering, IGI Global, 2020, ISBN 9781799821205, pp. 42–66 (Chapter 3).

CHAPTER 6

Deep learning methodology proposal for the classification of erythrocytes and leukocytes

Ana Carolina Borges Monteiro[1], Yuzo Iano[1],
Reinaldo Padilha França[1], Rangel Arthur[2]

[1]School of Electrical Engineering and Computing (FEEC) — State University of Campinas (UNICAMP), Campinas, São Paulo, Brazil; [2]Faculty of Technology (FT) — State University of Campinas (UNICAMP), Limeira, São Paulo, Brazil

1. Introduction

One of the areas of medicine benefiting most from technological advances is the diagnosis of blood smear digital imaging diseases, in which, since the first discoveries and research in this area, it has become easier to diagnose pathologies and establish the best management for each case. Since the scenario of digital imaging diagnosis of blood smears portrays constant evolution and improvement, encompassing conventional methodologies, ceasing to be applied only with its conventional foundations and gaining space in the electronic field, generating evolution, makes it this is the innovation with the best practical performance [1—3].

Blood smear imaging diagnostic methods are constantly renewing and incorporating new technologies; therefore the earlier the diagnosis, the greater the chances of curing patients. Consequently, imaging studies for complementary examinations and detection are important for effective disease prevention [4—12].

Performing a digital smear diagnosis of blood smears can be seen as one of the strategies to identify pathological nuances and direct the conduct of clinical professionals, and these tests also follow the evolution of clinical interventions already performed to show improvements or identify complications in diseases already diagnosed. Thus interdisciplinarity has been responsible for solving several problems in medical areas, because many of these are derived from the use of engineering techniques. One problem that affects a large part of the world's population is difficult access to good health, often caused by a lack of financial resources [13,14].

Trends in Deep Learning Methodologies
ISBN 978-0-12-822226-3
https://doi.org/10.1016/B978-0-12-822226-3.00006-4

Annually, 257,000 people in the world are diagnosed with leukemia. Leukemia is classified as a disorder in the production of blood cells inside the bone marrow, and can be triggered from genetic factors to external factors such as chemical agents and radiation. Its main laboratory finding is the presence of blast cells in the bloodstream, which can be easily detected by a hemogram, and early diagnosis is of great importance for an acceptable cure rate [7,15,16].

Treating a disease properly and detecting it early are equally important. It is undeniable that in recent times medicine has made great strides in both treatment and diagnosis. Much of this progress was due to the inter-disciplinarity between the areas of engineering and health, which were responsible for the present-day creation of tools of great value such as computed tomography, magnetic resonance, and ultrasound, among other medical equipment. However, developing new methodologies does not guarantee that all people have access to quality service, since quality is often a quantity directly proportional to the cost of the methodology [17,18].

Artificial intelligence has increasingly been able to bridge the gap between the abilities of machines and humans, performing well in many areas, such as computer vision. Advances in this area brought about by deep learning have been improved over time, especially the use of a particular algorithm, convolutional neural networks (CNNs) [19,20].

The commitment of this science is to allow machines to see and understand the world as humans do, and to use knowledge to perform a huge number of tasks such as image analysis, recognition and classification, language processing, and media recreation, among others. Machine learning is a technology area within artificial intelligence, as illustrated in Fig. 6.1, intended for the creation and enhancement of techniques and algorithms that grant the computer the ability to learn, with a strong connection with big data. This is the basis of predictive analysis, which is the use of data, techniques of machine learning, and statistical algorithms for the purpose of identifying the likelihood of future results and answers. It briefly creates algorithms capable of learning a compact representation of data, and predicting or generalizing patterns of unknown data from a known training set [21,22].

Deep learning is a component of machine learning, where its paradigm is to enable the computer to learn from data observation, mimicking the layered activity of human neurons. This technology is an advanced technique that allows artificial neural networks to learn, as illustrated in Fig. 6.2, making the computer "think, learn, and act" like a human being [23,24].

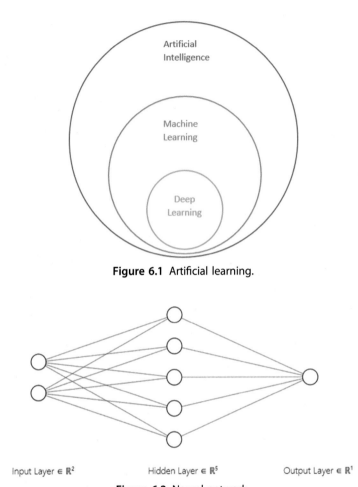

Figure 6.1 Artificial learning.

Input Layer $\in \mathbf{R}^2$ Hidden Layer $\in \mathbf{R}^5$ Output Layer $\in \mathbf{R}^1$

Figure 6.2 Neural network.

In this context, quantitative and qualitative evaluation of blood cells is an important parameter used to detect suspect pathologies, whether hematological or infectious. Considering that laboratory medical examinations are often costly and inaccessible to populations of underdeveloped and developing countries, it is of great importance to create tools that facilitate the obtaining of medical reports at low cost and of high reliability [25,26].

The present study aims to develop an algorithm that is able to perform the detection and classification of leukocytes through personal computers, conceiving a methodology more achievable to diverse populations. For this, Python 3.7 using a Jupyter notebook was developed. The experiments were conducted using a dataset containing 12,500 digital images of human blood smear fields, including nonpathological leukocytes. As a result, the accuracy of the approach was 86.17%, demonstrating the high reliability of the methodology.

In this way, the proposed methodology can be seen as the initial step for the development of blood classification from simple everyday tools, such as a computer, bringing benefits not only to patients through high-quality exams but also to medical professionals through an easy-to-use methodology that may even propel them to entrepreneurship.

2. Hematology background

Present throughout the body, blood, as well as everything that performs functions in the body, can also be afflicted by disease, so hematology is the area of medicine that studies all blood-related components of platelets, white blood cells, and red blood cells. It also investigates the organs where blood is produced, such as the spleen, lymph nodes, and bone marrow [1−3].

Hematology is a science that studies the histological structure, chemical composition, and physical properties of blood, the part of medicine that deals with diseases of the blood and hematopoietic organs. It deals with patients who have blood disorders and disorders of the tissues and organs that produce blood, and analyzes the quantitative and morphological variations of the figurative elements of blood. It is a subspecialty of internal medicine focused on the morphology, physiology, and pathology of blood and blood-forming tissues [27,28].

Blood, bone marrow, spleen, and lymph nodes are studied in the medical specialty of hematology. Blood is essential for life because it is responsible for carrying oxygen, hormones, nutrients, white cells, platelets, and various substances around the whole body. Blood consists of plasma and cells. Plasma is mostly protein and water. Blood cells have different functions. White blood cells or leukocytes perform the body's defense, platelets are responsible for coagulation, and red blood cells carry proteins to nourish the body. Each of these in the correct amount constitutes a healthy body; however, the lack or excess of these cells indicates that something is wrong. Blood count is the examination that gives this information together with clinical evaluation [29,30].

Red blood cells (erythrocytes) are blood cells responsible for carrying hemoglobin. They are also in charge of transporting oxygen from the lungs to the tissues and removing carbon dioxide to be eliminated by the lungs; they are the most common genus of cells observed in the blood, with every cubic millimeter of human blood comprising 4—6 million cells. Red blood cells are small enough to squeeze into the smallest blood vessels, and can circulate around the body for up to 120 days. They have a diameter of only 6 μm, and after the 120-day time period old or damaged red blood cells are withdrawn from circulation by specific cells, called macrophages, which are produced in the liver and spleen [31,32].

White blood cells (leukocytes) are in charge of defending the human body against infectious agents such as viruses or bacteria and also protect it from foreign substances. To properly defend the body, a sufficient amount of white blood cells must go where they are needed to kill and digest harmful organisms and substances. White blood cells come in different sizes and shapes. Some cells contain a large round nucleus, while others have nuclei with multiple lobes. Leukocytes contain granulocytes, which are bundles of granules in their cytoplasm. Like all blood cells, leukocytes are produced in the bone marrow. They originate from stem cells. Stem cells differentiate and mature into one of five major types: neutrophils, eosinophils, basophils, monocytes, and lymphocyte/leukocytes, as exemplified in Fig. 6.3. All types of white blood cells play a role in the body's immune response, despite their differences in appearance. They have an important

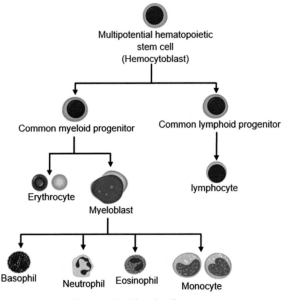

Figure 6.3 Blood cell types.

function in the body, which is to circulate in the blood until they receive a signal that a body part is damaged [10,33,34].

Platelets are pieces of large cells that make up the blood clotting system and act to prevent bleeding. They have a low platelet count in the blood. The reduced number of platelets may be due to a lack of production, use of certain drugs, or destruction [34].

On average there are 6 L of blood in an adult person's body. The blood leads nutrients and oxygen to live cells still removing their waste. Besides providing the ability of immune cells to cope with infections, it must be borne in mind that platelets have the ability to plug a damaged blood vessel to prevent blood loss. The circulatory system powered by the heart that pumps faster and faster provides more blood and therefore takes oxygen to the muscles, so the blood adapts to the body's needs. Regarding infection, the blood supplies more immune cells to the site of infection, accumulating and thus preventing harmful invaders [35−37].

Blood can be separated into two layers: plasma, which forms about 60% of blood; and another from cells like platelets, leukocytes, and erythrocytes, where these last two cell types represent two lower cell layers forming about 40% of blood. Plasma is mostly water; however, it also contains substances such as sugars (glucose), proteins (antibodies, enzymes, albumin, clotting factors, and hormones), and fat particles. All cells localized in the blood originate from the bone marrow, starting their life as stem cells and maturing into three major cell types: red blood cells, white blood cells, and platelets [38].

Through specific blood tests, it is possible to discover if there are any blood components from cells to nutrients that are altered and that may be causing different health problems; these tests are conducted in a hematology laboratory. Among the diseases treated are anemia, hemophilia, and sickle cell disease; however, this specialty is closely linked to oncology, because it can diagnose and treat lymphoma, leukemia, and myeloma cancers. The treatment plan for malignant cases may involve chemotherapy, radiotherapy, or bone marrow transplantation [39−41].

Thus hematology involves both the body's production of blood and the evaluation of all components that form and are involved with this fluid, including blood cells, bone marrow, veins, and free circulating substances. Blood testing is one of the simplest medical procedures and provides a lot of information for doctors about the health of patients. The blood count, in particular, describes in detail the condition of the cellular portion of the blood [5,40].

3. Deep learning concepts

With the evolution of computer science, artificial intelligence has also developed, with intelligent devices showing much progress in the area of computer analysis. Looking at its history, artificial intelligence research was meant to replicate the human way of thinking, but with the findings made during studies, it was realized that this science could go much further and develop electronic devices with greater capabilities such as self-improvement and the use of language recognition. Studies to develop artificial intelligence in machines are still incipient but the influence of technology in several sectors, such as health, agriculture, industry, and others, has already been noted [22,23].

Machine learning, as illustrated in Fig. 6.4, is a way of improving artificial intelligence. It is defined as the use of a series of algorithms for collecting, analyzing, and learning from system interactions, usually done together and supported by big data. It is also a combination of techniques, methods, and algorithms that improve the performance of software or hardware as they acquire more data, meaning that it learns from historical information and can predict future behaviors [19,23].

The concept of deep learning, as illustrated in Fig. 6.5, consists of learning through the implementation of neural networks, being a machine learning technique. Broadly speaking, deep learning makes artificial intelligence applicable and is extremely effective because it achieves a performance very close to humans [42].

One of the techniques used by deep learning is artificial neural networks, which is how the machine learns. It was developed similarly to the way brain neurons work, as well as using statistical techniques such as Bayesian hypotheses, decision trees, various regression tools, etc. Deep learning is a concept that is becoming increasingly relevant in the field of artificial intelligence, and is a subarea of machine learning that uses types and classes of neural networks to learn speech recognition, computer vision, and natural language processing, which are its main fields of activity [43,44].

Deep learning stands out compared to machine learning, because rather than being a system interconnecting with the various branches of the neuron, it analyzes the discrete layers of the artificial neural network, existing connections, and data directions. In addition to adopting the concept of layers, each layer consists of hidden units that perform mathematical operations to define which will be activated or not [45,46].

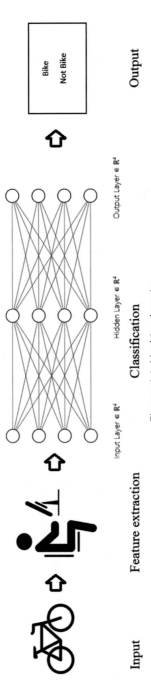

Figure 6.4 Machine learning.

Feature extraction + Classification

Figure 6.5 Deep learning.

In an image context, each attribute of this image can be recognized by a different neuron and each neuron will be assigned a percentage indicating the possibility of what this image may be, according to your prior knowledge. The end result of this system will be the junction of all the conclusions of the artificial neurons about what the particular image is, working with a probability vector, which calculates the percentages that have been attributed to it [47,48].

This exemplified context means that the more deep layers the neurons have, the more deep learning technology can provide solutions to increasingly complex questions. This underlines the literary meaning of "deep" which is directly linked to the number of layers that make up a neural network. Correspondingly, the more levels there are, the deeper the learning and the greater the ability to provide complex solutions [49].

Deep learning technology has helped to advance many areas of knowledge, as well as the development of several solutions, bringing significant advances to artificial intelligence, especially voice recognition, translation, and object perception. This practical and real development is already being used to improve advertising campaigns, filter spam, and recognize image and voice patterns, as well as analyze feelings expressed through texts on social networks, predict equipment failures, and detect fraud, among others. In addition it allows the creation of several practical applications for artificial intelligence, such as the development of autonomous cars and automated health diagnostics to support doctors [50].

Deep learning makes it possible to analyze a large volume of data, and to learn from it through algorithms that can predict future scenarios faster and more securely than humans do.

The advantage of deep learning algorithms lies in their ability to learn large amounts of data in a way that does not need to be supervised, such as machine learning, thus it is a valuable tool for big data where most data of this nature, also referred to as unstructured data, requires no further processing as in the case of machine learning. In this way, machines that apply the technique can learn complex abstractions of data through a hierarchical learning process very similar to what happens with the human brain [51,52].

Deep learning presents an innovative approach as it dispenses with much of the preprocessing by automatically generating invariant properties in its hierarchical representation layers, producing great results in different applications, including computer vision. This is ideal for medicine because deep learning algorithms allow the implementation of computer-aided artificial intelligence detection tools that can be integrated with archived images, which is very useful for tomography, magnetic resonance, and X-ray, as well as others that need to evaluate digital imaging results in a short time [21,42,47].

In short, machine learning, which is one of the consequences of artificial intelligence that enables the system to analyze data, makes predictions and learns without human interference during the process. Deep learning, in contrast, is a deepening of machine learning. This system has a different learning process and enables the analysis of voice and images, for example, expanding the ability of artificial intelligence to act [53].

4. Convolutional neural network

Image recognition is a definitive classification problem, and CNNs, as illustrated in Fig. 6.6, have a history of high accuracy for this problem. Basically, the main essence of a CNN is to filter lines, curves, and edges and in each layer to transform this filtering into a more complex image, making recognition easier [54].

A CNN is a deep learning algorithm able to capture a digital input image and carries relevance such as weight and bias to various features and objects of the image, which have the ability to differentiate each other, since, for a computer, a digital image is simply an array of pixel values [55].

The structure of convolutional networks consists of three main objectives: *feature extraction*, since from a receptive field of the previous layer each neuron receives input signals, allowing the extraction of local features, and making the exact position of each feature, the pixel, irrelevant, while its position related to neighboring characteristics is maintained. *Mapping characteristics*, since each computational layer of the network is composed of several characteristic maps that are regions where neurons share the same synaptic weights, called filters or kernels, giving the model robustness, and making it able to handle variations in image distortion, rotation, and translation. This is connected to *subsampling*; after each convolution layer a subsampling layer is applied, which is nothing more than a sampling of each feature map. This operation can be performed by averaging, by obtaining the sum, or by max pooling or min pooling the value of the region under analysis [56].

A pooling layer serves to simplify information from the previous layer. As with convolution, one unit of area is chosen. The most widely used method is max pooling, where only the largest number of units is passed to the output, serving to decrease the number of weights to be learned and

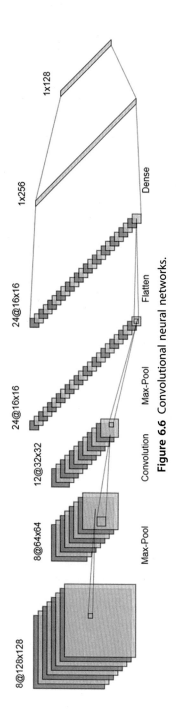

Figure 6.6 Convolutional neural networks.

also to avoid overfitting. Regarding image recognition and classification, the inputs are usually three-dimensional arrays with height and width relating to image dimensions and depth, determined by the number of color channels using the three channels, RGB, with the values of each pixel [45,53,54].

Convolutions work as filters that see small squares and "slip" all over the image capturing the most striking features. Convolution in reality, and in simple terms, is a mathematical operation applied to two functions to obtain a third. The depth of the output of a convolution is equal to the number of filters applied; the deeper the layers of the convolutions, the more detailed are the traces identified. The filter, or kernel, is made up of randomly initialized weights, which are updated with each new entry during the process [50,57].

Applications of a CNN in images are generally classification, assigning object categories to an image; detection with respect to the location of multiple objects (multiple bounding boxes and labels); location around the target object; as well as segmentation through contouring and labeling of the object of interest [58].

In addition to the filter size and the convolution stride as a hyperparameter, it is necessary to choose what the padding will look like, which serves to avoid the layers from shrinking much faster than is required for learning. This may be null, where the output of the convolution will be at its original size, or zero pad, which concerns where a border is added and filled with 0s. The preprocessing necessary in a CNN is much smaller compared with other classification techniques. In outdated methods filters are done literally by logic and manual implementation; however, a CNN has the ability to learn these filters alone or with features, and its architecture is similar to that of the neuron connection pattern in the human brain [55,56].

The novelty of CNN is the possibility and competence to learn automatically from a huge amount of filters in parallel specific performing training on a dataset under the limitations of a given predictive modeling problem, such as image recognition and classification, where its results are highly specific resources [58].

5. Scientific review

In 2011 the need was investigated for machine vision methods with the ability to extract information with details from imaging tests and active learning processes to overcome the dimensionality problem in drug development through the study of complex biological systems and this meant that advanced machine learning strategies would be crucial for drug development [59].

In 2012 it was shown that transcription optimizers could enhance/integrate the collaboration of various types of transcription factors (TFs) by orchestrating the numerous spatiotemporal gene expression applications during development. It was found that a molecular conception of optimizers with similar actions was required to identify shared and unique string resources. In this DNA-based context, the transcription factor binding site (TFBS) was analyzed, which governed the rewriting of a coexpressed gene pool, and the creation of phylogenetic profiles with an enhancer sequence classifier was combined. A small number of active enhancers were then assembled into the founding cells of *Drosophila melanogaster* muscles (CFs) just like other mesodermal cell categories. And employing the phylogenetic profile, the number of optimizers integrating orthologous, however, divergent sequences from other *Drosophila* species were increased. In practical experiments, even though there is an extensive evolutionary change in known TFBSs, it was revealed that divergent intensifying orthologs were active in patterns broadly similar to those of *D. melanogaster*. A classifier was then constructed and trained using this set of enhancers and complementary related optimizers identified based on the absence or presence of TFBSs. Finally, extensive variety in the formation of TFBSs was discovered within CF optimizers, revealing that combination plays a fundamental role in the cellular characteristics presented by the optimizers. So, machine learning linked with evolutionary sequencing analysis has been shown to facilitate the recognition of cognate TFs that determine cell-type-specific development of gene expression patterns as well as being useful for recognizing new TFBSs [60].

In 2013, an in-depth learning structure for the automatic detection of basal cell carcinoma cancer was presented and evaluated, integrating image representation learning, image classification, and interpretation of results. It expanded the deep learning structure to include an understandable layer that highlights the visual patterns contributing to the discrimination of normal and carcinogenic tissue patterns, with execution similar to digital coloring that highlights important regions of the image for decision making. A set of 1417 images derived from 308 regions of interest of skin histopathology slides was used to determine the presence and absence of basal cell carcinoma. Different image representation strategies were evaluated for comparison, including Haar-based wavelet transform, discrete cosine transform, resource bag (bag of features [BOF]), and representations learned from the data. The results showed that there was an improvement of about 3% related to the corresponding BOF representation and 7% related to canonical representations, which were derived from a large set of histological imaging data highlighting the performance (91.4% in balanced accuracy and 89.4% in the F-measure) [61].

In 2014, a segmentation method based on a superpixel and CNN was developed to segment cervical cancer cells. Because cytoplasm and background contrast were not clear, cytoplasm segmentation was performed, with CNN-based deep learning explored for detection of regions of interest, and coarse-to-fine nucleus segmentation was developed for cell segmentation cervical cancer and best improvement. Results showed that an accuracy of 0.9143 ± 0.0202, just like 94.50% to core region detection, and a recovery of 0.8726 ± 0.0008 for core cell segmentation were achieved, and through thorough comparative analysis it was shown that the developed method surpassed the relative methods [62].

In 2015 it was shown that the administration of small pulmonary nodules observed on computed tomography (CT) was conflicting due to the uncertain properties of the tumor resulting in a poor prognosis of lung cancer when early and unresectable lesions were not diagnosed. However, a traditional computer-aided diagnostic (CAD) scheme required pattern recognition and various image processing phases to obtain a quantitative result of tumor recognition and differentiation. In this ad hoc image analysis pipeline, each step was dependent on the execution of the previous step, and adjusting classification in a traditional CAD structure was very laborious. Deep learning methods have been found to have an intrinsic advantage of uniform performance tuning and an automatic scanning feature. The study simplified the conventional CAD image analysis pipeline with deep learning techniques, introducing modeling of a CNN and a deep belief network, in the scope of nodule recognition and classification in CT images. Two baseline procedures with resource computation steps were also employed for comparison, and results suggested that deep learning techniques can produce improved promising and classifying results in the CAD application environment [63].

In 2016 it was seen that unlabeled cell analysis was fundamental for specific genomics, drug development, and cancer diagnosis, avoiding implications of staining reagents on cell signaling and viability. However, nowadays available unlabeled cell tests are not sufficiently differentiated and rely primarily on a single resource, taking into account that the sample size analyzed is limited regarding its low yield. In this sense, deep learning and resource extraction with high-yield quantitative images, made possible by the photonic period of time, reached high accuracy in the classification of unlabeled cells. The system captured quantitative phase and optical intensity images by extracting various biophysical resources from cells, where biophysical measurements formed a hyperdimensional characteristic space where supervised learning could be employed for cell classification. Several learning techniques were also compared, encompassing artificial neural network, support vector machine, logistic regression, and a new deep learning pipeline, which adopted the overall optimization of receiver operating peculiarities. The classification of leukocyte T cells against colon cancer cells was shown, and the sensitivity and specificity of the developed system were validated and algal strains that accumulate lipids for biofuel production were analyzed. The system, implemented according to the authors, generated a better comprehension of heterogeneous gene expressions in these cells and opened a new way for data-based phenotypic diagnosis [64].

In 2017 it was shown that deep CNN bound with nonlinear dimension reduction can provide the reconstruction of biological processes related to raw image data. Jurkat cell cycle reconstruction and disease advancement in diabetic retinopathy have been demonstrated, where a further examination of Jurkat cells detected and separated an unsupervised dead cell subpopulation. By generating discrete stage classification of the cell cycle, a sixfold decrease in error rate was achieved compared to a current approach regarding enhanced imaging capabilities. Deep learning predictions are fast for on-the-fly analysis on an image flow cytometer as seen in contrast to previous research methods [65].

In 2018, one of the indispensable procedures employed by pathologists to evaluate the stage, subtype, and type of lung tumors, as well as visual inspection of histopathological slides, was studied. Squamous cell carcinoma of the lung (LUSC) and lung adenocarcinoma (LUAD) are the most predominant subtypes of lung cancer, and their differentiation requires visual inspection by an experienced pathologist because of their complexity. In this context, a deep CNN was implemented and trained in full slide images acquired from the Cancer Genome Atlas with a focus on precision and automatic classification in LUSC and LUAD, or healthy lung tissue. The network performance was analogous to that of pathologists. With a mean area below the curve area under the curve (AUC) of 0.97, the model approved on independent embedded tissue, frozen tissue, and paraffin and biopsy datasets. It was also possible to perform network training to predict the 10 most common mutated genes in LUAD, and it was noticed that six of them, FAT1, SETBP1, STK11, KRAS, EGFR, and TP53, can have a prediction from digital pathology images, with an AUC of 0.733—0.856 according to measurement in an isolated population. The results suggest that deep learning models have features to help pathologists detect genetic mutations or lung cancer subtypes [66].

In 2019 it was shown that in developing and underdeveloped countries, breast cancer was the main cause of death in women, but its classification and detection in the early stages allowed patients to receive appropriate medication and treatment. In this context, a deep learning framework was proposed for the classification and detection of breast cancer focused on digital breast cytology images implementing the logic of transfer learning . Deep learning architectures are built for problem-specific purposes and are executed separately, in contrast to the traditional learning paradigms that were developed and produced separately. Thus transfer learning has the purpose of using the knowledge acquired in the course of the resolution of a problem embedded in another problem. In the deep learning framework, the resources of the images were extracted through pretrained CNN architectures, visual geometry cluster networks, residual networks, and GoogLeNet, and then fed into a fully connected layer to classify benign cells. and malignant with the use of average pool ratings. For performance evaluation, experiments were performed on standard reference datasets, noting that the presented structure surpassed all other deep learning architectures in the matter of tumor classification and accuracy in breast tumor detection in cytology images [67].

6. Methodology proposal

A blood cell count and detection [68] dataset consisting of 12,500 enlarged blood cell images subdivided into four cell morphology-related classes, monocytes, lymphocytes, neutrophils, and eosinophils, with a chained denial logic for basophil classification, was used with 2400 images for training, as shown in Figs. 6.7, and 6.8 more classes using 600 images for testing.

Kera's environment with Python 3.7 language, with the structure developed on a Jupyter notebook version 0.35.4 on a hardware platform composed of an Intel Core i3 processor with 4 GB of RAM, was used to

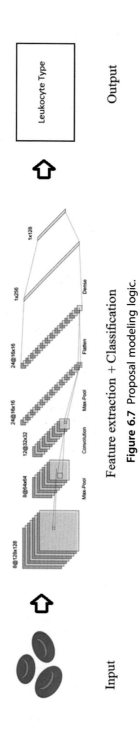

Figure 6.7 Proposal modeling logic.

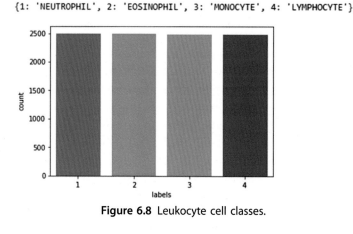

Figure 6.8 Leukocyte cell classes.

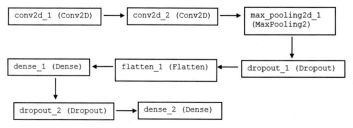

Figure 6.9 Convolutional neural network architecture.

perform the training. To facilitate or train each image the size was reduced to $60 \times 80 \times 3$ and loaded as numerical arrays in the neural network, or using Kera's libraries for preprocessing such images as methods and objects for dataset processing. Thus a CNN was constructed, which is a particular class of neural network commonly used for image classification, which contains a set of convolution layers and a feed-forward network connected to it.

The dataset was a composite of color images of cells represented by a three-dimensional matrix, as previously stated, storing a combination of red, green, and blue colors. Thus the CNN had its main role in shaping convolution operations to extract edges from an image used to extract important resources from cell images. This is a difficult process, and it is not possible for a simple network to learn the unique resources present in each class of the cell dataset that was worked and processed. The CNN architecture used is shown in Fig. 6.9.

7. Results and discussion

As stated earlier, the model was run on a hardware structure consisting of a 4 GB RAM Intel Core i3 processor. The model was then trained for 40 epoch seasons and reached an accuracy of 86.17%, as can be seen in Fig. 6.10, which is a relevant result due to the complexity of the structure.

To validate the accuracy obtained by the network, Fig. 6.11 was analyzed according to the trained CNN model, confirming the network's accuracy and learning in classifying the cell in the image as a leukocyte, monocyte type, as can be seen in Fig. 6.12.

The area of medical diagnosis has evolved significantly over the years, and artificial intelligence has brought about technological advancement with more space and high growth in healthcare. Thus new methodologies for examinations of this nature with new technologies such as deep learning increasingly help medicine in the discovery and classification of diseases, bringing greater security to both doctors and patients for better treatment.

Being fully linked to the technological advancement of the modern world, the diversity of technology-assisted examinations has enabled medical specialists to visualize more accurately and have greater certainty of diagnosis than without this technology. Thus in parallel with this technological evolution, which offers the best in new methodologies to help medicine and generate better welfare for patients, the detection of diseases and consequently the increase in chances of better treatment have become easier.

Advances in imaging technology have been essential to the development of medicine. The evolution of the use of imaging in medical treatment has been so significant in imaging diagnosis, aiding in the accuracy of its outcome. Also, diagnoses of major, serious, and frequent diseases such as sinusitis, brain clots, and breast and bowel cancer can be analyzed by imaging. Images have also been helpful at other times, and are essential in tracking the evolution of certain diseases, such as cancer progression.

The results achieved in this study are promising for medical areas. Sections of the world population live in situations of extreme poverty, with little or no government assistance. This includes those with poor incomes and the homeless. The vast majority of pathologies are more likely to be cured when discovered at the early stages. Thus this method can be seen as a technique that solves problems, such as blood tests and procedures that have fewer side effects. This is because traditionally blood cell count is dependent

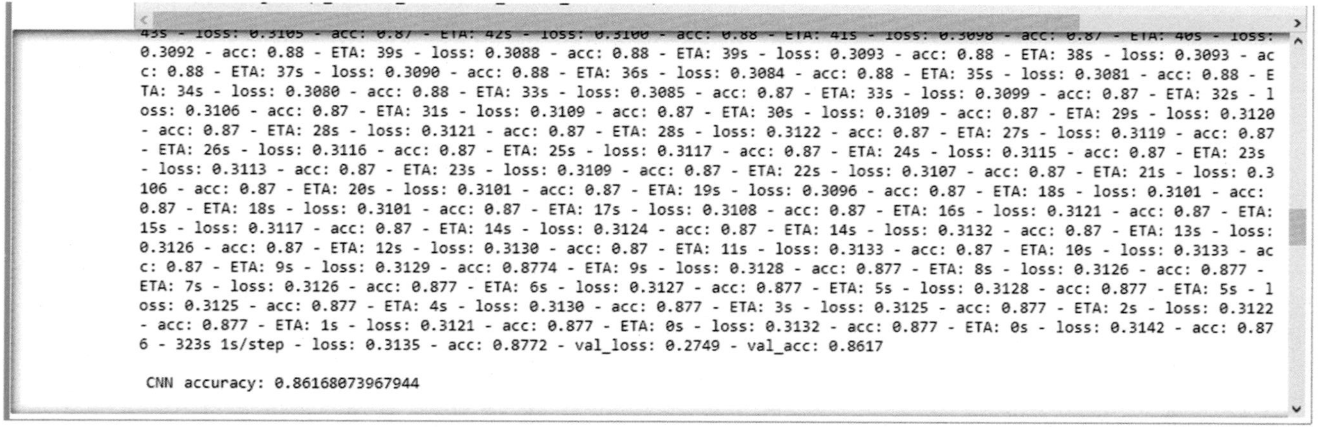

```
...3s - loss: 0.3105 - acc: 0.87 - ETA: 42s - loss: 0.3100 - acc: 0.88 - ETA: 41s - loss: 0.3098 - acc: 0.87 - ETA: 40s - loss:
0.3092 - acc: 0.88 - ETA: 39s - loss: 0.3088 - acc: 0.88 - ETA: 39s - loss: 0.3093 - acc: 0.88 - ETA: 38s - loss: 0.3093 - ac
c: 0.88 - ETA: 37s - loss: 0.3090 - acc: 0.88 - ETA: 36s - loss: 0.3084 - acc: 0.88 - ETA: 35s - loss: 0.3081 - acc: 0.88 - E
TA: 34s - loss: 0.3080 - acc: 0.88 - ETA: 33s - loss: 0.3085 - acc: 0.87 - ETA: 33s - loss: 0.3099 - acc: 0.87 - ETA: 32s - l
oss: 0.3106 - acc: 0.87 - ETA: 31s - loss: 0.3109 - acc: 0.87 - ETA: 30s - loss: 0.3109 - acc: 0.87 - ETA: 29s - loss: 0.3120
 - acc: 0.87 - ETA: 28s - loss: 0.3121 - acc: 0.87 - ETA: 28s - loss: 0.3122 - acc: 0.87 - ETA: 27s - loss: 0.3119 - acc: 0.87
 - ETA: 26s - loss: 0.3116 - acc: 0.87 - ETA: 25s - loss: 0.3117 - acc: 0.87 - ETA: 24s - loss: 0.3115 - acc: 0.87 - ETA: 23s
 - loss: 0.3113 - acc: 0.87 - ETA: 23s - loss: 0.3109 - acc: 0.87 - ETA: 22s - loss: 0.3107 - acc: 0.87 - ETA: 21s - loss: 0.3
106 - acc: 0.87 - ETA: 20s - loss: 0.3101 - acc: 0.87 - ETA: 19s - loss: 0.3096 - acc: 0.87 - ETA: 18s - loss: 0.3101 - acc:
0.87 - ETA: 18s - loss: 0.3101 - acc: 0.87 - ETA: 17s - loss: 0.3108 - acc: 0.87 - ETA: 16s - loss: 0.3121 - acc: 0.87 - ETA:
15s - loss: 0.3117 - acc: 0.87 - ETA: 14s - loss: 0.3124 - acc: 0.87 - ETA: 14s - loss: 0.3132 - acc: 0.87 - ETA: 13s - loss:
0.3126 - acc: 0.87 - ETA: 12s - loss: 0.3130 - acc: 0.87 - ETA: 11s - loss: 0.3133 - acc: 0.87 - ETA: 10s - loss: 0.3133 - ac
c: 0.87 - ETA: 9s - loss: 0.3129 - acc: 0.8774 - ETA: 9s - loss: 0.3128 - acc: 0.877 - ETA: 8s - loss: 0.3126 - acc: 0.877 -
ETA: 7s - loss: 0.3126 - acc: 0.877 - ETA: 6s - loss: 0.3127 - acc: 0.877 - ETA: 5s - loss: 0.3128 - acc: 0.877 - ETA: 5s - l
oss: 0.3125 - acc: 0.877 - ETA: 4s - loss: 0.3130 - acc: 0.877 - ETA: 3s - loss: 0.3125 - acc: 0.877 - ETA: 2s - loss: 0.3122
 - acc: 0.877 - ETA: 1s - loss: 0.3121 - acc: 0.877 - ETA: 0s - loss: 0.3132 - acc: 0.877 - ETA: 0s - loss: 0.3142 - acc: 0.87
6 - 323s 1s/step - loss: 0.3135 - acc: 0.8772 - val_loss: 0.2749 - val_acc: 0.8617

CNN accuracy: 0.8616808739967944
```

Figure 6.10 Convolutional neural network accuracy.

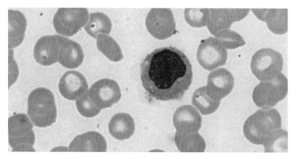

Figure 6.11 Monocyte test image.

Figure 6.12 Convolutional neural network monocyte classification.

on high-cost hematological equipment and specific reagents that restrict the ability to purchase from resellers to users [4,8,9].

Through blood cell counting by methods related to deep learning, counts can be made via computer or cell phone, with the entire process of counting and identifying cells being managed on a cloud platform. Considering the execution of cloud computing, it must be considered that examinations may be performed by low-cost methodologies that avoid locking the devices due to incompatibility with the operating system [5,7,10].

In addition to the cost, we must consider that, in mainly underdeveloped and developing countries, cell counting and the entire preparation of biological materials for analysis are the sole responsibility of human beings. Such methodology presents much lower costs when compared with automated methodologies. However, we must consider that humans are subject to errors, especially when we consider that many health professionals may be subject to long working hours and inadequate remuneration. Thus tiredness and dissatisfaction are two drawbacks of the reliability of tests performed manually [11].

Using the methodology presented in this study formedical routine is synonymous with reliability and low cost for less-favored populations and also for populations in developed countries. In the scenario of populations with a more advantageous economic situation, our methodology can be used as a confirmatory tool for the results of counts that are outside the reference values [6].

Naturally, when the patient has leukocytosis (an increase in the total amount of leukocytes per cubic millimeter of blood), the presence of infection or inflammation is suspected. In this case, the professional usually reconfirms this change by manual methods. Knowing that the greater the accuracy, the greater the reliability of the examination, exchanging manual methodology for a technique that employs deep learning decreases the possibility of false-positive and false-negative tests in medical routines [12].

8. Conclusions

Through dataset training, it was seen that the deep learning structure developed in Python for learning white cells obtained excellent results with 86.17% accuracy. This was due to the complexity of the studied problem and obtaining a satisfactory performance, because of the accuracy in the classification of cells, which is crucial during the completion of laboratory diagnosis.

With respect to the CNN developed, the deep learning structure implemented was effective in detecting and differentiating blood cell subtypes, where it can be concluded that the structure modeling parameters allowed a good distinction in the classification between different blood subtypes. As can be noted, the positive exploitation of the CNN's advantage of maintaining the spatial characteristics of an image, such as height, width, and even colors, as long as they receive the images as input, where these images are interpreted by the computer, is nothing more than values stored in an array, making processing easier.

Confirming the diagnosis or even performing laboratory tests using artificial intelligence through deep learning gives higher reliability concerning the results for both health professionals and patients, since the structure employed reduces the possibilities of human failure. There is a similarity of operation with the human brain, concluding that this tool is highly viable for distinguished realities and laboratory types, and can contribute directly to the access to health of economically disadvantaged populations.

Health is a vast area related to medical diagnostics by images. In this context, the methodology developed with deep learning enables the results, suggestive or not, of serious pathologies to be archived in digital files for later consultation, eliminating the generation of physical space for storage.

In laboratories and hospitals, for data storage the automation of laboratory tests is still a distant reality for some laboratories in underdeveloped and developing countries. However, the creation of new methodologies, such as the one presented in this chapter using artificial intelligence structures for image recognition and classification, results in a reduction in equipment costs without loss of quality and accuracy of hematological diagnoses.

9. Future research directions

Considering the wide applicability and importance of the proposed methodology, coupled with the constant need for advances in the medical field to create and optimize cell detection and counting systems for faster and more accurate diagnostics, this work has its continuity related to the development of algorithms in Python. Deep learning structures are increasingly able to perform recognition and classification of white blood smear platelet cells, as well as further refining the level of detail of cell types such as the differentiation of T-lymphocytes and B-lymphocytes [69,70].

The methodology can be further expanded to develop algorithms capable of classifying and detecting pathological blood cells, and identifying each of the leukocyte subtypes can be done based on machine learning techniques such as generative adverse networks (GANs), which are a recent innovation in machine learning, GANs are generative models that create new instances of data that resemble the training data. This technique has the characteristics of achieving realism when paired with a generator, learning to produce the desired output, and with a discriminator, learning to distinguish the generator output from true data, and it attempts to mislead the discriminator while trying to avoid the mistake [71–73].

The structure developed in this chapter can be further improved by increasing its accuracy through the implementation of the optimization algorithm, the addition of better libraries that perform data processing more efficiently, and the further refining of the developed structure, which include attempts to reduce image size to improve training time without affecting model performance.

References

[1] L.C.U. Junqueira, et al., Biología Celular Y Molecular, McGraw-Hill Interamericana, 1998.
[2] G. Karp, Biologia Celular Y Molecular: Conceptos Y Experimentos, sixth ed., McGraw Hill Mexico, 2011.
[3] L.C. Junqueira, C. José, Histologia básica, tenth ed., 2004. Rio de Janeiro.

[4] A.C.B. Monteiro, Y. Iano, R.P. França, Detecting and counting of blood cells using watershed transform: an improved methodology, in: Brazilian Technology Symposium (pp. 301—310), Springer, Cham, December 2017.

[5] A.C.B. Monteiro, Y. Iano, R.P. França, An improved and fast methodology for automatic detecting and counting of red and white blood cells using watershed transform, VIII Simpósio de Instrumentação e Imagens Médicas (SIIM)/VII Simpósio de Processamento de Sinais da UNICAMP (2017).

[6] A.C.B. Monteiro, Y. Iano, R.P. França, R. Arthur Applied Medical Informatics in the Detection and Counting of Erythrocytes and Leukocytes through an Image Segmentation Algorithm.

[7] A.C.B. Monteiro, Y. Iano, R.P. França, R. Arthur, V.V. Estrela, A.D. Rodriguez, S.L.L. Assumpção, Development of Digital Image Processing Methodology WT-MO: An Algorithm of High Accuracy in Detection and Counting of Erythrocytes, Leucocytes, Blasts, 2019.

[8] A.C.B. Monteiro, Y. Iano, R.P. França, R. Arthur, Methodology of high accuracy, sensitivity and specificity in the counts of erythrocytes and leukocytes in blood smear images, in: Brazilian Technology Symposium (pp. 79—90), Springer, Cham, 2018, October.

[9] A.C.B. Monteiro, Y. Iano, R.P. França, R. Arthur, V.V. Estrela, A comparative study between methodologies based on the hough transform and watershed transform on the blood cell count, in: Brazilian Technology Symposium (pp. 65—78). (Springer, Cham), 2018, October.

[10] A.C. Borges Monteiro, Y. Iano, R.P. França, R. Arthur, Medical-laboratory algorithm WTH-MO for segmentation of digital images of blood cells: a new methodology for making hemograms, Int. J. Simul.—Syst. 20 (2019). Science & Technology.

[11] A.C.B. Monteiro, Y. Iano, R.P. França, N. Razmjooy, WT-MO algorithm: automated hematological software based on the watershed transform for blood cell count, in: Applications of Image Processing and Soft Computing Systems in Agriculture (pp. 39—79), IGI Global, 2019.

[12] A.C.B. Monteiro, Proposta de uma metodologia de segmentação de imagens para detecção e contagem de hemácias e leucócitos através do algoritmo WT-MO, 2019.

[13] L.E. Silberstein, J. Anastasi, Hematology: Basic Principles and Practice E-Book: Basic Principles and Practice, Elsevier Health Sciences, 2017.

[14] E.M. Keohane, C.N. Otto, J.M. Walenga, Rodak's Hematology-E-Book: Clinical Principles and Applications, Elsevier Health Sciences, 2019.

[15] P. Fortina, E. Londin, J.Y. Park, L.J. Kricka (Eds.), Acute Myeloid Leukemia: Methods and Protocols, Humana Press, 2017.

[16] O. Abla, F.L. Coco, M.A. Sanz (Eds.), Acute Promyelocytic Leukemia: A Clinical Guide, Springer, 2018.

[17] A. Mullally, The treatment of myeloid malignancies with kinase inhibitors, in: An Issue of Hematology/Oncology Clinics of North America, E-Book, vol. 31, Elsevier Health Sciences, 2017.

[18] E. Ishii (Ed.), Hematological Disorders in Children: Pathogenesis and Treatment, Springer, 2017.

[19] P. Harrington, Machine Learning in Action, Manning Publications Co., 2012.

[20] P.M. Domingos, A few useful things to know about machine learning, Commun. ACM 55 (2012) 10.

[21] I. Goodfellow, Y. Bengio, A. Courville, Deep Learning, MIT Press, 2016.

[22] Y. LeCun, Y. Bengio, G. Hinton, Deep learning, Nature 521 (2015) 7553, 436444.

[23] L. Deng, Y. Dong, Deep learning: methods and applications, Found. Trends® Signal Process. 7 (3—4) (2014) 197—387.

[24] Y. Bengio, I. Goodfellow, A. Courville, Deep Learning, vol. 1, MIT press, 2017.

[25] R.F. Grace, R.E. Ware, Pediatric hematology, Hematol. Oncol. Clin. 33 (3) (2019) xiii—xiv.

[26] A. Pecci, Diagnosis and treatment of inherited thrombocytopenias, Clin. Genet. 89 (2) (2016) 141—153.

[27] B. Ciesla, Hematology in Practice, FA Davis, 2018.

[28] A.H. Schmaier, Introduction to hematology, in: Concise Guide to Hematology (pp. 1—3), Springer, Cham, 2019.

[29] B.J. Bain, D.M. Clark, B.S. Wilkins, Bone Marrow Pathology, Wiley-Blackwell, 2019.

[30] F. Fend, Book Review—Diagnostic Pathology: Blood and Bone Marrow, 2018.

[31] A.C.B. Monteiro, et al., Sickle cell anemia, a genetic disorder characterized by the change in shape of red blood cells, Saúde em Foco, Edição no (2015) 07.

[32] L.J. Estcourt, P.M. Fortin, S. Hopewell, M. Trivella, Red blood cell transfusion to treat or prevent complications in sickle cell disease: an overview of Cochrane reviews, Cochrane Database Syst. Rev. 2016 (2) (2016).

[33] A. Wahed, A. Quesada, A. Dasgupta, Hematology and Coagulation: A Comprehensive Review for Board Preparation, Certification and Clinical Practice, Academic Press, 2019.

[34] J.A. Reese, J.D. Peck, J.J. McIntosh, S.K. Vesely, J.N. George, Platelet counts in women with normal pregnancies: a systematic review, Am. J. Hematol. 92 (11) (2017) 1224—1232.

[35] C.L. VanPutte, J.L. Regan, A.F. Russo, Seeley's Anatomy & Physiology, McGraw-Hill Education, 2017, p. 1264.

[36] G.N. Levine, Cardiology Secrets E-Book, Elsevier Health Sciences, 2017.

[37] K.T. Patton, G.A. Thibodeau, Anthony's Textbook of Anatomy & Physiology-E-Book, Mosby, 2018.

[38] D. Sturgeon, Introduction to Anatomy and Physiology for Healthcare Students, Routledge, 2018.

[39] R.A. McPherson, M.R. Pincus, Henry's Clinical Diagnosis and Management by Laboratory Methods E-Book, Elsevier Health Sciences, 2017.

[40] D. Kixmüller, N. Gässler, R. Junker, Hematological diagnostics, in: Point-of-Care Testing (pp. 155—158), Springer, Berlin, Heidelberg, 2018.

[41] M. Zakaria, T. Hassan, Introductory chapter: contemporary pediatric hematology and oncology, in: Contemporary Pediatric Hematology and Oncology, IntechOpen, 2019.

[42] S. Samarasinghe, Neural Networks for Applied Sciences and Engineering: From Fundamentals to Complex Pattern Recognition, Auerbach publications, 2016.

[43] S. Walczak, Artificial neural networks, in: Advanced Methodologies and Technologies in Artificial Intelligence, Computer Simulation, and Human-Computer Interaction (pp. 40—53), IGI Global, 2019.

[44] I.N. Da Silva, D.H. Spatti, R.A. Flauzino, L.H.B. Liboni, S.F. dos Reis Alves, Artificial Neural Networks, Springer International Publishing, Cham, 2017.

[45] N. Garg, P. Nikhitha, B.K. Tripathy, An insight into deep learning architectures, in: Encyclopedia of Information Science and Technology, fourth ed., IGI Global, 2018, pp. 4528—4534.

[46] A. Voulodimos, N. Doulamis, A. Doulamis, E. Protopapadakis, Deep Learning for Computer Vision: A Brief Review, Computational intelligence and neuroscience, 2018.

[47] P. Mamoshina, A. Vieira, E. Putin, A. Zhavoronkov, Applications of deep learning in biomedicine, Mol. Pharm. 13 (5) (2016) 1445—1454.

[48] M. Kubat, An Introduction to Machine Learning, vol. 2, Springer International Publishing, Cham, Switzerland, 2017.

[49] M. Van Gerven, S. Bohte, Artificial neural networks as models of neural information processing, Front. Comput. Neurosci. 11 (2017) 114.

[50] L. Lu, Y. Zheng, G. Carneiro, L. Yang, Deep learning and convolutional neural networks for medical image computing, in: Advances in Computer Vision and Pattern Recognition, Springer, New York, NY, USA, 2017.

[51] E. Charniak, Introduction to Deep Learning, The MIT Press, 2019.

[52] W. Meiyin, L. Chen, Image recognition based on deep learning, in: 2015 Chinese Automation Congress (CAC), IEEE, 2015.

[53] S. Raschka, V. Mirjalili, Python Machine Learning, Packt Publishing Ltd, 2017.

[54] Y. Kim, Convolutional Neural Networks for Sentence Classification, 2014 arXiv preprint arXiv:1408.5882.

[55] B. Hu, et al., Convolutional neural network architectures for matching natural language sentences, Adv. Neural Inform. Process. Syst. (2014).

[56] L. Xu, J.S. Ren, C. Liu, J. Jia, Deep convolutional neural network for image deconvolution, Adv. Neural Inform. Process. Syst. (2014) 1790−1798.

[57] P. Li, et al., Deep convolutional computation model for feature learning on big data in Internet of Things, IEEE Trans. Ind. Inform. 14 (2) (2017) 790−798.

[58] J.-E. Bibault, P. Giraud, A. Burgun, Big data and machine learning in radiation oncology: state of the art and future prospects, Cancer Lett. 382 (1) (2016) 110−117.

[59] R.F. Murphy, An active role for machine learning in drug development, Nat. Chem. Biol. 7 (6) (2011) 327.

[60] B.W. Busser, et al., A machine learning approach for identifying novel cell type-specific transcriptional regulators of myogenesis, PLoS Genet. 8 (2012) 3, e1002531.

[61] A.A. Cruz-Roa, et al., A deep learning architecture for image representation, visual interpretability and automated basal-cell carcinoma cancer detection, in: International Conference on Medical Image Computing and Computer-Assisted Intervention. Springer, Berlin, Heidelberg, 2013.

[62] Y. Song, et al., A deep learning based framework for accurate segmentation of cervical cytoplasm and nuclei, in: 2014 36th Annual International Conference of the IEEE Engineering in Medicine and Biology Society, IEEE, 2014.

[63] K.-L. Hua, et al., Computer-aided classification of lung nodules on computed to-mography images via deep learning technique, OncoTargets Ther. 8 (2015).

[64] C.L. Chen, et al., Deep learning in label-free cell classification, Sci. Rep. 6 (2016) 21471.

[65] P. Eulenberg, et al., Reconstructing cell cycle and disease progression using deep learning, Nat. Commun. 8 (1) (2017) 463.

[66] N. Coudray, et al., Classification and mutation prediction from non−small cell lung cancer histopathology images using deep learning, Nat. Med. 24 (10) (2018) 1559.

[67] S.U. Khan, et al., A novel deep learning based framework for the detection and classification of breast cancer using transfer learning, Pattern Recogn. Lett. 125 (2019) 1−6.

[68] GitHub − Shenggan/BCCD_Dataset: BCCD Dataset is a small-scale dataset for blood cells detection. BCCD Dataset is under MIT license. (Online). Available: https://github.com/Shenggan/BCCD_Dataset.

[69] A. Ratley, J. Minj, P. Patre, Leukemia disease detection and classification using ma-chine learning approaches: a review, in: 2020 First International Conference on Power, Control and Computing Technologies (ICPC2T) (pp. 161−165), IEEE, 2020, January.

[70] Y. Chen, A. Janowczyk, A. Madabhushi, Quantitative assessment of the effects of compression on deep learning in digital pathology image analysis, JCO Clin. Cancer Inform. 4 (2020) 221−233.

[71] F. Yang, Z. Wang, J. Li, R. Xia, Y. Yan, Improving generative adversarial networks for speech enhancement through regularization of latent representations, Speech Commun. 118 (2020) 1–9.

[72] M. Karimi, A. Hasanzadeh, Network-principled Deep Generative Models for Designing Drug Combinations as Graph Sets, 2020 arXiv preprint arXiv:2004.07782.

[73] Z. Liu, K. Xiao, B. Jin, K. Huang, D. Huang, Y. Zhang, Unified generative adversarial networks for multiple-choice oriented machine comprehension, ACM Trans. Intell. Syst. Technol. 11 (3) (2020) 1–20.

CHAPTER 7

Dementia detection using the deep convolution neural network method

B. Janakiramaiah[1], G. Kalyani[2]

[1]Department of Computer Science & Engineering, Prasad V. Potluri Siddhartha Institute of Technology, Vijayawada, Andhra Pradesh, India; [2]Department of Information Technology, Velagapudi Ramakrishna Siddhartha Engineering College, Vijayawada, Andhra Pradesh, India

1. Introduction

Dementia is a disorder that manifests as a decrease in memory as well as a decline in other cognitive areas like language and vision [1]. Numerous maladies can be the reason for the disorder of dementia. Most of the individuals who have dementia also have a neurodegenerative illness or cerebrovascular ischemia as the fundamental reason. Somewhere in the range of 60%−70% of individuals who have dementia also have Alzheimer's malady; around 20%−30% contain blended vascular and Alzheimer's sickness. A small proportion of people have different causes, like Lewy body dementia, frontal dementia, and Parkinson's disease [2,3]. General history and physical assessments are not generally used to analyze dementia during doctor visits. Numerous investigations in the United States show that dementia identification by primary doctors is very low [4]. More than half of patients with dementia have never been analyzed by physicians [5]. This raises the likelihood that viable screening tests may have the option to recognize individuals with dementia at the start of the disease, permitting the plausibility of prior mediation.

Globally, there are nearly 900, million individuals aged 60 years or more. The number of older adults drastically increases among populace because of an increase in lifespan. Approximately 46 million individuals had dementia in 2015. Roughly, this value doubles every 20 years. By 2030 the number of people with dementia could rise to 74 million, and by 2050, that number could be 131 million (World Alzheimer Report, 2015), as shown in Fig. 7.1.

Even though research in molecular chemistry has been ongoing with dementia, various reports indicate that neuroimaging may recognize

Trends in Deep Learning Methodologies
ISBN 978-0-12-822226-3
https://doi.org/10.1016/B978-0-12-822226-3.00007-6

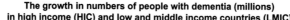

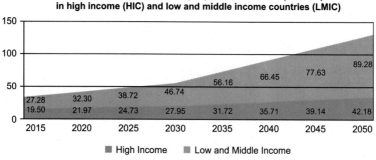

Figure 7.1 Worldwide development of Alzheimer's dementia.

functional and structural changes in the mind [6,7]. Evaluation and treatment for dementia patients are multimodal, which relies on the phase of the sickness. At every stage, doctors ought to be cautious, support sufferers and their relatives, and be wary of potential side effects. Although controlling dementia is possible, reducing dementia development is not straightforward considering the physiological components [8].

Neuroimaging can categorize dementia, like dementia by Lewy bodies and Alzheimer's illness, etc. Treatment in the early stages of these problems is significant from a predictive as well as a restorative point of view, and to recognize them exactly is clinically indispensable. Neuropsychological appraisals are essential for premature identification of dementia and for checking the development of dementia in clinical and investigative ways. Significant expensive neuroimaging-based findings, like magnetic resonance imaging (MRI) and positron emission tomography (PET), are used to detect dementia [9].

The anticipation is that there may be a 300% expansion in dementia in the next 40–50 years. Mild cognitive impairment (MCI) is an early phase of dementia. If problem identification is possible at the MCI stage, diagnosis can be made and can forestall the movement to dementia; therefore the determination of MCI is imperative in forestalling the onset of dementia. The primary indication at the MCI stage is the decrease in psychological aptitudes. Patients will have the option to do ordinary tasks even though the loss of mental capacities occurs.

Recognizing dementia with corresponding biomarkers by artificial intelligence (AI) [10] at an early stage helps in timely treatment and avoidance of worsening of the disease. Use of AI techniques in the characterization of normal control, MCI, and Alzheimer's by utilizing neuroimaging information from MRI, PET, single-photon emission computed tomography, neuropsychological scores, and genetic biomarkers is significant in developing regions of research. A few investigations have used necessary MRI, PET, cerebrospinal fluid (CSF) biomarker, and genetic data for separation of Alzheimer's and MCI. However, a few examinations have utilized neuropsychological information alone for treating the disease [11].

Current research has demonstrated that a mix of both neuroimaging information and neuropsychological information is critical for accomplishing higher precision in the separation of Alzheimer's, normal control, and MCI. Four-class separation of normal control, early MCI, late MCI, and Alzheimer's dementia has been investigated by consolidating neuropsychological information and MRI. Thus a coordinated methodology with numerous biomarkers from neuroimaging and neuropsychological information appraisal is vital and can be studied for viable multiclass separation of different stages in Alzheimer's with AI techniques.

Machine learning has given fantastic performance in different fields, especially in health care [12]. Machine learning is a domain that is a combination of statistics, AI, visualization, database frameworks, etc. [13]. It concentrates on finding new essential patterns in a vast dataset and gives the data in the required format. Notably, deep learning has come about to handle enormous amounts of information and to have increased computing potential for enhancing performance. Deep learning is proficient in identifying intricate patterns from information to find an excellent portrayal. The drawbacks of conventional techniques are defeated using deep learning. Besides, deep learning has extraordinary commitments to significant improvements in various domains such as bioinformatics and health care [14–16]. Even though an enormous amount of neuropsychological evaluation information has amassed, concealed examples in the data have not yet been entirely analyzed. For investigating neuropsychological evaluation information, machine learning by utilizing deep learning procedures is a reasonable methodology.

Deep learning has been considered widely [17,18] over the last couple of years. Ongoing advanced techniques in AI regarding understanding the picture have prompted extraordinary advances concerning distinguishing, characterizing, and evaluating examples of medicinal descriptions, particularly utilizing deep learning. Notably, the usage of various practical demonstrations adapted exclusively with information rather than physically highlighted, which depend on explicit domain information, is at the center of this advancement [18–20].

2. Related work

The fundamental part of deep learning, i.e., a deep convolutional neural network (CNN), is used to automatically retrieve the features that have surprisingly enhanced the performance of image identification and classification [21,22]. A few mechanisms that depend on deep learning have been projected to perceive and classify Alzheimer's and moderate intellectual impedance [23].

Lui et al. [24] projected a methodology for four-class characterization of Alzheimer's by utilizing LASSO-chosen gray matter highlights with MRI and PET images. The authors performed four-class characterizations with a cross-validation technique by applying it 10-fold and achieving an enhancement of 3.6% in accuracy contrasted with the conventional method based on the support vector machine (SVM) model. The creators do not utilize any technique that may avoid overtraining, and their strategy uses two scanning reports, e.g., MRI and PET, for investigation.

A deep neural network (DNN) was employed with three levels to include learning and combination structure for MRI, PET, and inherited information as foreseen in [25,26], with the underlying level including the learning of latent portrayals of every methodology and the final standard for the learning of joint latent highlights. At every level, a DNN was utilized, which was comprised of a few completely associated hidden layers and finally an output layer with softmax function.

Qureshi et al. [27] isolated Alzheimer's patients who had a clinical dementia rating of 0.5—3 into two categories by considering the severity of dementia. The first category was extremely mellow/gentle, which had a rating score of 0.5—1, and moderate to extreme dementia with a rating score of 2—3, which comprised 77 and 56 subjects, respectively. The author's utilized resting-state functional magnetic resonance imaging (rs-fMRI) to separate useful features, identified with independent component analysis, and completed automated categorization based on severity. They used 3D-convolutional neural systems based on deep learning. Rs-fMRI information demonstrated average frontal, precise control, and related visual systems for the most part connected with dementia seriousness. The proposed clinical dementia rating-based novel order utilizing rs-fMRI was a satisfactory target seriousness pointer. Even though trained neuropsychologists were not available, dementia seriousness can be unbiasedly and precisely characterized by utilizing a 3D deep learning system with rs-fMRI autonomous parts.

Payan and Montana [28] used 2D and 3D convolution neural systems and reported that the accuracy of classification in the classes Alzheimer's, MCI, and cognitive normal (CN) was 89% by utilizing their own approval set. Nevertheless, the work does not report cross–approval or dismisses correctness; along these lines, their exactness was exclusively founded on 10% of their haphazardly chosen 100 subject datasets.

The methodology projected in [29] utilizes a deep-stacked autoencoder with three kinds of highlights: gray color tissue volume from MRI, PET power, and CSF biomarkers. The highlights were further categorized based on a stacked autoencoder with the number of hidden layers as three for binary categorization. Tong et al. [30] consolidated correlative multimodal highlights from PET, MRI, and CSF biomarkers, and hereditary highlights utilizing nondirect chart highlights. An advantage of the strategy was that it did not need to prepare weights. With the Alzheimer's Disease Neuroimaging Initiative dataset, they accomplished 60.2% accuracy for Alzheimer's disease, MCI, and CN characterization. Administering multimethodology and utilizing just basic MRI, they achieved 56.6% Alzheimer's disease, MCI, and CN accuracy by using fourfold cross-validation.

D. Cardenas-Pena et al. [31] designed a deep network by utilizing focal bit arrangement. They accomplished 47.6% accuracy on a stacked autoencoder with three hidden layers and 63.8% accuracy on a stacked autoencoder combined with principal component analysis. With the stacked autoencoder, they achieved 38.1%, 33.1%, and 73.4% as the true-positive rate for Alzheimer's disease, MCI, and CN, respectively. This way, the model might be improved further for better characterization precision.

A deep Boltzmann machine (DBM) is built up by loading more than one restricted Boltzmann machine (RBM) as the main blocks to locate level-wise suppressed features. The layers of DBMs are like an undirected generative model subsequent to the RBM stack. DBMs can manage uncertain sources of information more strongly by consolidating top-down input. However, joint streamlining is tedious in DBMs, and perhaps inconceivable for massive datasets [32,33]. Suk et al. discovered that a significant-level 3D portrayal acquired through DBM was progressively sensitive to noise. At the same time, a multimodular DBM of a PET scan obtained its highlights from matched patches of changed estimations of MRI scans (a straight SVM as a classifier) [34].

A recurrent neural network (RNN) is not as profound as DNNs or CNNs as far as the quantity of layers is concerned, and in terms of issues when remembering extended input information. Luckily, replacing the generally used hidden nodes with progressively complex units like long short-term memory (LSTM) or gated recurrent unit (GRU), which work as memory units, solves the issues related to memory. Cui et al. built and trained an RNN model with two GRU layers to catch longitudinal changes from the data based on time sequences [35]. In the investigation, the GRUs used the features of the picture and separated longitudinal highlights. To encourage disease determination, Gao et al. planned an architecture based on LSTM [36] to separate longitudinal highlights and identified pathological changes.

A comparison of the different methods used in the related work in this section is summarized in terms of strengths and weaknesses in Table 7.1.

3. Basics of a convolution neural network

A CNN or ConvNet is an exceptional sort of multilayer neural network. A CNN mostly takes images as input, which permits the user to encode a few properties of the network model, thus reducing the number of parameters. Generally, there are three main layers in a simple ConvNet: convolution layer, pooling layer, and fully connected layer. The **input layer** holds the image data. Fig. 7.2 demonstrates the general structural design of a CNN with various layers.

3.1 Convolution layer

The principal layer in a CNN is the convolution layer, in which every neuron is related to a specific region of the area in the input called the receptive field. The main aim of convolution concerning ConvNet is to remove the features from the given image. This layer does most of the computation in a ConvNet. The result of every convolution layer is a set of feature maps, created by a solitary kernel filter of the convolution layer. These maps consolidate the characteristics of the input to the succeeding layer.

A convolution is an algebraic operation that slides a function over other space and measures the essentials of their location-based multiplication of a value-wise product. It has profound associations with Fourier and Laplace transforms and is intensely utilized in processing the signals. Convolution layers use cross-relationships, which are fundamentally the same as convolutions. In terms of mathematics, convolution is an operation with two functions that deliver another feature—that is, the convoluted form of one of the input functions. The generated feature gives the integral of the value-wise product of the two given features as an element of the sum when one of the given input functions is deciphered.

Table 7.1 Comparison of the methods used in the related work.

Models	Strengths	Limitations
Conventional SVM	- Performs well with unorganized and semiorganized data like text and images - By using a suitable kernel function, any complex problem can be solved - Scales generally well to high dimensional information	- Difficult to choose a "good" kernel function - Training takes more time for massive datasets - Complex to comprehend and infer the final model - Difficulty in tuning the hyperparameters
DNN	- Excellent for vector-based problems - Handles massive datasets that contain an enormous number of records - Discovers complex nonlinear relationships	- Training consumes more time
AE	- Exceptionally nonlinear and intricate patterns can be represented - Efficient in reducing dimensions - Simple to implement	- Captures as much information as feasible instead of relevant information
DBM	- Can learn a perfect generative model - Able to generate patterns even though missing data existed	- Heavy computational process in training the network
RNN	- Excellent for sequential data in 2D images	- Vanishing/exploding gradients problem
2D CNN	- Performs well in extracting the local features of the image - Simple to train	- Unable to handle 3D images
3D CNN	- Performs well in extracting the local features of the image - Captures 3D information from the 3D scan images	- Heavy computational procedure in training the network

2D CNN, Two-dimensional convolution neural network; *3D CNN*, three-dimensional convolution neural network; *AE, auto encoder; DBM*, deep Boltzmann machine; *DNN*, deep neural network; *RNN*, recurrent neural network; *SVM*, support vector machine.

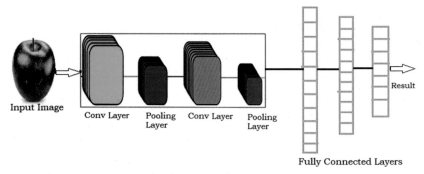

Figure 7.2 Conceptual architecture of a convolution neural network.

The architectural design of ConvNet enables the system to focus on low-level highlights in the first layer, and afterward collect them into more significant-level highlights in the following hidden layer, etc. This type of various leveled structure is consistent in natural pictures, which is the reason for the functioning of CNNs for recognizing the images. Adding a convolution layer in Keras produces the following syntax:

Conv2D(filters, kernel_size, strides, padding, activation="relu", input_shape).

Arguments in the foregoing syntax have the following implications:

- Filters: The number of filters.
- Kernel_size: A number specifying both the height and width of the (square) convolution window. Some additional optional arguments have existed, which are changed if required.
- Strides: The stride of the convolution. If the user does not specify anything, the default value is 1.
- Padding: This is either "valid" or "same." If the user does not specify anything, the default value is "valid."
- Activation: This is generally "relu." If the user does not specify anything, no activation is applied. It is strongly advised to add a ReLU activation function to every convolutional layer in the networks.

It is possible to represent both kernel_size and strides as either a number or a tuple. When using the convolution layer as a first layer (appearing after the input layer) in a model, you must provide an additional input_shape argument—input_shape. It is a tuple specifying the height, width, and depth (in that order) of the input. Make sure that the input_shape argument is not needed if the convolution layer is not the first layer in the network.

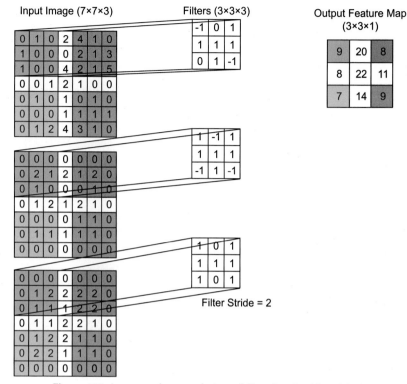

Figure 7.3 An example convolution of filter 3 × 3 with stride 2.

Fig. 7.3 illustrates an example of convolution with filter size 3 × 3 and stride, also like 2.

The behavior of the convolution layer is controlled by specifying the number of filters and dimensions for each filter. The number of nodes in a convolution layer is increased by increasing the filters. The dimensions of the filter are increased to enlarge the size of the pattern. There are also a few other hyperparameters that can be tuned. One of them is the stride of the convolution. Stride is the amount by which the filter slides over the image. The stride of 1 moves the filter by 1 pixel horizontally and vertically. Here, the size of the convolution becomes the same as the width and depth of the given input image. The stride of 2 makes a convolution layer half the given input dimension. If the kernel filter moves outside the image, then we can either ignore these unknown values or replace them with zeros.

3.2 Pooling layer

As we have seen, a convolution layer retrieves the feature maps, with one feature map for each filter. More filters increase the dimensionality of convolution. Higher dimensionality indicates more parameters. So, the pooling layer controls overfitting by progressively minimizing the spatial size of the feature map to lower the parameters as well as calculations. The pooling layer often takes the convolution layer as input. Every neuron in the pooling layer is linked to a few neurons of the preceding layer, which are in a receptive field, i.e., specified as a rectangular region. However, size, stride, and type of padding are determined for that region. In other words, the aim of using pooling is to reduce a load of computation, usage of memory, and the number of parameters by subsampling the input image. It helps the model to avoid overfitting in the phase of training. Lessening the image size of the input additionally causes the neural system to endure a slight picture shift. The spatial semantics of the convolution operations rely upon the scheme of padding picked.

The operation of padding is to expand the size of the information. On account of 1D data, a constant is added to the array; in 2D information, the constants are used surrounding the input matrix. In n-dimensional data, the n-dimensional hypercube is surrounded by a constant. To a maximum extent, the constant used in the padding is "0." Hence, it is called "zero" padding. There exist other types of padding techniques like "VALID" padding and "SAME" padding. "VALID" padding drops the rightmost columns or bottom-most rows. In the case of "SAME" padding, data is padded evenly on the right and left. If the padded columns are odd, then an additional column is appended on the right.

Selecting the operation for pooling plays a significant role in the pooling layer. The pooling operation is like applying the filter to the feature map. Hence, the filter size should be less than the feature map size. Explicitly, it is quite often 2×2 size, with stride 2. This implies that the pooling layer will consistently diminish the size of every feature map to half of its original size. The most generally utilized pooling approach is max pooling. Along with max pooling, pooling layers can also implement other pooling operations like mean pooling and min pooling.

The most extreme pooling, i.e., max pooling, considers the highest or most significant pixel value in each filter patch of the feature map. The outcomes are the features that correspond to the brightest element in the filter patch. Max pooling selects the sparkling highlights in the given image.

By using image classification in the domain of computer vision, max pooling presents the enhanced results when contrast to the other pooling operations. Max pooling gives an improved outcome if the image is white on a black background. Fig. 7.4 illustrates the process of max pooling.

Average or mean pooling performs the calculation of the mean of all the values in a filter patch, which are applied to the feature map. This implies that each 2 × 2 square of the filter is examined to the usual incentive in the square. The mean pooling technique smooths out the picture, and thus the sharp highlights may not be recognized when using this pooling strategy. Fig. 7.5 illustrates the operation of mean pooling.

The minimum pooling or min pooling operation considers the minimum or smallest value in every patch of the feature map. Min pooling provides an enhanced outcome in the case of black images on a white background. Fig. 7.6 illustrates the operation of min pooling.

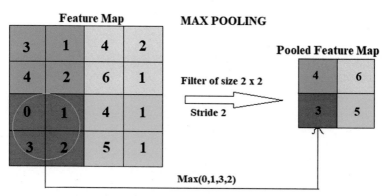

Figure 7.4 Illustration of max pooling.

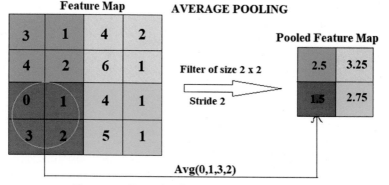

Figure 7.5 Example of average or mean pooling.

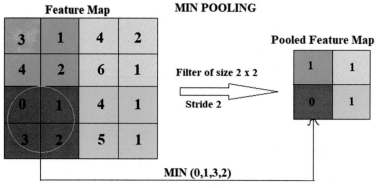

Figure 7.6 Illustration of min pooling.

Fig. 7.7 shows the difference between these three pooling methods with an example picture resulting in max pooling, average pooling, and min pooling for a given original picture.

Figure 7.7 Comparison of the different pooling operations results.

3.3 Fully connected layer

The set of convolution and pooling layers acts as the feature extraction part in the CNN. The retrieved features are processed to classify or detect the objects in the image. The final few layers of the ConvNet are fully connected layers for detection purposes. Fig. 7.8 illustrates the fully connected layers.

Fully connected layers simply work as a feed-forward network. The result of the last pooling is in the form of a matrix. It is converted into a vector with a technique called "flattened" and is considered as input to the fully connected layer. The process of flattened is demonstrated in Fig. 7.9.

Fully connected layers compute the mathematical operations as follows:

$$A(W*X+b)$$

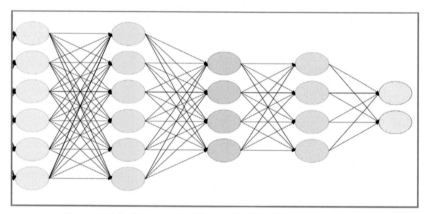

Figure 7.8 Fully connected layers for identification of objects.

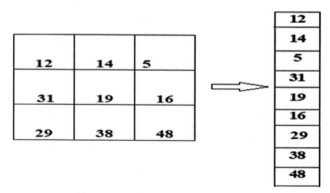

Figure 7.9 The process of flattened.

where A stands for activation function

W indicates weight matrix of dimension $M \times N$

M indicates neurons of the preceding layer

N stands for neurons of the succeeding layer

X represents the input vector obtained from the flattened process of size $N \times 1$

b denotes the vector of bias.

The computation is carried out in every layer. All fully connected layers utilize ReLu as the activation function. After processing through all the fully connected layers, in the final layer instead of ReLu the softmax function is implemented. This function gives probabilities of the input related to every class. The highest probability node indicates the class label of the considered input data.

4. Materials and methods

This part explores the methodology for identifying dementia people by using MRI scan reports. The model is based on a deep CNN.

4.1 Dataset description

Open Access Series of Imaging Studies (OASIS) [37] is a platform planned for creating MRI scan reports of the brain that can be unreservedly accessible to scientific researchers. In this chapter for experimentation of the projected methodology, we use "Cross-sectional MRI Data in Young, Middle-Aged, Non-demented, and Demented Older Adults" (OASIS-1) dataset images. This assortment is a collection of 416 people of both sexual orientations, whose age is in the range of 18—96. The dataset incorporates 100 patients (aged 60 or more) with a medical determination of dementia problem at a very mild to modest level. Table 7.2 demonstrates the features of the OASIS-1 dataset.

4.2 Deep Learning methodology for dementia detection

This section explores the projected methodology for detecting dementia. The procedure is based on deep CNNs.

Deep learning systems "learn" from a lot of inputs, disseminate the learned data through the system from the input to the output layer, estimate the error at the output layer, and propagate the error back. Then, deep learning systems alter their weights and repeat the process until the error

Table 7.2 Specifications of people in the OASIS-1 dataset.

Age	# of people	Statistics of dementia people			Statistics of nondementia people		
		Male	Female	# of people	Male	Female	# of people
<20	19	0	0	0	10	9	19
20–39	135	0	0	0	62	73	135
40–59	64	0	0	0	21	43	64
60–79	123	26	28	63	17	43	60
80–99	75	15	22	37	9	29	38
TOTAL	416	41	59	100	119	197	316

becomes negligible. Finally, the trained system is utilized to anticipate the class of new data. Various architectures of deep learning are used in different application domains. CNNs are a unique sort of feed-forward neural system that is first intended to process pictures with various mutilations. The outline structural design of a CNN is illustrated in Fig. 7.10. As shown in Fig. 7.10, a general CNN contains convolution and pooling layers one after the other, which will extract the features of the given input image. The extracted features are provided as input to fully connected layers for processing. The output layer is used to identify the associated result of the input image. The convolution layer extracts the features as a "feature map." A

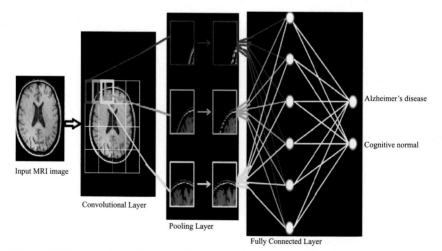

Figure 7.10 General architecture of the convolution neural network. *MRI*, Magnetic resonance imaging.

nonlinear activation is used to change the negative values n of the feature map to zero. ReLu is the generally used nonlinear activation, which is rapid in terms of training. Nonlinear activation was followed by the pooling layer to downsample the unwanted features.

For dementia detection, we used pretrained network Inception V3 from Keras framework [38]. Inception-V3 is a deep learning network for identifying natural images. The Inception-V3 architecture is shown in Fig. 7.11. Inception-V3 contains 48 layers and can classify 1000 objects in an image. Hence, the network has learned efficient feature maps for several images. The system considers an image of size 299 × 299 as input. The configuration of the layers is shown in Table 7.3. Inception-V3 uses "RMSProp" Optimizer, Factorized 7 × 7 convolutions, Batch Norm in the Auxillary Classifiers, and Label Smoothing. The Inception-V3 model mainly comprises two phases: a part that extracts the features with convolution and pooling layers and a part that classifies with fully connected layers and softmax layers. By using the concept of transfer learning, the network is retrained for OASIS-1 dataset images. In transfer learning, when retraining a model to classify the given dataset, extracting the features with

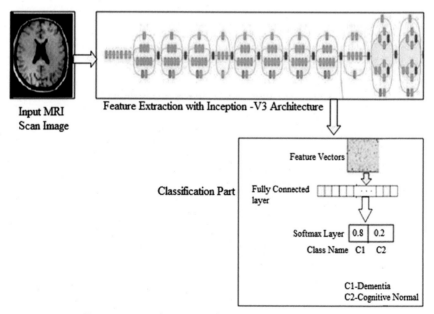

Figure 7.11 architecture of the Inception-V3 network.

Table 7.3 Layers configuration of the Inception-V3 model.

Name of layer	Stride	7 × 7	1 × 1	3 × 3-reduce	3 × 3	5 × 5-reduce	5 × 5	O/P size
		# of filters						
Convolution	2	64	—	—	—	—	—	112 × 112 × 64
Max pooling	2	—	—	—	64	—	—	56 × 56 × 64
Convolution	1	—	—	—	192	—	—	56 × 56 × 192
Max pooling	2	—	—	—	192	—	—	28 × 28 × 192
Inception–3a	—	—	64	96	128	16	32	28 × 28 × 256
Inception–3b	—	—	128	128	192	32	96	28 × 28 × 480
Max pooling	2	—	—	—	480	—	—	14 × 14 × 480
Inception–4a	—	—	192	96	208	16	48	14 × 14 × 512
Inception–4b	—	—	160	112	224	24	64	14 × 14 × 512
Inception–4c	—	—	128	128	256	24	64	14 × 14 × 512
Inception–4d	—	—	112	144	288	32	64	14 × 14 × 528
Inception–4e	—	—	256	160	320	32	128	14 × 14 × 832
Max pooling	2	—	—	—	832	—	—	7 × 7 × 832
Inception–5a	—	—	256	160	320	32	128	7 × 7 × 832
Inception–5b	—	—	384	192	384	48	128	7 × 7 × 1024
Avg pooling	1	1024	—	—	—	—	—	1 × 1 × 1024
Softmax	—	—	—	—	—	—	—	1 × 1 × 1000

convolution and pooling is reused, and we retrain the layers used for classification with the new dataset. Since there is no need to train the feature extraction part, the model is trained with fewer computational resources and within a short time.

5. Experimental results

Experimentation is performed with K-fold validation strategy with a k value of 10 for unbiased results validation. The dataset is initially separated as training and test set with a ratio of 90:10. The training data is partitioned into 10 folds. Among the 10 folds, nine folds are used to train the network, and the leftover folds are utilized to check the accuracy of the trained model. The experimentation is done 10 times. Hence, every input image is used for training the model as well as to test the model. Finally, with the test data, the model will be estimated with performance parameters.

To prove the efficiency of dementia detection with the proposed model the experimental results are compared with two existing methods. One is an ensemble method, which is a set of deep belief networks (DBNs) proposed by A. Ortiz et al. [39], and the second is a multimodal and multiscale DNN proposed by D. Lu et al. [40]. Comparison is done by using the standard parameters of the classification task, i.e., accuracy, sensitivity, specificity, and F-measure. We evaluate these parameters as follows:

$$\text{Accuracy} = \frac{TP + TN}{DP + NP}$$

$$\text{Sensitivity} = \frac{TP}{TP + FN}$$

$$\text{Specificity} = \frac{TN}{TN + FP}$$

$$\text{F1 Score} = \frac{2 * \text{Sensivity} * \text{Specificity}}{\text{Sensitivity} + \text{Specificity}}$$

where DP is the number of dementia persons, NP is the count of normal people, TP is the correctly identified dementia persons, TN indicates the correctly identified normal persons, FP is the number of the dementia patients identified as normal patients, and FN is the number of normal patients identified as dementia patients. The flowchart of the experimentation is shown in Fig. 7.12.

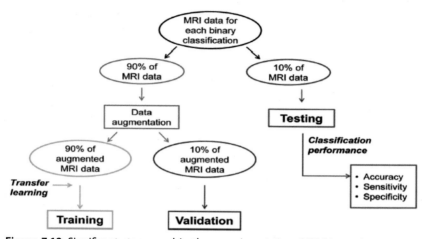

Figure 7.12 Significant steps used in the experimentation. *MRI*, Magnetic resonance imaging.

The resultant confusion matrix of the validations is shown in Fig. 7.13. In the confusion matrix, the number 89 indicates the true positives, i.e., 89 people who have dementia identified as dementia by the retrained network. The value 302 indicates the true negatives, i.e., 302 people who are normal cognitive means no dementia and are also identified as normal by the retrained network. The value 11 indicates the false negatives, i.e., people who have dementia are identified as cognitive normal by the retrained network. The value 14 indicates the false positives, i.e., people who are normal cognitive (not having dementia) identified as dementia people.

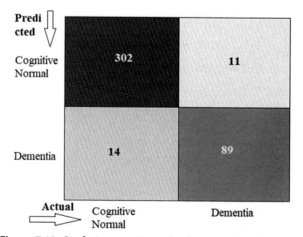

Figure 7.13 Confusion matrix result of proposed architecture.

By considering the confusion matrix shown in Fig. 7.13, the performance parameters are evaluated. The retrained model is given an accuracy of 93%, a sensitivity value of 89%, a specificity of 95%, and an F-measure of 91.9%. The parameter values are shown in Table 7.4.

Comparison of accuracy is shown in Fig. 7.14 which demonstrates clearly that accuracy has the values 0.846, 0.9, and 0.93 for multimodal and multiscale DNNs, DBNs, and the proposed method, respectively. Comparison of sensitivity is shown in Fig. 7.15 which demonstrates clearly that sensitivity has the values 0.802, 0.86, and 0.89 for multimodal and multiscale DNNs, DBNs, and the proposed method, respectively. Comparison of specificity is shown in Fig. 7.16 which demonstrates clearly that accuracy has the values 0.918, 0.94, and 0.95 for multimodal and multiscale DNNs, DBNs, and the proposed method, respectively. Comparison of the F1 score is shown in Fig. 7.17 which demonstrates clearly that accuracy has the

Table 7.4 Outcome of the performance measures.

Method	Accuracy	Sensitivity	Specificity	F1 score
Multimodal and multiscale DNNs consist of seven DNNs	0.846	0.802	0.918	0.855
A set of DBNs for all ROIs and SVM	0.9	0.86	0.94	0.898
Proposed architecture	0.93	0.89	0.95	0.919

DBNs, Deep belief networks; *DNNs*, deep neural networks; *ROIs, region of interest*; *SVM*, support vector machine.

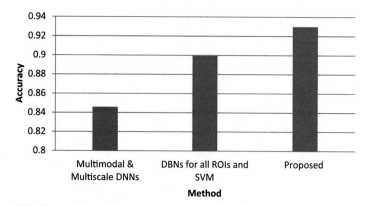

Figure 7.14 Comparison of accuracy measure. *DBNs*, Deep belief networks; *DNNs*, deep neural networks; *ROIs*, region of interest; *SVM*, support vector machine.

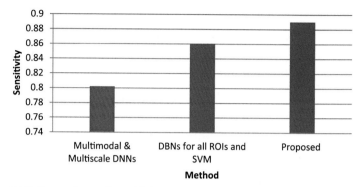

Figure 7.15 Comparison of sensitivity measure. *DBNs*, Deep belief networks; *DNNs*, deep neural networks; *ROIs*, region of interest; *SVM*, support vector machine.

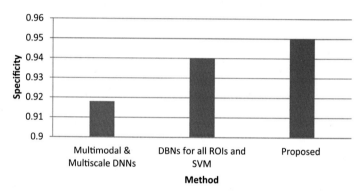

Figure 7.16 Comparison of specificity measure. *DBNs*, Deep belief networks; *DNNs*, deep neural networks; *ROIs*, region of interest; *SVM*, support vector machine.

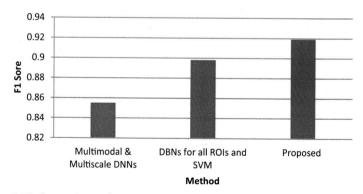

Figure 7.17 Comparison of F1 score measure. DBNs, Deep belief networks; DNNs, deep neural networks; *ROIs*, region of interest; *SVM*, support vector machine.

values 0.855, 0.898, and 0.919 for multimodal and multiscale DNNs, DBNs, and the proposed method, respectively. From the experimental results it is clear that the proposed architecture for dementia detection has improved results when compared to existing methods.

6. Conclusion

Dementia is a disorder that manifests as a decrease in memory as well as a decline in other cognitive skills like language and vision and is a widespread problem in older people. Generally, dementia detection is not possible in routine health checkups. But early detection of dementia can be treated with proper diagnosis. Hence, we proposed an efficient automated detection of dementia at the early stages. The model was developed based on deep CNNs to detect whether a person has dementia or not based on MRI scan report images. The model is developed based on pretrained network Inception-V3 from the Keras framework. Subsequently, the network was retrained based on the concept of transfer learning for medical MRI scan images. Validation of the retrained model was performed with the test dataset. The experimental results ensured an accuracy of 93% in early detection of dementia for better survival. The developed model identified dementia but not the level of dementia for better treatment. The future scope of this work relies on detecting the level of dementia for better and correct treatment. In the future, the project can also be extended to identifying the type of dementia, such as Lewy body dementia, vascular dementia, Parkinson's disease, frontotemporal dementia, etc.

References

[1] L. Calvó-Perxas, et al., Incidence and characteristics of uncommon dementia subtypes: results from 10 years of clinical surveillance by the Registry of Dementia of Girona, Alzheimer's Dementia 15 (2019) 917—926, https://doi.org/10.1016/j.jalz.2019.03.017.
[2] J. Lan, Acupuncture for cognitive impairment in vascular dementia, alzheimer's disease and mild cognitive impairment: a systematic review and meta-analysis, Eu. J. Integr. Med. 35 (2020), https://doi.org/10.1016/j.eujim.2020.101085.
[3] L.C.P. Banning, I.H.G.B. Ramakers, K. Deckers, F.R.J. Verhey, P. Aalten, Apolipoprotein E and affective symptoms in mild cognitive impairment and Alzheimer's disease dementia: a systematic review and meta-analysis, Neurosci. Biobehav. Rev. 96 (2019), https://doi.org/10.1016/j.neubiorev.2018.11.020.

[4] M.T. Ruthirakuhan, N. Herrmann, D. Gallagher, A.C. Andreazza, A. Kiss, N.P.L.G. Verhoeff, S.E. Black, K.L. Lanctôt, Investigating the safety and efficacy of nabilone for the treatment of agitation in patients with moderate-to-severe Alzheimer's disease: study protocol for a cross-over randomized controlled trial, Contemp. Clin. Trials Commun. 15 (2019), https://doi.org/10.1016/j.conctc.2019.100385.

[5] M. Mofizul Islam, A. Parkinson, K. Burns, M. Woods, L. Yen, A training program for primary health care nurses on timely diagnosis and management of dementia in general practice: an evaluation study, Int. J. Nurs. Stud. 105 (2020), https://doi.org/10.1016/j.ijnurstu.2020.103550.

[6] O. Dekhil, M. Ali, R. Haweel, Y. Elnakib, M. Ghazal, H. Hajjdiab, L. Fraiwan, A. Shalaby, A. Soliman, A. Mahmoud, R. Keynton, M.F. Casanova, G. Barnes, A. El-Baz, A comprehensive framework for differentiating autism spectrum disorder from neurotypicals by fusing structural MRI and resting state functional MRI, Semin. Pediatr. Neurol. 34 (2020), https://doi.org/10.1016/j.spen.2020.100805.

[7] D.H. Lee, P. Lee, S.W. Seo, J.H. Roh, M. Oh, J.S. Oh, S.J. Oh, J.S. Kim, Y. Jeong, Neural substrates of cognitive reserve in Alzheimer's disease spectrum and normal aging, Neuroimage 186 (2019), https://doi.org/10.1016/j.neuroimage.2018.11.053.

[8] J. Cummings, N. Fox, Defining disease-modifying therapy for Alzheimer's disease, J. Prev. Alzheimer's Dis. 4 (2017) 109−115.

[9] H.C. Rossetti, C. Munro Cullum, L.S. Hynan, L.H. Lacritz, The CERAD neuro-psychologic battery total score and the progression of Alzheimer disease, Alzheimer Dis. Assoc. Disord. 24 (2) (2010) 138−142.

[10] F. Falahati, E. Westman, A. Simmons, Multivariate data analysis and machine learning in Alzheimer's disease with a focus on structural magnetic resonance imaging, J. Alzheimer's. Dis. 41 (3) (2014) 685−708.

[11] H. Etayash, K. Jiang, S. Azmi, T. Thundat, K. Kaur, Real-time detection of breast cancer cells using peptide-functionalized microcantilever arrays, Sci. Rep. 5 (2015), 13967.

[12] J. Iavindrasana, G. Cohen, A. Depeursinge, H. Müller, R. Meyer, A. Geissbuhler, Clinical data mining: a review, Yearbook of Med. Info. 18 (1) (2009) 121−133.

[13] J. Han, M. Kamber, J. Pei, Data Mining: Concepts and Techniques, third ed., Morgan Kaufmann Publishers Inc., San Francisco, 2011.

[14] S. Kwon, S. Yoon, Deepcci: end-to-end deep learning for chemical-chemical inter-action prediction. ACM-BCB'17, in: Proceedings of the 8th ACM International Conference on Bioinformatics, Computational Biology, and Health Informatics, ACM, New York, 2017.

[15] S. Park, S. Min, H.-S. Choi, S. Yoon, Deep recurrent neural network-based identi-fication of precursor microRNAs, in: I. Guyon, U.V. Luxburg, S. Bengio, H. Wallach, R. Fergus, S. Vishwanathan, R. Garnett (Eds.), Advances in Neural Information Processing Systems, vol. 30, Curran Associates, Inc., 2017, 2891−900.

[16] H. Kim, S. Min, M. Song, S. Jung, J.W. Choi, Y. Kim, S. Lee, S. Yoon, H. Kim, Deep learning improves prediction of crispr−cpf1 guide rna activity, Nat. Biotechnol. 36 (3) (2018) 239.

[17] Y. Gal, Z. Ghahramani, Dropout as a Bayesian approximation: representing model uncertainty in deep learning, in: Proceedings of the 33rd International Conference on Machine Learning (New York, NY: ACM), 2016, pp. 1050−1059.

[18] S. Amiri, M.A. Mahjoub, I. Rekik, Bayesian network and structured random forest cooperative deep learning for automatic multi-label brain tumor segmentation, in: Proceedings of the 10th International Conference on Agents and Artificial Intelligence Volume 2, 183−190, 2018.

[19] M. Raju, V. Pagidimarri, R. Barreto, A. Kadam, V. Kasivajjala, A. Aswath, Development of a deep learning algorithm for automatic diagnosis of diabetic retinopathy, Stud. Health Technol. Inf. 245 (2017) 559−563.

[20] D. Shen, G. Wu, H.-I. Suk, Deep learning in medical image analysis, Annu. Rev. Biomed. Eng. 19 (2017) 221−248, https://doi.org/10.1146/annurev-bioeng-071516-044442.

[21] Y. LeCun, Y. Bengio, G. Hinton, Deep learning, Nature 521 (2015) 436−444.

[22] M. Liu, D. Zhang, D. Shen, Alzheimer's Disease Neuroimaging Initiative, Hierarchical fusion of features and classifier decisions for Alzheimer's disease diagnosis, Hum. Brain Mapp. 35 (2014) 1305−1319.

[23] A. Krizhevsky, I. Sutskever, G.E. Hinton, ImageNet classification with deep convolutional neural networks, Adv. Neural Inf. Process. Syst. (2012) 1097−1105.

[24] S. Liu, et al., Multimodal classification of Alzheimer's disease and mild cognitive impairment, in: IEEE 11th International Symposium on Biomedical Imaging, Beijing, 2014.

[25] T. Zhou, K.-H. Thung, X. Zhu, D. Shen, Feature learning and fusion of multimodality neuroimaging and genetic data for multi-status Dementia diagnosis, in: Proceedings of the International Workshop on Machine Learning in Medical Imaging, Springer, 2017, pp. 132−140.

[26] T. Zhou, K.H. Thung, X. Zhu, D. Shen, Effective feature learning and fusion of multimodality data using stage- wise deep neural network for dementia diagnosis, Hum. Brain Mapp. 40 (3) (2019) 1001−1016.

[27] M.N.I. Qureshi, et al., Evaluation of functional decline in Alzheimer's dementia using 3D deep learning and group ICA for rs-fMRI measurements, Front. Aging Neurosci. 11 (2019).

[28] A. Payan, G. Montana, Predicting Alzheimer's Disease: A Neuroimaging Study with 3D Convolutional Neural Networks, arXiv preprint, 2015.

[29] H. Suk, et al., Latent feature representation with stacked auto-encoder for AD/MCI diagnosis, Brain Struct. Funct. 220 (2) (March 2015) 841−859.

[30] T. Tong, et al., Nonlinear graph fusion for mult-modal classification of Alzheimer's disease, Lect. Notes Comput. Sci. 9352 (2015) 77−84.

[31] D. Cardenas-Pena, et al., Centered kernel alignment enhancing neural network pre-training for MRI-based dementia diagnosis, Comput. Math. Methods Med. 2016 (2016), 9523849, https://doi.org/10.1155/2016/9523849.

[32] M.I. Razzak, S. Naz, A. Zaib, Deep learning for medical image processing: overview, challenges and the future, in: Classification in BioApps, Springer, 2018, pp. 323−350.

[33] Y. Guo, Y. Liu, A. Oerlemans, S. Lao, S. Wu, M.S. Lew, Deep learning for visual understanding: a review, Neurocomputing 187 (2016) 27−48.

[34] H.-I. Suk, S.-W. Lee, D. Shen, the Alzheimer's Disease Neuroimaging Initiative, Hierarchical feature representation and multimodal fusion with deep learning for AD/MCI diagnosis, Neuroimage 101 (2014) 569−582.

[35] R. Cui, M. Liu, G. Li, Longitudinal analysis for Alzheimer's disease diagnosis using RNN, in: Proceedings of the IEEE 15th International Symposium on Biomedical Imaging, ISBI), 2018, pp. 1398−1401.

[36] L. Gao, et al., Brain disease diagnosis using deep learning features from longitudinal MR images, in: Proceedings of the Joint International Conference on Web and Big Data Asia-Pacific Web (APWeb) and Web-Age Information Management (WAIM), 2018, pp. 327−339.

[37] D.S. Marcus, et al., Open Access Series of Imaging Studies (OASIS): cross-sectional MRI data in young, middle-aged, non-demented, and demented older adults, J. Cognit. Neurosci. 19 (9) (2007) 1498−1507.

[38] C. Szegedy, et al., Rethinking the inception architecture for computer vision, in: Proceedings of the IEEE Conference on Computer Vision and Pattern Recognition, 2016, pp. 2818–2826.

[39] A. Ortiz, J. Munilla, J.M. Gorriz, J. Ramirez, Ensembles of deep learning architectures for the early diagnosis of the Alzheimer's disease, Int. J. Neural Syst. 26 (07) (2016).

[40] D. Lu, K. Popuri, G.W. Ding, R. Balachandar, M.F. Beg, Multimodal and multiscale deep neural networks for the early diagnosis of Alzheimer's disease using structural MR and FDG-PET images, Sci. Rep. 8 (1) (2018). Art. no. 5697.

CHAPTER 8

Deep similarity learning for disease prediction

Vagisha Gupta[1], Shelly Sachdeva[1], Neha Dohare[2]
[1]Department of Computer Science and Engineering, National Institute of Technology Delhi, New Delhi, India; [2]Department of Information Technology, Maharaja Surajmal Institute of Technology, New Delhi, India

1. Introduction

Deep learning has gained tremendous popularity, and has become a highly sought-after research area over the past decade. Even though deep learning has received great attention recently, it has been around for several years. The reason for the sudden popularity is the improvement in processing power of computers as well as the availability of large amounts of good quality data. Deep learning has proven to be useful in many areas, including but not limited to image recognition, stock market prediction, automated text generation, and automated machine translation. Deep learning has also yielded fruitful results in the healthcare domain. It is being actively used for drug discovery, precision medicine, medical imaging, and disease prediction [1]. Deep learning offers huge potential for application in the field of disease prediction. It is essentially a part of the vast field of machine learning, whose functionality aims to mimic the working of the human brain. Deep learning aims to search for solutions to certain trivial tasks that humans find intuitive. These tasks cannot be formally described by rules or mathematical functions but are rather inherent or automatic like identifying objects, animals, or faces. Deep learning models gather knowledge by experience and do not need humans to supply them with formal rules to do so.

Deep learning teaches computers to learn by examples, the same way an infant learns to identify a cat or a dog by looking at several real-life examples. Given a large set of labeled data, deep learning algorithms make predictions based upon the patterns identified between the given input/output pairs by using artificial neural networks (ANNs). These networks try to minimize the difference between the predicted and the actual correct output. By learning patterns present in a dataset, deep learning algorithms can generalize to previously unseen inputs. For example, consider Fig. 8.1, which is a neural network with four layers. The dataset consists of labeled

Trends in Deep Learning Methodologies
ISBN 978-0-12-822226-3
https://doi.org/10.1016/B978-0-12-822226-3.00008-8
183

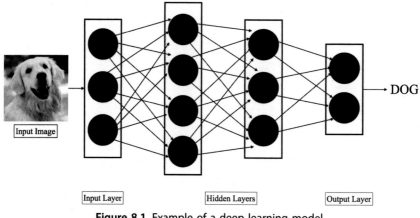

Figure 8.1 Example of a deep learning model.

images of cats and dogs. The deep learning network identifies the features of the images of cats and dogs (like facial features, shape of ears, etc.) from the given dataset and makes a prediction when a new image of a dog is shown to it. In actuality, the layers in a deep learning model may range from several hundred to several thousand as well. Thus the name "deep" learning refers to creating deep neural networks (neural networks with large numbers of layers).

Deep learning models use neural networks for finding associations between inputs and outputs. A neural network contains three types of layer: the input layer, the hidden layers, and the output layer (Fig. 8.1). Every layer consists of several nodes or neurons. Hidden layers perform most of the computation. Each layer is associated with weight and bias parameters that can be tuned. These parameters are associated with the learning process of a deep learning algorithm. The model predicts a complete pass of inputs, from input to the output layer. This predicted output is then compared with the actual output using a loss function. One of the simplest loss functions, "mean squared error" loss function [2], is given by the following equation:

$$MSE = \sum_{i=1}^{n} \left(Y_i - \widehat{Y}_i\right)^2 \qquad (8.1)$$

where $\widehat{Y}$ represents the prediction, Y represents the expected output, and n is the sample size. The goal of the network is to minimize the loss by tuning the weight and bias parameters (this is done through back-propagation). The learning stops when the loss is minimized and reaches an optimal value or after a specified number of iterations are completed.

Deep learning architectures can be classified into different types, namely, convolutional neural networks (CNNs) [3], autoencoders [4], adversarial networks [5], restricted Boltzmann machine (RBM) [1], recurrent neural networks (RNNs) [6], and radial basis function neural networks [1,15]. All these are summarized in Table 8.1. The table talks about all these different types of deep learning architectures: their network model, training type, implementation sample, and common applications. All machine learning models are of two types: discriminative and generative. Broadly speaking, discriminative models model the decision boundary between classes, whereas generative models model the actual distribution of each class. In both these cases the training type or learning can be supervised and/or unsupervised. In the case of supervised learning, the model learns the mapping between input and output, given the input/output pairs. However, in the case of unsupervised learning, the goal is to learn about the data from the given input data. In this case, there is no corresponding output data.

Some popular deep learning architectures are discussed in detail next.

1. Convolutional neural network

CNN is a deep learning architecture that is most commonly used for visual tasks [3]. A CNN consists of neurons or nodes that have learnable weights and biases. Every node performs a convolution operation (dot product with filters) on the received input, which may be followed with a nonlinearity. Three kinds of layers build up a CNN: convolution layers, pooling layers, and fully connected layers (same as regular neural networks). These are stacked together to form a CNN or ConvNet. CNNs have applications in several areas like image recognition, image classification, video recognition, and natural language processing (NLP). The major advantage of CNNs is that the preprocessing required is much less as compared to other similar deep learning networks. Where in other primitive techniques filters are hand engineered, in CNNs characteristics are learned by the network during the training.

2. Recurrent neural networks

An RNN is a type of ANN in which the connections between the nodes form a directed graph along a sequence [6]. RNNs are deep learning networks that possess dynamic temporal behavior. They are neural networks with memory. All the inputs in the case of RNNs are related, contrary to other neural networks where they are independent. RNNs find their application in places where some context is needed from the previous inputs. They are popularly used in next word prediction, speech recognition, etc.

Table 8.1 Deep learning architectures.

Architecture	Network model	Training type	Implementation sample	Common application
CNN	Discriminative	Supervised	Siamese network, deep CNN	Image recognition/classification
Autoencoder	Generative	Unsupervised	Sparse autoencoders	Dimensionality reduction; encoding
Adversarial network	Generative and discriminative	Unsupervised	Generative adversarial network	Reconstruction of 3D models; image improvement
RBM	Generative and discriminative	Unsupervised	Deep belief network; deep Boltzmann machine	Dimensionality reduction; feature learning
RNN (LSTM)	Discriminative	Supervised	Deep RNN; neural machine translation	NLP; language translation
RBF	Discriminative	Supervised and unsupervised	Radial basis function NN	Function approximation; time series prediction
Kohonen self-organizing NN	Generative	Unsupervised	Kohonen self-organizing NN	Dimensionality reduction; optimization problems

CNN, Convolutional neural network; *LSTM*, long short-term memory; *NLP*, natural language processing; *NN*, neural network; *RBF*, radial basis function neural network; *RBM*, restricted Boltzmann machine.

3. Multilayer perceptron

Multilayer perceptron (MLP) [7] is a feed-forward neural network that examines how a straightforward model of biological brains can be used to solve challenging computational tasks like predictive analysis tasks. The goal is not to develop realistic models of the brain, but instead to produce robust algorithms and data structures that can be used to represent hard problems. An MLP contains three types of layers, which consist of input layers, hidden layers, and output layers. The first layer is known as the input layer, the last layer is known as the output layer and all the middle layers are called the hidden layers. In this deep learning network, the information flows in a single direction only, that is, from the input to the output. The computations are all done along the forward pass path.

4. Autoencoders

Autoencoders [4] are deep learning architectures where the input is the same as the output. These are feed-forward neural networks that basically compress input and then reconstruct the output using this feature/representation. Autoencoders consist of two types of networks: the encoder and the decoder network. The former compresses input and creates what can be called an intermediate code and the latter uses this intermediate code to generate the output. The encoder and decoder are comprised of several layers of RBMs stacked together. Autoencoders are very useful in dimension reduction techniques.

There are several deep learning libraries like TensorFlow [8], Keras [9], Microsoft Cognitive Toolkit (previously CNTK) [10], PyTorch [11], Apache MXNet [12], Caffe [13], deeplearning4j, and Theano [14]. Table 8.2 summarizes these libraries. CNN and RNN are supported by all these libraries. Since GPU is significantly helpful in speeding up the matrix computation, most of them also support graphics processing unit (GPU) via the interface provided by NVIDIA CUDA deep neural network library (CuDNN).

Deep learning, despite its tremendous potential, poses many challenges. Deep learning models are assessed based on their outputs and it is not clear how that output has been reached. Most deep learning techniques are black box techniques. Another challenge faced by deep learning is the lack of labeled data. Even though there is an enormous amount of data, with more data being added day by day, there is not enough labeled data as it is not humanly possible to go through all this data. Another possible big challenge faced by deep learning is the computational power and resources required. It is not possible to reduce complexity without losing critical information

Table 8.2 Deep learning libraries.

Library	Initial release	Developed by	Core language	Interface support	License
TensorFlow	November 2015	Google Brain Team	Python, C++, CUDA	Python, C/C++, Java, Go	Apache License 2.0
Keras	March 2015	Developed as part of project ONEIROS	Python	Python	MIT License
Microsoft Cognitive Toolkit (previously CNTK)	January 2016	Microsoft	C++	C++, Python, Brain Script	MIT License
PyTorch	October 2016	Facebook's AI Research Lab	Python, C++, CUDA	Python, C/C++, and Lua	BSD
Apache MXNet	December 2016	Apache Software Foundation	C++	C++, Python, R, Scala, Perl, Julia, etc.	Apache License 2.0
Caffe	September 2015	Berkeley Vision and Learning Center	C++	Python and MATLAB	BSD
deeplearning4j	November 2013	Eclipse deeplearning4j Development Team	Java	Java, Scala, and Python	Apache License 2.0
Theano	2007	Montreal Institute for Learning Algorithms, University of Montreal	Python	Python	BSD

needed for classification. As a result of this, deep learning models are fairly expensive. Deep learning has done well in areas like visual data processing, NLP, image recognition, etc. However, the application of deep learning in several fields like healthcare has not yet been explored to the fullest.

In this chapter, one such field, that is, disease prediction, has been explored. We have proposed a deep learning model for disease prediction based on similarity learning, which is a subpart of supervised learning. First, a deep learning architecture is used to obtain an effective representation that contains important characteristics of the patient data. Then, similarity probability between a pair of patients is measured to indicate the risk of having the same disease between two patients. Using the similarity information, disease prediction is performed by classifying the patients into the category of diseases.

The chapter is organized in the following way. In Section 2, we put our work in a broader context by examining the state of the art in the current domain. Section 3 presents an architecture of a deep similarity learning model with the performed steps and a case study for disease prediction using the model. Section 4 presents the performance evaluation of different deep learning architectures on a sample dataset. In Section 5 we discuss why our proposed model can help in an expert decision support system to better facilitate patients, and look at directions for further work.

2. State of the art

There have been several surveys of deep learning. In [1,15], a general survey of deep learning algorithms, architectures, and applications has been discussed. Various deep neural network architectures are compared based on the network model, training type, training algorithm, implementation sample, application area, sample dataset, and deep learning framework. In [3], an overview and application of CNN in radiology insights imaging has been studied. There has also been a significant amount of work with a focus on disease diagnosis in the healthcare domain. For example, in [16], a regularized stacked denoising autoencoder has been used to perform clinical risk prediction. Deep Patient [17] aims to predict multiple diseases like severe diabetes, schizophrenia, and various types of cancers. It accomplishes this with the help of a three-layer stack of denoising autoencoders, which capture the hierarchical regularities and dependencies in the electronic health records (EHRs). Deep Record [18] has been built to predict unplanned readmission after discharge. It provides an end-to-end deep learning system that learns to extract features from medical records and predict the future automatically. DeepCare [19] is a deep dynamic neural network, based on long short-term memory (LSTM), that aims to read medical records and predict future outcomes. The authors in their earlier research evaluated the presence of kidney disease in patients on a nephrology dataset through a deep learning technique, namely, feed-forward network [21]. Similarity learning [22] deals with measuring the similarity between a pair of images and objects, and has application in tasks related to classification and regression.

Learning patient similarity is an important area in the medical domain to improve decision support and help medical experts to provide better medical facilities. The traditional similarity learning methods directly measure the similarity on input feature vectors without learning the parameters on the input vector. Therefore in recent research [23], softmax and triplet loss framework have been proposed to measure similarity learning based on the length of the visits of a patient by appropriately representing the medical records. Using softmax-based framework, pairwise labels are classified into one of the classes and using a triplet loss framework a margin is learned to separate the patients into positive class and negative class.

In recent years, significant research has been done that employs deep learning in the field of disease prediction. The state of the art in the domain of deep learning and disease prediction is shown in Table 8.3. Various methods such as CNN, regularized stacked denoising auto-encoder – softmax layer (RSDAE-SM), stacked denoising auto-encoder (SDAE), and LSTM have been used in disease prediction. In [31], generative adversarial networks have been used for disease prediction using (EHRs). Mehta et al. [32] present a technical report on sampling for a deep learning model diagnosis. In [33], chronic disease prediction has been performed using the medical notes of a patient. Some research has also been done on the application of deep learning techniques for prediction of kidney diseases in recent years. A deep neural network method is proposed in [20] that predicts the presence or absence of chronic kidney disease. The model outperforms other machine learning classifiers. In [34] the risk of kidney disease in hypertension patients has been found using bidirectional LSTM. An article on the employment of artificial intelligence for the improvement of kidney care [35] discusses the tremendous potential of artificial intelligence in the domain. Deep learning techniques like ANNs have been proven to outperform machine learning techniques like support vector machines in the prediction of chronic kidney disease [36]. These along with

Table 8.3 State of the art in the domain of deep learning and disease prediction.

Title of research	Method	Application domain	Data source	Results
Application of CNN in radiology [3]	CNN	Radiology tasks	ImageNet	Knowledge about CNN is needed to leverage it in radiology research
Risk prediction of acute coronary syndrome [16]	RSDAE–SM	Acute coronary syndrome	EHR data from the Chinese People's Liberation Army General Hospital	AUC = 0.868 Accuracy = 0.73
Proposing a novel unsupervised deep feature learning model for predicting the future of patients [17]	SDAE	Future disease prediction	EHR from the clinical data warehouse	Results obtained on future disease prediction were better than other feature learning models AUC = 0.773 Accuracy = 0.929
Proposing a novel deep learning model, Deepr, for future risk prediction [18]	CNN	Prediction of future risks and unplanned readmission after discharge	Data was collected from an Australian hospital chain	Deepr can extract features from medical records and predict future risk
Proposing a novel dynamic memory model, DeepCare, for predictive learning [19]	LSTM	Mental health and diabetes	Data was collected from a large Australian hospital over 12 years	Results were competitive when compared to the state of the art F-score = 79.1%

Continued

Table 8.3 State of the art in the domain of deep learning and disease prediction.—cont'd

Title of research	Method	Application domain	Data source	Results
Use of similarity learning for personalized healthcare [23]	CNN_softmax, CNN_tripletloss	Disease prediction based on visit length of patients	Real-world dataset over 2 years	CNN_softmax outperforms state-of-the-art learning methods in the domain
Disease prediction from EHR [31]	Auxillary classifier GAN (AC-GAN)	Generalized disease prediction model	Breast Cancer Wisconsin (Diagnostic) dataset	AC-GANs gave the best results in comparison to machine learning algorithms (SVM, Adaboost, decision tree, random forest, etc). Accuracy = 97.77% AUC–ROC = 98.89%

AUC-ROC, area under curve - receiver operator characteristic; *CNN*, convolutional neural network; *EHR*, electronic health record; *GAN*, generative adversarial network; *LSTM*, long short-term memory; *RSDAE-SM*, regularized stacked denoising auto-encoder - softmax layer; *SDAE*, stacked denoising auto-encoder; *SVM*, support vector machine.

all the other state of the art are summarized in Table 8.4. The results of using various deep learning techniques are presented along with the datasets used during experimentation.

After rigorous analysis, the state of the art shows that there exists plenty of work done on disease prediction using deep learning approaches (some are detailed in Table 8.3). Also, many similarity learning methods have been proposed to find relationships between a pair of patients. The current study presents a model to jointly learn patient feature representations using a deep learning architecture and measure pairwise similarity for disease prediction.

Data for the evaluation of the current study has been acquired from the OpenEHRBenchmark Dataset (ORBDA), which is a standardized dataset based on OpenEHR (a standard for semantic interoperability of electronic health records) [24,25]. A domain-specific (kidney-related) dataset has been explored. Table 8.4 discusses the use of various deep learning techniques on kidney-specific data and their results.

3. Materials and methods

This section presents the architecture of a deep similarity learning model. The steps involved for disease prediction are data gathering, data pre-processing, splitting the data, training the model, evaluation, and prediction. A case study involving the prediction of kidney-related disease on an EHR dataset is also presented. Combining deep learning with similarity learning results in a model called deep similarity learning model. Fig. 8.2 presents an architecture diagram of a deep similarity learning model involving various steps.

3.1 Data gathering

This step is of immense importance as the performance of our predictive model will be determined by the quality and quantity of our data. Healthcare data helps in providing a comprehensive view of patients, personalized healthcare, and improved communication between patients and doctors. Healthcare data can be gathered in two data sources, which are categorized as primary and secondary data sources [26]. Primary data is the data collected for the first time directly from observations of patients, interviews, and surveys. Secondary data is the data already collected and examined by someone else, e.g., online data (EHRs, electronic medical records, research data, and libraries).

Table 8.4 State of the art in the domain of disease prediction (kidney specific).

Title of research	Deep learning technique	Application domain	Data source	Results
Prediction of chronic kidney disease [20]	ANN	Chronic kidney disease	Chronic kidney disease dataset from UCI Machine Learning Repository	Accuracy = 97.76%
Prediction of kidney diseases [21]	Feed-forward neural network	Kidney disease	ORDBA dataset	Accuracy = 98.7%
Proposing a framework, DeepEHR, for chronic disease prediction using medical notes [33]	Different hierarchical structures and their comparison with CNN and LSTM	Heart failure, kidney failure, and stroke	PubMed Dataset, NYU Langone Center medical notes	Deep learning models with notes outperform all baseline models by a large margin
Prediction of kidney disease in hypertension patients using EHR [34]	Initial modeling of the problem as a binary classification task, then proposal of a hybrid neural network incorporating BiLSTM and autoencoder networks	Kidney disease	Dataset based on a large number of raw EHR data from hospitals in China	Proposed model received 89.7% accuracy
Analysis of AI approaches to improve kidney care [35]		Acute kidney injury and chronic kidney disease		AI has great potential for improving kidney care
Comparison of ANN and SVM for prediction of chronic kidney disease [36]	ANN	Chronic kidney disease	Chronic kidney disease dataset obtained from UCI Machine Learning Repository	ANN outperformed SVM

AI, Artificial intelligence; ANN, artificial neural network; BiLSTM, bidirectional LSTM; CNN, convolutional neural network; EHR, electronic health record; LSTM, long short-term memory; ORBDA, OpenEHRBenchmark Dataset; SVM, support vector machine.

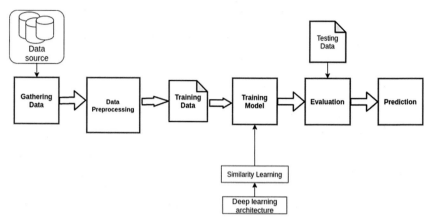

Figure 8.2 Architecture of a deep similarity learning model.

EHRs can be used to evaluate clinical similarities between patients. An EHR is individual health information stored digitally, instantly, and securely available to authorized users. EHRs consist of the patient's diagnoses, medications, allergies, treatment plans, radiology images, and test results. An important consideration while working on deep similarity learning architecture is collecting large volumes of EHR data.

3.2 Data preprocessing

A huge amount of healthcare data exists in the world. After gathering this data, it cannot be directly used by medical experts, researchers, or any applications. Data preprocessing is a way of converting this raw data into a much-desired form so that useful information can be derived from it, which is fed into the training model for successful medical decisions, diagnoses, and treatments. It aims to remove outliers from data, normalize the data, find relations between data, and extract important features from the data. Data preprocessing involves several techniques like data cleaning, data integration, data transformation, and data reduction. These techniques are shown in Fig. 8.3.

Inaccurate or inconsistent records are replaced, modified, or deleted from the data by the process of data cleaning. Due to the increasing volume of data, integrating the data becomes an important step. The data from multiple data sources is unified to a single source with the help of data integration. Data transformation plays a significant role in converting unprocessed data into an understandable form. Data reduction is performed to obtain a reduced representation of the data that is significantly smaller in

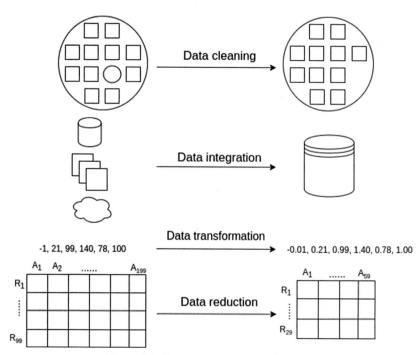

Figure 8.3 Data preprocessing techniques.

volume but maintains the original quality. Data preprocessing is an important task while dealing with healthcare data due to different challenges such as data collection from different sources, handling missing values, data heterogeneity, and high dimensionality data. Patient data is collected in different forms such as patients' diagnoses, medications, allergies, treatment plans, radiology images, and test results, and then integrated into a single data source (or a database). Sensitive patient data is then cleaned by using appropriate techniques like interpolation, multiple imputations, or expectation maximization. The data is transformed by using strategies like aggregation, generalization, and normalization. Dimensionality is reduced by using data reduction techniques like feature extraction and feature selection.

3.3 Splitting the data

After bringing our data into the desired form using preprocessing techniques, it is split into two sets: a training set and a test set. The training set contains known output values. The model or the algorithm trains on this training data and is generalized to other data later on. After the model has been trained on the training data, the test data (or subset) is used to evaluate our model's prediction on this subset.

3.4 Model training

Training a model means teaching a machine or an algorithm to memorize patterns in the dataset and capture these patterns to map the input features to the target output using a function. Model training improves the ability of the model to predict the objective output. The training of a model involves supplying training data to a learning algorithm. But, for training the model the first important step is to choose the right model. We categorize our input and output values and then the model is chosen depending on the algorithm. It is a supervised learning algorithm if the input data is labeled, and an unsupervised algorithm if the input data is unlabeled. If the objective function is optimized by interaction with an environment, it is a reinforcement learning problem. Depending on the output of the model, it is a regression problem if the output is a number, a classification problem if the output is a class, and a clustering problem if the output is a group of inputs. Also, many models have been created by data scientists and researchers over the years, some of which are well equipped for image, sequence (like music), numerical, and text-based data. The training model process involves initialization of some random values for weights W and biases b, and concatenating them with our input values x for prediction of the output using those values. Sometimes, the prediction is very poor. This can be improved by comparing our model's predictions with the required output and simultaneously modifying the values in W and b such that we have better predictions. This is repeated several times and each iteration is referred to as a training step.

We explore many different deep learning architectures that can potentially be used to train our model for optimal representation learning of our data to perform disease prediction. We further present the idea of implementing representation learning, similarity learning to learn local important features and relationships among patient vectors, and obtain a similarity score to perform disease prediction.

3.4.1 Representation learning

Representation of information can make a computational task very easy or very difficult. Representation learning [27] refers to techniques by which a system can automatically discover representations or features from the input data. A feed-forward neural network, trained using supervised learning, can be thought to perform representation learning in the sense that the entire network learns a representation to pass to the last layer, which is a linear classifier. In the case of supervised learning, a representation is obtained at every hidden layer (specifically the topmost hidden layers), which makes the learning task easier. For instance, consider the task of identifying vehicles on a road. In this case, the representation passed to the last layer can separate vehicle images from nonvehicle images.

The core idea of representation learning is to make the same representation useful for similar tasks. It is essentially a way to extract features from raw unlabeled data by training a neural network on a secondary learning task. The general idea is to use the data from a primary task and use it for learning or making predictions for a second similar task. By using representation learning it is also possible to learn good representations for unlabeled data (which is usually abundant) and then use it for supervised learning tasks. This overcomes the problem of overfitting arising if supervised learning is performed on the limited labeled data available. Recently, some deep learning architectures like CNNs, RNNs, and autoencoders have been widely chosen for representation learning where the output of each layer can be considered as a representation. Each hidden layer represents the next layer, i.e., each output is a representation.

Deep learning networks based on these architectures have also been employed for performing disease prediction, the topic of discussion in this chapter. CNNs and autoencoders have been the most widely used ones [15,16]. In [19], a deep learning network, DeepCare, has been developed for reading medical records of patients, storing and analyzing previous as well as current illnesses, and predicting future outcomes using a neural network based on LSTM. In this chapter, a case study on the prediction of kidney disease has been done using the ORDBA dataset, as well as three deep learning architectures (namely CNNs, RNNs, and MPL).

3.4.2 Similarity learning

Similarity learning [22] deals with measuring the similarity between a pair of images and objects, and has application in tasks related to classification and regression. The aim is to learn the similarity function that finds an optimal relation between two relatable or similar objects in a quantitative way. Some applications of finding similarity measures are handwritten text recognition, face identification, search engines, signature verification, etc. Typically, similarity learning involves giving a pair of images as input and discovering how similar they are to each other. The output can be a nonnegative similarity score between 0 and 1, 1 if the two images are completely similar to each other, otherwise 0. Fig. 8.4 shows the calculation of the similarity score between two images. The images are embedded into vector representation using a deep learning architecture for learning the

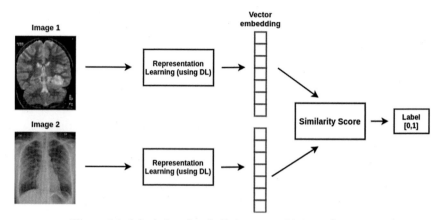

Figure 8.4 Calculating the similarity score. *DL,* Deep learning.

representation of features of the images followed by passing it to the similarity metric learning function, which measures the similarity score between two images, usually a value between 0 and 1.

Consider two vectors of features, x and y; some of the similarity calculation measures are:

1. *Cosine similarity:* This measures the similarity using the cosine of the angle between two vectors in a multidimensional space. It is given by:

$$\text{similarity}(x, y) = \cos(\theta) = \frac{x \cdot y}{|x||y|} \tag{8.2}$$

2. *Euclidean distance:* This is the most common similarity distance measure and measures the distance between any two points in a euclidean space. It is given by:

$$d(x, y) = \sqrt{\sum_{i=1}^{n} (x_i - y_i)^2} \tag{8.3}$$

3. *Manhattan distance:* This is a similarity distance measure in which the distance between two points is calculated by the sum of the absolute differences of the points. It is given by:

$$d(x, y) = \left| \sum_{i=1}^{n} (x_i - y_i) \right| \tag{8.4}$$

Some research [23] shows disease prediction using the traditional similarity learning methods (cosine, euclidean) directly measuring the similarity on input feature vectors without learning the parameters on the input vector. They do not perform well on original data, which is highly dimensional, noisy, and sparse. Therefore we follow an approach used in [28] to measure the similarity between patients by first learning the parameters on the input value. We call this novel approach the *softmax-based framework* for calculating the similarity between a pair of vectors.

4. *Softmax-based supervised classification framework:* This method performs classification on the learned representation by measuring a similarity probability between pairs of objects and using it as a score for ranking the similarity. To ensure that pairwise labels are classified correctly, a fully connected softmax layer is added. The similarity is calculated by using a bilinear distance given by:

$$\text{sim}(x, y) = W_k x_i \oplus W_k y_i, \qquad (8.5)$$

where $W_k \in R$ and $\oplus$ is a bitwise addition.

3.5 Evaluation and prediction

After training the model using representation learning and similarity learning, local important features and relationships among patient vectors are learned and a similarity score is obtained. New patients are then ranked according to their similarity score and disease prediction is performed using a classification-based approach to predict the disease from which a patient might be suffering. An accuracy score is calculated for the evaluation performance. Deep learning has shown good results in the prediction of kidney disease [20,21]. In [23] it has been shown that the incorporation of similarity learning with deep learning can yield good results as well. Hence, in this study, both have been combined to see the results on disease prediction.

Case study for a deep similarity learning model: Medical experts are continuously trying to take into consideration many parameters to discover the unique characteristics of a patient. Many deep learning approaches have been presented for disease prediction in the healthcare domain to discover important characteristics of patients and provide personalized treatments. However, deep learning approaches ignore finding the relationships between different patients. Therefore there is a need for developing methods that jointly learn the patient representations and find the relationship between the patients using pairwise similarity. In this study, one such field for disease prediction has been explored. The case study aims to derive important insights and knowledge from the healthcare dataset and apply it to the deep similarity model for predicting kidney-related diseases. The data is gathered from the ORBDA dataset. It is then preprocessed by removing missing values, maintaining heterogeneity in the data, and using one-hot encoding for the output values. Assuming there are N patients, the nth patient p_n having kidney disease can be represented by a sequence of input features denoted by x_1, x_2, ..., x_{12}. Medical codes are captured indicating the disease suffered or treatment received by the patient. These codes are mapped to the International Classification of Diseases (ICD-10) for statistical classification of diseases and related health problems [29]. The medical codes from the EHR data are denoted as c_1, c_2, ..., $c_{|c|}$ where $|c|$ is the number of unique medical codes that correspond to the output label or prediction and is termed main_diagnosis.

The model is trained by using three deep learning architectures, ANN (MLP), CNN, and RNN (LSTM), for optimal representation of patient data. The idea is fist to derive important local patient information using representation learning and then measure similarity among patients using a softmax-based supervised classification framework. This is done using the ability of best suitable deep learning architecture as per the requirement of the model. After deriving the learned representations, a patient similarity score is computed using a softmax-based framework. After training the model, disease prediction is done to predict the disease from which a patient might be suffering. For each new patient that is being hospitalized, the distance from each training patient is calculated for classification purposes after mapping the representation matrix to another hyperplane. Training patients are then ranked according to their similarity score from new patients in ascending order.

4. Results and discussion

This section discusses the experimental results by evaluating the model on EHR data.

Dataset description: The dataset used in this study is known as ORBDA. It was developed using data supplied by the Brazilian Public Health System through the SUS (DATASUS) Database Department of Informatics. The source dataset used in this study encodes two kinds of healthcare data, hospitalization and high-complexity procedures, accessible in the Hospital Admission Authorization (AIH) (5.73 million records) and

High Complexity Procedure Authorization (APAC) (9.56 million records) databases, respectively. An entry in the AIH database is created whenever a medical institution generates a hospitalization request. On the other hand, medical service providers create documents in the APAC database to record approved high complexity processes for accounting purposes. While AIH data is recorded in a single file, occurrences recorded in the APAC database are further split into six distinct classifications: bariatric surgery, chemotherapy, medicine, nephrology, radiotherapy, and outpatient miscellaneous. The dataset is filtered into a nephrology dataset (containing 5.07% records) from the APAC database and used in evaluating the model for the current study. After analyzing the dataset and performing preprocessing steps, 12 input patient features are taken into consideration, which are owner_id, HIC_antibodies, HIV, HbsAg, age, healthcare_unit, procedure, reason_-for_discharge, state, urea_reduction_rate, venous_fistula_amount, and volume. The output or the prediction is made on main_diagnosis, which contains 10 output classes following ICD-10 codes for kidney-related diseases (E10_2—Type 1 diabetes mellitus with kidney complications, E14_2—Unspecified diabetes mellitus with renal complications, I10—Essential primary hypertension, I12_0—Hypertensive chronic kidney disease, N03_9—Chronic nephritic syndrome with unspecified morphologic changes, N08_3, N08_8—Glomerular disorders in diseases classified elsewhere, N18_0—Chronic kidney disease, N18_8—End-stage renal disease, N18_9—Chronic kidney disease, unspecified).

Software and hardware configuration: For performance evaluation and metric calculation on CPU, a Dell-Inspiron with operating system Ubuntu 18.04 LTS, 1.70 GHz Intel Core i5 with four core processor and 4GB RAM is used. The frameworks are implemented with TensorFlow [8] and Keras [9]. Adam [30] is used to optimize the parameters of the model.

Performance evaluation: In this section, the results obtained after evaluating the model on a real EHR dataset are presented. The dataset used belongs to nephrology and it has been randomly divided into training and test sets having a ratio of 0.80:0.20. To optimally represent the health data for each patient, various deep learning architectures are implemented, which is effective in deriving important features from fixed-length segments of the complete dataset. The performance of a deep learning model on the nephrology dataset for disease prediction accuracy as a measure is calculated as follows:

Accuracy

$$= \frac{\text{True Positive } + \text{ True Negative}}{\text{True Positive } + \text{ False Negative } + \text{ False Positive } + \text{ True Negative}}$$

The model is trained by using three deep learning architectures, ANN (MLP), CNN, and RNN (LSTM), for optimal representation of patient data. As can be seen from Table 8.5, the MLP model achieved an effective training accuracy of 98.74%, whereas CNN and RNN achieved training accuracies of 98.72% and 96.71%, respectively. Although MLP gives slightly better results than CNN, the layers in CNN are sparsely connected rather than fully connected as in MLP, hence making the CNN architecture go deeper rather than grow bigger. Also, CNN is considered best for a classification-based supervised task where medical data features need to be optimally represented by finding the patterns using filters. Exploring some deep learning approaches helped us to discover the important characteristics of patients and provide personalized treatments. However, deep learning approaches ignore finding the relationships between different patients. Therefore there is a need to develop methods that jointly learn the patient representations and find the relationship between the patients using pairwise similarity learning.

5. Conclusions and future work

With recent advancements, deep learning techniques have been found to play an important role in disease diagnosis, risk assessment, drug development, and providing personalized healthcare to patients. In the current study, a deep similarity learning model for disease prediction was proposed. As an initial work, the model was trained by using three deep learning architectures, ANN (MLP), CNN, and RNN (LSTM), for optimal representation of patient data. The idea was first to derive important local patient information using representation learning and then measure similarity

Table 8.5 Measure of performance model.

Deep learning architecture	Accuracy	Loss
MLP	98.74	8
CNN	98.72	12.7
RNN	96.71	15.28

CNN, Convolutional neural network; MLP, multilayer perceptron; RNN, recurrent neural network.

among patients using a softmax-based supervised classification framework. This was done using the ability of best suitable deep learning architecture as per the requirement of the model. After deriving the learned representations, a patient similarity score could be computed using a softmax-based similarity learning framework. After training the model, disease prediction was done to predict the disease from which a patient might be suffering. The model was trained on a standardized nephrology dataset and experimental results obtained encouraged us to use one of the suitable models in calculating similarity as future work. The deep similarity learning model can further be enhanced where large complex models and training on large datasets become necessary for improving the performance. An effective methodology can be proposed to increase the scalability of the deep similarity learning model.

References

[1] A. Shrestha, A. Mahmood, Review of deep learning algorithms and architectures, IEEE Access 7 (2019) 53040–53065. https://doi.org/10.1109/ACCESS.2019.2912200.

[2] A. Ghosh, H. Kumar, P. Sastry, Robust Loss Functions under Label Noise for Deep Neural Networks, 2017.

[3] R. Yamashita, M. Nishio, R.K.G. Do, K. Togashi, Convolutional neural networks: an overview and application in radiology, Insights Imaging (2018).

[4] P. Vincent, H. Larochelle, I. Lajoie, Y. Bengio, P.-A. Manzagol, Stacked denoising autoencoders: learning useful representations in a deep network with a local denoising criterion, J. Mach. Learn. Res. 11 (2010) 3371–3408.

[5] I. Goodfellow, J. Pouget-Abadie, M. Mirza, B. Xu, D. Warde-Farley, S. Ozair, A. Courville, Y. Bengio, Generative adversarial networks, Adv. Neural Inf. Process. Syst. 3 (2014).

[6] P. Liu, X. Qiu, X. Huang, Recurrent Neural Network for Text Classification with Multi-Task Learning, 2016.

[7] F. Murtagh, Multilayer perceptrons for classification and regression, Neurocomputing 2 (1991) 183–197.

[8] M. Abadi, et al., TensorFlow: Large-Scale Machine Learning on Heterogeneous Distributed Systems, 2016 (Online). Available: https://arxiv.org/abs/1603.04467.

[9] F. Chollet, Keras, 2015. https://github.com/fchollet/keras.

[10] F. Seide, A.C. Agarwal, Microsoft's open-source deep-learning toolkit, in: Proceedings of the 22Nd ACM SIGKDD International Conference on Knowledge Discovery and Data Mining (New York, NY, USA, 2016), KDD'16, ACM, 2016, 2135–2135.

[11] A. Paszke, S. Gross, S. Chintala, G. Chanan, E. Yang, Z. DeVito, Z. Lin, A. Desmaison, L. Antiga, A. Lerer, Automatic differentiation in pytorch, in: NIPS-W, 2017.

[12] T. Chen, M. Li, Y. Li, M. Lin, N. Wang, M. Wang, T. Xiao, B. Xu, C. Zhang, Z. Zhang, MXNet: A Flexible and Efficient Machine Learning Library for Heterogeneous Distributed Systems, 2015.

[13] Y. Jia, E. Shelhamer, J. Donahue, S. Karayev, J. Long, R.B. Girshick, S. Guadarrama, T.C. Darrell, Convolutional architecture for fast feature embedding, CoRR abs/1408 (2014) 5093.

[14] J. Bergstra, F. Bastien, O. Breuleux, P. Lamblin, R. Pascanu, O. Delalleau, G. Desjardins, D. Warde-Farley, I. Goodfellow, A. Bergeron, et al., Theano: deep learning on GPUs with python, in: NIPS 2011, BigLearning Workshop, Granada, Spain, vol. 3, Citeseer, 2011, pp. 1−48.

[15] S. Pouyanfar, S. Sadiq, Y. Yan, H. Tian, Y. Tao, M.P. Reyes, M.L. Shyu, S.C. Chen, S.S. Iyengar, A survey on deep learning: algorithms, techniques, and applications, ACM Comput. Surv. 51 (5) (2018) 92:1−92:36.

[16] Z. Huang, et al., A regularized deep learning approach for clinical risk prediction of acute coronary syndrome using electronic health records, IEEE Trans. Biomed. Eng. 65 (5) (2017) 956−968.

[17] R. Miotto, L. Li, B.A. Kidd, J.T. Dudley, Deep patient: an unsupervised representation to predict the future of patients from the electronic health records, Sci. Rep. 6 (2016) 26094. April.

[18] P. Nguyen, T. Tran, N. Wickramasinghe, S. Venkatesh, Deepr: a convolutional net for medical records, IEEE J. Biomed. Health Inform. 21 (2016) 22−30. https://doi.org/10.1109/jbhi.2016.2633963.

[19] T. Pham, T. Tran, D. Phung, S. Venkatesh, Deepcare: a deep dynamic memory model for predictive medicine, Adv. Knowl. Discov. Data Min. (2016) 1−27, arXiv, no. i.

[20] H. Kriplani, B. Patel, S. Roy, Prediction of Chronic Kidney Diseases Using Deep Artificial Neural Network Technique, 2019, 10.1007/978-3-030-04061-1_18.

[21] N. Dohare, S. Sachdeva, Evaluation of nephrology dataset through deep learning technique, in: U. Batra, N. Roy, B. Panda (Eds.), Data Science and Analytics. REDSET 2019. Communications in Computer and Information Science, vol. 1229, Springer, Singapore, 2020.

[22] S. Melacci, L. Sarti, M. Maggini, M. Bianchini, A Neural Network Approach to Similarity Learning, 2008, pp. 133−136, 10.1007/978-3-540-69939-2_13.

[23] Q. Suo, F. Ma, Y. Yuan, M. Huai, W. Zhong, J. Gao, A. Zhang, Deep patient similarity learning for personalized healthcare, IEEE Trans. NanoBiosci. 17 (3) (2018) 219−227. https://doi.org/10.1109/TNB.2018.2837622.

[24] Generation of a Public Base for Evaluation of Persistence Mechanisms of Electronic Health Records Systems Based on the openEHR Foundation Specifications « L@MPADA/UERJ -InformáticaMédica, Lampada.uerj.Br, 2019 (Online). Available: http://www.lampada.uerj.br/en/orbda/. (Accessed 17 April 2019).

[25] S. Sachdeva, S. Bhalla, Semantic interoperability in standardized electronic health record databases, J. Data Inform. Qual. 3 (2012) 1.

[26] C.R. Kothari, Research Methodology: Methods and Techniques.

[27] Y. Bengio, A. Courville, P. Vincent, Representation Learning: A Review and New Perspectives. IEEE Transactions on Pattern Analysis and Machine Intelligence, vol. 35, 2013, pp. 1798−1828, 10.1109/TPAMI.2013.50.

[28] A. Bordes, J. Weston, N. Usunier, Open question answering with weakly supervised embedding models, in: Machine Learning and Knowledge Discovery in Databases. Springer, 2014, pp. 165−180.

[29] Government of India, Placing the Report on National Digital Health Blueprint (NDHB) in Public Domain for Comments/views Regarding, 2019. https://mohfw.gov.in/sites/default/files/National_Digital_Health_Blueprint_Report comments_invited.pdf.

[30] D.P. Kingma, J. Ba, Adam: A Method for Stochastic Optimization, 2014 (Online). Available: https://arxiv.org/abs/1412.6980.

[31] U. Hwang, S. Choi, S. Yoon, Disease Prediction from Electronic Health Records Using Generative Adversarial Networks, 2017.

[32] P. Mehta, S. Portillo, M. Balazinska, A. Connolly, Sampling for Deep Learning Model Diagnosis (Technical Report), 2020.

[33] J. Liu, Z. Zhang, N. Razavian, Deep EHR: Chronic Disease Prediction Using Medical Notes, 2018. Available: https://arxiv.org/pdf/1808.04928.pdf.

[34] Y. Ren, H. Fei, X. Liang, et al., A hybrid neural network model for predicting kidney disease in hypertension patients based on electronic health records, BMC Med. Inf. Decis. Making 19 (2019) 51. https://doi.org/10.1186/s12911-019-0765-4.

[35] P. Rashidi, A. Bihorac, Artificial intelligence approaches to improve kidney care, Nat. Rev. Nephrol. 16 (2020) 71–72. https://doi.org/10.1038/s41581-019-0243-3.

[36] N. Almansour, H. Syed, N. Khayat, R. Altheeb, R. Juri, J. Alhiyafi, S. Alrashed, S. Olatunji, Neural network and support vector machine for the prediction of chronic kidney disease: a comparative study, Comput. Biol. Med. 109 (2019). https://doi.org/10.1016/j.compbiomed.2019.04.017.

CHAPTER 9

Changing the outlook of security and privacy with approaches to deep learning

Shweta Paliwal, Vishal Bharti, Amit Kumar Mishra
Department of Computer Science and Engineering, DIT University, Mussoorie, Uttarakhand, India

1. Introduction

A significant hike in the usage of Internet of Things (IoT) devices has created an awareness for the designing of efficient and reliable network security systems. Information technology is evolving day by day, thus unfolding new innovations and at the same time opening up new ways for attackers and intruders. Consequently, cyber security and privacy have become the need of the hour [1−3]. Attackers and intruders are using synchronized and orchestrated ways of initiating attacks and targeting high-profile organizations.

Security attacks have increased significantly according to the latest statistics, and the security industry has become the fastest evolving industry in the world. Figs. 9.1 and 9.2 show how active and passive attacks are being carried out by an intruder.

The term security and privacy is no longer limited to securing hardware devices but now includes the electronic data that is being shared online between two peers through either a trusted or a third-party transmission

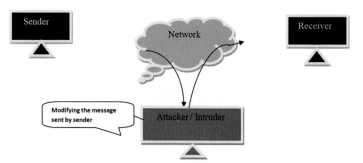

Figure 9.1 Phenomena of an active attack.

Trends in Deep Learning Methodologies
ISBN 978-0-12-822226-3
https://doi.org/10.1016/B978-0-12-822226-3.00009-X

207

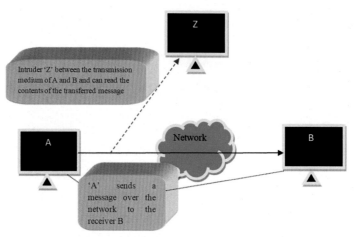

Figure 9.2 Phenomena of a passive attack.

channel [4]. This process is subject to data breaches where millions of unique identities are exposed on the web. Fig. 9.3 shows the dimensions of security that are of foremost importance and the level of security that is expected to be provided.

Confidentiality encompasses authorization and authentication of data along with nonrepudiation.

1. **Confidentiality:** This term in relation to information security defines the rules that safeguard the information from being accessed from an unauthorized user and at the same time ensures that only authorized users access the information. Data breaches fall under the category of confidentiality when one fails to safeguard the information.

2. **Integrity:** This ensures that the security of the data is not comprised, which means that information constraints are not being altered.

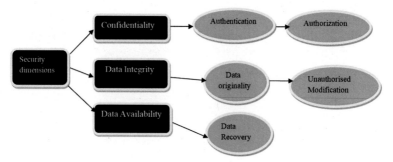

Figure 9.3 Dimensions of security.

The terms that come under integrity are correctness of data and validation of data along with the measure of quality assurance.

3. **Availability:** This ensures that the information is available to authorized users. Denial of service (DOS) is a security attack where the availability of data is comprised, thus making it unavailable for legitimate users. Failure recovery is a term that falls under this category.

There are several categories of network security attacks that can be launched onto a network. Security attacks are defined as an attempt to gain unauthorized access to a database. Security attacks are classified into active attacks and passive attacks. In active attacks, attempts are made to access data available on the target, whereas passive attacks target the system's information where the ultimate goal is to access the information that is being transmitted onto the network. The following are points that describe a broad classification of security attacks:

- Data breach: An incident where the information is accessed without authorization. In the execution of a data breach, an intruder first identifies the vulnerabilities in a network and then triggers a network attack.
- Point of vulnerabilities: A defect in the code that turns out to be a potential point for compromising. A point can either be application programming interface (API) vulnerability or Web browser vulnerability.
- Session hijacking: A technique that grants the control of a user's session, which in turns provides access to resources.
- Internet Protocol (IP) spoofing attack: A technique where IP addresses are forged.
- Botnet attack: A botnet is a group of IoT devices connected together. Here, IoT devices are infected by a malware through which attackers can control these devices.
- Phishing attack: A technique where an attacker pretends to be a trusted entity and dumps a victim to steal confidential information (Fig. 9.4).
- Man-in-the-middle attack: Here, a malicious intruder inserts itself into the transmission medium between two parties to gain access to information (Fig. 9.5).
- DOS: Here, an attempt is made to shut down the network to make it inaccessible to its legitimate users.
- Distributed denial of service (DDOS) attack: DDOS is an attack that is focused on disrupting the normal traffic of a targeted network by flooding its network infrastructure with unwanted traffic.

Today, technologies laid down by artificial intelligence have made it possible to design network solutions that can trigger an alert as soon as

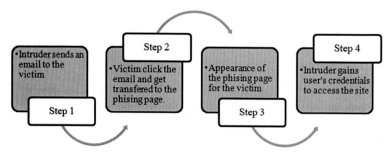

Figure 9.4 Illustration of a phishing attack.

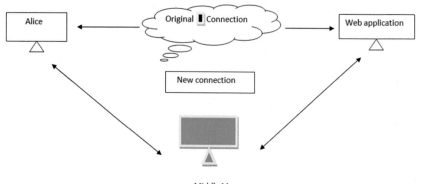

Figure 9.5 Illustration of a man-in-the-middle attack.

something malicious is observed on the network. The transformation in network intrusion detection systems is based on machine learning and its subset technologies by inspecting the packets that have been transmitted over the network. This chapter deals with the research that is being carried out in the field of cyber security using deep learning, which is a subset of machine learning, and how the frameworks and algorithms of deep learning are contributing to combating attacks against privacy and offering individuals and organizations a better networking solution.

2. Birth and history of deep learning

Deep learning designs the networks that are able to learn from unstructured data and forms a subset within the domain of machine learning in artificial intelligence. Machine learning is an application of artificial intelligence that allows the system to learn automatically from experiences to eliminate the need for programming systems explicitly, whereas deep learning is based on the concept of interconnected networks where the result from the previous layer forms the output of the next layer; such networks can also be termed deep neural networks (Fig. 9.6).

The term deep learning emerged in 1943 when a system was designed based on neural networks by Warren McCulloch and Walter Pitts [5,6]. Thereafter several efforts were made to improve the activation functions to yield better algorithms. Fig. 9.7 describes the basic functionality of deep learning.

Deep learning differs from the method of traditional machine learning in terms of how patterns can be drawn from the raw data, thus allowing the designing of computational models based on multiple layers of neural networks for processing, offering multiple levels of abstraction. Deep learning frameworks provide more hidden layers and have the ability to draw meaningful abstractions of the provided input; these features differ from artificial neural networks [7]. Hence, deep learning algorithms can also be termed representation-based algorithms.

3. Frameworks of deep learning

1. **Tensorflow:** Tensorflow developed by Google was first released in 2015 and the final and stable version came into existence in 2017.

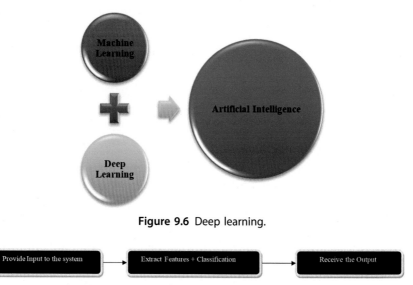

Figure 9.6 Deep learning.

Figure 9.7 Basic functionality of deep learning.

Tensorflow operated on a multidimensional array and operates in three phases: phase 1 consists of preprocessing the data; phase 2 consists of model building; and the third phase comprises training and estimation of the model. The following are the steps involved while working with Tensorflow [8].

Step 1: Defining the variable: A placeholder node is created at the beginning and is assigned a user name; let us say Z_1 and Z_2 are the input nodes, then the placeholder nodes will be Z1 and Z2:

import numpy as np
import Tensorflow as tf
Z_1= tf.placeholder(tf.float32, name = "Z_1")
Z_2= tf.placeholder(tf.float32, name = "Z_2")

Step2: Defining the computation: Here, the nodes are linked to perform the desired computation.

Step3: Executing the operation: To execute the desired operation a session is created using tf.Session().

2. **PyTorch:** This provides the creation of serializable and optimization models. PyTorch offers distributed training to perform parallel computation so that the computation time can be reduced. Moreover, PyTorch offers the creation of dynamic computation graphs [9].

3. **Sonnet:** Sonnet is designed on the top of Tensorflow. It offers high-level object-oriented libraries that provide abstraction for the algorithms of the neural networks.

4. **MXNet:** This was released by Apache and is an open-source deep learning-based framework used for the training and deployment of deep neural networks. It can run parallel with multiple machines and can support several languages such as C++, Python, JavaScript, and others. It has the ability to solve complex computational models quickly and at the same time generates a clear code.

5. **Gluon:** This is used for the creation of more sophisticated models and develops interfaces that are flexible in nature.

Deep learning-based frameworks have taken neural networks to a different level by making generalizations and inferences, by discovering the hidden patterns in a dataset, and by modeling the relations between variables that are nonlinear in nature, thus improving the decision process [11]. The research performed in this area of security has revealed that artificial neural networks have successfully designed an intrusion detection system that identifies attacks in scenarios where the rules have yet to be discovered. They detect malicious activities in a more consistent manner and offer more reliability and security. Neural networks are discussed in detail in the next section.

4. Statistics behind deep learning algorithms and neural networks

Linear algebra belonging to applied mathematics is an expedient requirement for understanding deep learning algorithms. The field of linear algebra includes scalars, vectors, matrices, and tensors. In the context of deep learning a combination of a matrix and a vector variable results in another matrix. Let us assume that X denotes the representation for a matrix and Y denotes the representation for a vector quantity:

$$Z = X + Y \tag{9.1}$$

$$Z(i \cdot j) = X(i,j) + Y(j) \tag{9.2}$$

where $Z(i, j)$ represents the new resultant matrix and I and j represent rows and columns, respectively. It is understood that vector Y has been added to each row of the matrix.

The next mathematical measures in deep learning algorithms include the concept of eigen decomposition comprising eigenvectors and eigenvalues. For a square matrix X an eigenvector is termed a nonzero vector v, which states that multiplication by X changes only the scale of v represented by Eq. (9.3). The function numpy() in Python helps in the normalization of eigenvectors.

$$Xv = \lambda v \tag{9.3}$$

The term neural networks was coined back in 1958 by Frank Rosenblatt. This neural network was termed a "perceptron," which was designed for the modeling of the processing of visual data performed by the human brain. The pattern-matching ability made artificial neural networks more popular because of their vibrant nature when addressing complex computational problems. The architecture of neural networks is made up of an artificial neuron, which is grouped into different layers. These consist of three basic layers named an input layer, a hidden layer, and an output layer [10].

Artificial neural networks are based on the same process of communication that is followed by neurons of the human brain. They perform the simulation of the learning procedure by using algorithms of complex qualities. Every connection that forms the network has a weight associated with it that can be either positive or negative. Neurons are activated if the associated weights are of positive value and are constrained if the associated weight has a negative value. At each iteration the neuron computes the weighted average of the values of the vector z denoted as Eq. (9.4):

$$x = w_1 z_1 + w_2 z_2 + \ldots + w_n z_n \qquad (9.4)$$

The key element of a neural network is its activation function because without an activation function the neural network becomes a sequence of linear functions. Activation functions are mathematical statistical functions that result in the output of the neural network and perform normalization for the output between (1 and 0) and (1 and −1). Binary step function, linear activation function, and nonlinear activation function form the three categories of activation functions. A threshold value-based function is known as a binary activation function. For any input value above or below the threshold value the same signal is being transferred to the next layer by the respective neuron. In the case of a linear activation function the input is multiplied by the weight of each neuron and the resultant signal is proportional to the input signal. Today, neural networks use nonlinear activation functions as they allow for complex mappings to be made between input and output.

The next important function in a neural network is the loss function. The value of the loss function demonstrates the growth of the learning process. The loss function in general describes an idea of how far we are from the ideal situation. Minimization of the loss function is the foremost objective for the learning process of the neural network and this minimization is performed with the help of gradient descent. An algorithm that trains a complicated gradient is termed backpropagation and is used to train the architecture of the neural networks. The gradient of each weight parameter has been computed through feed-forward and backpropagation procedures.

5. Deep learning algorithms for securing networks

Intrusion detection systems are further classified into the following categories: network-based intrusion detection system, which is planted into the network at a fixed point to examine the incoming traffic from all the devices connected to the network, and host-based intrusion detection system, which monitors incoming and outgoing traffic from the connected devices and issues alerts for malicious activities. The frameworks based on deep learning for designing enhanced intrusion detection systems are mainly of two types: generative deep and discriminative deep architectures. The discriminative deep architecture deals with the identification of suitable patterns using supervised learning, whereas the generative deep architecture is focused on the use of deep neural networks. Convolutional neural networks (CNNs) and recurrent neural networks (RNNs) have been used for making effective intrusion detection and prevention systems.

Spam detection and spam filtering have been made possible with one of the most reliable deep learning algorithms known as natural language processing (NLP). Belonging to a subfield of linguistics, NLP is focused on the analysis and representation of normal text to carry out the interaction between computers and humans. Figs. 9.8 and 9.9 describes a few basic steps for building a spam classifier.

- **CNN:** This is an algorithm of deep learning that takes the input and differentiates it on the basis of assigned importance (Fig. 9.10). The architecture of the CNNs is based on the visual cortex and the error gradient method is employed to achieve the results for pattern recognition. The convolution layers, the pooling layers, and the fully connected layers form three layers of CNNs.

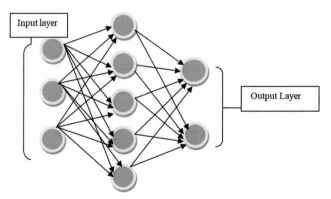

Figure 9.8 Artificial neural networks.

Figure 9.9 Steps for building a spam classifier.

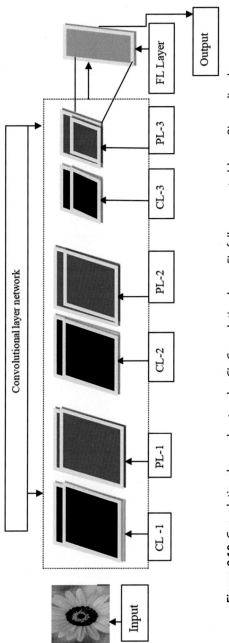

Figure 9.10 Convolutional neural networks. *CL*, Convolution layer; *FL*, fully connected layer; *PL*, pooling layer.

The convolution layer comprises several kernels, whereas the pooling layer is responsible for the reduction of spatial dimensions of the volume of input required for the next convolution layer [12,13]. Neurons embedded in a fully connected layer gain full control over the activation of the previously connected layers. CNNs provide methods for the implementation of ideal security systems by improving accuracy in detection rates and generalization. For the classification of malicious traffic, syntactic and semantic structures do not work, therefore CNNs are used because they do not have predefined knowledge regarding the matter.

- **Deep belief networks:** These belong to the category of deep neural networks that are comprised of multiple hidden units that establish a connection between layers without establishing a connection between units of each layer.
- **Deep autoencoders:** These are made up of two deep belief networks that are of a symmetrical nature (Fig. 9.11). They are implemented for either a high- or low-dimensional representation of data. Autoencoders come under the category of unsupervised neural networks. If the space dimensionality of a hidden layer is less than the input and output layer, then the network performs the data encoding [14].
- **RNNs:** In RNNs, output of the previous layer serves as the input for the current layer. RNNs are used in several areas of security such as fraud detection and incident detection and also provide malware classification.
- **Generative adversarial networks:** These belong to the class of neural networks that deals with unsupervised learning and were developed in 2014. Generative adversarial networks comprise a generator and a discriminator. False data samples are being generated by the generator

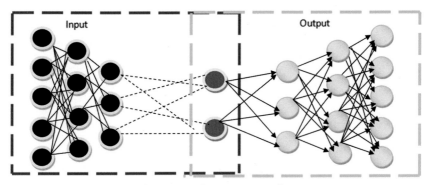

Figure 9.11 Deep autoencoder.

and the task of the discriminator is to identify and differentiate the real and false data samples. Deep neural networks are used to accomplish this purpose.

6. Performance measures for intrusion detection systems

Intrusion detection systems are further classified into the following categories: network-based intrusion detection system, which is planted into the network at a fixed point to examine the incoming traffic from all the devices connected to the network, and host-based intrusion detection system, which monitors incoming and outgoing traffic from the connected devices and issues alerts for malicious activities.

Performance metrics measure the deep neural networks on the basis of certain parameters. These parameters are as follows:

- **Accuracy:** This is defined as the ratio of all the classified samples to all the samples present in the dataset.

TP, true positive, TN, true negative, FP, false positive, and FN, false negative form these performance measures.

$$Accuracy = \frac{TP + TN}{TP + TN + FP + FN}$$

- **Precision:** This is the ratio between all items correctly classified as Class A to all the items that were classified as Class A.

$$Precision = \frac{TP}{TP + FP}$$

- **Recall:** This is the ratio of all the items correctly classified as Class A to all the items that were actually belonging to Class A. Recall is also known as the true positive rate.

$$Recall = \frac{TP}{TP + FN}$$

- **False alarming rate (FAR):** This is defined as ratio of items incorrectly classified as Class A to the items that do not belong to Class A.

$$FAR = \frac{FP}{TN + FP}$$

7. Security aspects changing with deep learning

The quantity of modern-day attacks is increasing at a constant pace; new malware attacks are being launched against high-profile target organizations by exploiting their loopholes or their points of vulnerabilities. The building ability of generalized models by deep learning offers an opportunity to detect malware autonomously in a network. Deep learning-based detection of intrusion in applications is designed based on a collection of static and dynamic features. Learning-based deep-Q networks are proving helpful in the analysis of security issues related to IoT. Systems can analyze various attacks at an intermediate level and discard unauthorized access to IoT devices; deep learning neural networks like CNN and RNN can detect malware by identifying dynamic features with the help of API kernels.

Ferdowsi and Saad [15] proposed a framework for signal authentication for IoT devices. Security attacks such as data injection and DOS are major security threats; hence, a deep learning approach has been developed with the help of long short-term memory structure and it has been observed that messages with this framework can be transmitted with reliability.

Random neural networks have been used for the identification of network attacks that are being launched against IoT devices. Brun et al. [16] designed a deep learning-based framework on random neural networks that proved to be helpful in detecting packets transmitted.

Intrusion detection systems help in the detection of suspicious activities, monitor the network against malicious activities, and generate a trigger when any such activity is encountered. DOS is the major security threat that creates major problems by completely shutting down the target machine, thus making it unavailable to its legitimate or authorized users [17]. Fig. 9.12 describes a DOS attack.

Yin et al. [18] proposed a deep learning RNN-based framework for the detection of DOS attacks This model resulted in higher accuracy detection rates and the results were compared with the existing machine learning algorithms (J48, support vector machines). These machine learning classification models were based on binary and multiclass classification. It has been observed that the framework for the detection of DOS attacks in IoT-based devices has performed better in terms of accuracy and FAR, and provides a greater extent of scalability as compared to the traditional approaches of machine learning-based frameworks. In this approach a pre-stacked autoencoder was used in the process of feature engineering and a publicly available dataset was used.

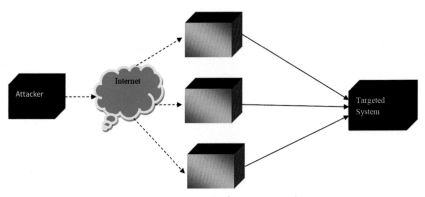

Figure 9.12 Denial of service attack.

Deep learning-based malware detectors have been developed that were based on the feeding of API calls into random neural networks for the procedure of feature extraction. These extracted features were then transferred into CNNs and were able to achieve higher detection rates with an accuracy of 96% [19].

Opcodes were also used for the purpose of detecting malware injection onto the packets being transmitted over the network; processing of these opcodes is achieved by the embedding layers and are then fed into the CNN network. There is a possibility that the algorithms laid by deep learning may differ in their precision, and FARs depend on the size of the data that has been used. Deep neural networks also helped in the identification of malicious traffic over the network.

An insider threat is defined as a threat that is generated from individuals within an organization and these sorts of threats have emerged as serious cyber threats. These insiders could either be former employees of the organizations or current employees. Deep learning has successfully emerged in combating these insider threats. Unsupervised deep learning networks were designed on the logged data of the system and deep learning networks and RNNs were tested using the mechanism of feature selection vector. A network framework based on deep learning networks and RNNs performed satisfactorily when the analyzed results were compared with approaches of machine learning like principal component analysis and support vector machines [20].

The deep learning technique deep belief network has been employed to design an effective anomaly-based intrusion detection system and classify intrusions into five accuracy-based classes. Stacked autoencoders and stacked restricted Boltzmann machines are two techniques of deep learning that have been implemented in designing intrusion detection systems. A deep learning-based technique self-taught learning has been implemented for designing an efficient intrusion detection system. The system provides better performance metrics, which includes precision, recall, and F-measure.

There are certain challenges that affect the development of intrusion detection systems: one is the selection of suitable feature selection methodology. Features that have been identified for a particular class may not be suitable for other attacks as they are continuously evolving in nature. The next problem faced by researchers includes identification of a traffic-labeled dataset that includes a real-time network dataset [21]. Flow-based intrusion detection systems are gaining popularity because they are capable of classifying malicious traffic effectively with a high accuracy rate. If compared with the techniques of machine learning where feature identification is manual, the techniques of deep learning are based on identification of features automatically and features are represented in abstract form at each layer. To make this research more effective a deep neural network has been designed where initiation parameters are designed at batch size 10. The performance metrics of the developed network intrusion detection system is evaluated in terms of precision and recall [22].

In the domain of network security, the foundation of a robust intrusion detection system poses a challenge. With regard to significant advances, maximum solutions are still focused on signature-based intrusion detection systems. As an alternative to the current situation, where reliance on such techniques leads to ineffective analytic solutions, a novel deep learning model has been proposed that is a combination of deep and shallow learning. This is a combination of a nonsymmetric deep autoencoder and a random forest. The proposed intrusion detection system has been evaluated against a GPU-enabled tensor flow framework [23].

DDOS attacks are catastrophic attacks over the internet as they are focused on the disruption of bandwidth. Hence, a deep learning-based approach has been designed to combat these attacks. This deep defense intrusion detection system is based on RNNs and 20 best features have been identified from the network dataset. Future work is focused on an increase in diversity of DDOS attacks and testing the model in robust environments [24].

DDOS attacks can be said to be based on the cooperative model because intruders use puppets or bots to launch a synchronized attack. The resources of the system and bandwidth collapsing or exhaustion remain the ultimate targets of the attacker. The DDOS detection model is applied to open flow-based software-defined networking. This detection model results in high accuracy and reduces the degree of dependence on software and hardware environments [25].

In the Open System Interconnection model the application layer is most prone to DOS and DDOS attacks. Several detection methods have been employed for the mitigation of security attacks launched on Transmission Control Protocol and IP layers. Attacks at the application layer comprise request flooding, session flooding, and asymmetric attacks. A research approach based on the concept of an autoencoder has been proposed and is observed to be better than other existing systems. Features are extracted from the web server log and after data preprocessing the features are converted to numeric form. The work is focused on learning more abstract features by applying multiple layers of autoencoders. Finally, logistic regression is applied to classify the incoming traffic into normal and attack [26].

Software-defined networking (SDN) is an approach focused on making the network more intelligent and centrally controlled. A multivector deep learning-based framework has been proposed for the mitigation of DDOS attacks in an SDN environment. The approaches based on the deep learning methodology provide reduction of features in a dataset of high dimensions. The framework proposed has been implemented in the form of a network application on the top of the SDN controller for the monitoring of traffic over the network and the framework after implementation provides high accuracy with a low false positive rate [27].

IoT is facing a tremendous rise in soft targets for DDOS attacks. A bot net-based detection framework based on deep learning is implemented in a secured sandboxed environment, which contains a command and control server and scan loader server. The model is based on a bidirectional long short-term memory-based RNN and a dataset contains bot net traffic. The implemented model provides high accuracy and low loss metrics [28].

The extended expansion in network communication technology has made the detection of DDOS attacks a primary research area. If we consider the traditional architecture of the network, then DDOS attacks have been classified using characteristics of the traffic and traffic anomaly, whereas an SDN environment offers flexible and rapid development. The SDN controller is held responsible for the management and collection of traffic information [29]. Identification of the points of vulnerabilities in a network is a serious challenge for network analysts. Deep autoencoders are made up of two symmetrical deep belief networks where half of the layers represent the encoding and the other half represent decoding. A deep learning approach based on a deep autoencoder has been designed for anomaly detection. The proposed model is trained on the greedy-based approach for avoiding overfitting and the proposed model has provided improvement in terms of accuracy, detection rate, and FAR [30].

Hypertext transfer protocol (HTTP) is one of the most vulnerable protocols to security attacks belonging to the application layer. An immense volume of traffic is experienced by datacenters and hence due to the popularity of the protocol attackers launch several DOS attacks, which include SYN flood attacks, HTTP fuzzers, and reverse bandwidth floods. A web application firewall framework has been proposed and an approach interpreting HTTP traffic and dimensionality reduction has been performed using a sparse autoencoder. Subsequently, an isolation forest was applied for the detection of anomalies in traffic [31]. Deep belief neural networks have emerged as a promising algorithm from the set of deep neural nets stacked on a restricted Boltzmann machine. Advanced persistent threats are the fastest growing threats to a network. Therefore a model has been proposed for improving the classification rate for known and unknown attacks. The training set has been modeled using a restricted Boltzmann machine in which stochastic and binary pixels are integrated with stochastic binary feature detectors using weighted connections [32].

8. Conclusion and future work

Cyber threats and security attacks are increasing rapidly. Attackers and intruders are launching modern vector attacks and targeting high-profile organizations. In the process of initiating attacks there are several indicators that are distributed all over the network and the identification of these indicators is a great challenge to cyber security experts. To quell these security attacks, deep learning came to the rescue. The advent of deep learning in cyber security helps in the identification of patterns, correlation of events, and identification of suspected behaviors and patterns.

Deep learning-based frameworks perform classification and detection of malware in the packet transmission over the network and identification of fake data injections. Deep learning-based frameworks are proving better as compared to the traditional methods of machine learning, and perform far better when compared with the existing intrusion detection systems based on a signature-based approach. The performance of deep learning frameworks varies according to the size of the dataset because deep learning deals with large datasets. True positive rates vary from 94.01% to 98.06% for some frameworks. The main advantage of deep learning that has been observed after comparing with traditional approaches is its ability to execute the task of feature engineering.

Deep learning is also able to transfer the data to a higher level and provide abstraction. Neural networks open up gateways of detection of any misuse happening in a network and offer system administrators protection for their organizational network. In the cyber security domain, obtaining a real-time dataset is a problem and the scope has been limited due to less publicly available datasets, thus future research should be primarily focused on designing new datasets that include modern-day security attacks, so that new deep learning approaches combined with machine learning can be developed for the accurate detection and prediction of security attacks.

References

[1] G. Apruzzese, M. Colajanni, L. Ferretti, A. Guido, M. Marchetti, On the effectiveness of machine and deep learning for cyber security, in: 2018 10th International Conference on Cyber Conflict (CyCon), IEEE, 2018, May, pp. 371—390.

[2] M.Z. Alom, T.M. Taha, Network intrusion detection for cyber security using unsupervised deep learning approaches, in: 2017 IEEE National Aerospace and Electronics Conference (NAECON), IEEE, 2017, June, pp. 63—69.

[3] J.A. Cox, C.D. James, J.B. Aimone, A signal processing approach for cyber data classification with deep neural networks, Proc. Comput. Sci. 61 (2015) 349—354.

[4] R. Von Solms, J. Van Niekerk, From information security to cyber security, Comp. Secur. 38 (2013) 97—102.

[5] J. Schmidhuber, Deep Learning. Encyclopedia of Machine Learning and Data Mining, 2016, pp. 1—11.

[6] L. Deng, An Overview of Deep-Structured Learning for Information Processing, 2011.

[7] R. Miotto, F. Wang, S. Wang, X. Jiang, J.T. Dudley, Deep learning for healthcare: review, opportunities and challenges, Brief. Bioinf. 19 (6) (2017) 1236—1246.

[8] N. Ponomareva, S. Radpour, G. Hendry, S. Haykal, T. Colthurst, P. Mitrichev, A. Grushetsky, Tf boosted trees: a scalable tensorflow based framework for gradient boosting, in: Joint European Conference on Machine Learning and Knowledge Discovery in Databases, 2017, September, pp. 423—427 (Springer, Cham).

[9] A. Paszke, S. Gross, F. Massa, A. Lerer, J. Bradbury, G. Chanan, T. Killeen, Z. Lin, N. Gimelshein, L. Antiga, A. Desmaison, PyTorch: an imperative style, high-performance deep learning library, Adv. Neural Inf. Process. Syst. (2019) 8024—8035.

[10] J. Cannady, Artificial neural networks for misuse detection, in: National Information Systems Security Conference, vol. 26, 1998, October.

[11] D.S. Berman, A.L. Buczak, J.S. Chavis, C.L. Corbett, A survey of deep learning methods for cyber security, Information 10 (4) (2019) 122.

[12] R. Polishetty, M. Roopaei, P. Rad, A next-generation secure cloud-based deep learning license plate recognition for smart cities, in: 2016 15th IEEE International Conference on Machine Learning and Applications (ICMLA), IEEE, 2016, December, pp. 286–293.

[13] Y. Liu, S. Liu, X. Zhao, Intrusion detection algorithm based on convolutional neural network, DEStech Trans. Eng. Technol. Res. (2017) (iceta).

[14] W. Wang, M. Zhao, J. Wang, Effective android malware detection with a hybrid model based on deep autoencoder and convolutional neural network, J. Ambient Intell. Humaniz. Comput. 10 (8) (2019) 3035–3043.

[15] A. Ferdowsi, W. Saad, Deep learning-based dynamic watermarking for secure signal authentication in the Internet of Things, in: 2018 IEEE International Conference on Communications (ICC), IEEE, 2018, May, pp. 1–6.

[16] O. Brun, Y. Yin, E. Gelenbe, Deep learning with dense random neural network for detecting attacks against IoT-connected home environments, Proced. Comput. Sci. 134 (2018) 458–463.

[17] A. Bakshi, Y.B. Dujodwala, Securing cloud from DDoS attacks using intrusion detection system in virtual machine, in: 2010 Second International Conference on Communication Software and Networks, IEEE, 2010, February, pp. 260–264.

[18] C. Yin, Y. Zhu, J. Fei, X. He, A deep learning approach for intrusion detection using recurrent neural networks, Ieee Access 5 (2017) 21954–21961.

[19] A. Azzouni, G. Pujolle, NeuTM: a neural network-based framework for traffic matrix prediction in SDN, in: NOMS 2018-2018 IEEE/IFIP Network Operations and Management Symposium, IEEE, 2018, April, pp. 1–5.

[20] A. Tuor, S. Kaplan, B. Hutchinson, N. Nichols, S. Robinson, Deep learning for unsupervised insider threat detection in structured cybersecurity data streams, in: Workshops at the Thirty-First AAAI Conference on Artificial Intelligence, 2017, March.

[21] A. Javaid, Q. Niyaz, W. Sun, M. Alam, A deep learning approach for network intrusion detection system, in: Proceedings of the 9th EAI International Conference on Bio-inspired Information and Communications Technologies (formerly BIO-NETICS), May 24, 2016, pp. 21–26.

[22] T.A. Tang, L. Mhamdi, D. McLernon, S.A. Zaidi, M. Ghogho, Deep learning approach for network intrusion detection in software defined networking, in: 2016 International Conference on Wireless Networks and Mobile Communications (WINCOM), IEEE, October 26, 2016, pp. 258–263.

[23] N. Shone, T.N. Ngoc, V.D. Phai, Q. Shi, A deep learning approach to network intrusion detection, IEEE Trans. Emerg. Top. Comput. Intell. 2 (1) (January 22, 2018) 41–50.

[24] X. Yuan, C. Li, X. Li, DeepDefense: identifying DDoS attack via deep learning, in: 2017 IEEE International Conference on Smart Computing (SMARTCOMP), IEEE, May 29, 2017, pp. 1–8.

[25] C. Li, Y. Wu, X. Yuan, Z. Sun, W. Wang, X. Li, L. Gong, Detection and defense of DDoS attack–based on deep learning in OpenFlow-based SDN, Int. J. Commun. Syst. 31 (5) (March 25, 2018) e3497.

[26] S. Yadav, S. Subramanian, Detection of application layer DDoS attack by feature learning using stacked autoencoder, in: 2016 International Conference on Computational Techniques in Information and Communication Technologies (ICCTICT), IEEE, March 11, 2016, pp. 361–366.

[27] Q. Niyaz, W. Sun, A.Y. Javaid, A Deep Learning Based DDoS Detection System in Software-Defined Networking (SDN), November 22, 2016 arXiv preprint arXiv:1611.07400.

[28] C.D. McDermott, F. Majdani, A.V. Petrovski, Botnet detection in the internet of things using deep learning approaches, in: 2018 International Joint Conference on Neural Networks (IJCNN), IEEE, July 8, 2018, pp. 1–8.

[29] J. Ye, X. Cheng, J. Zhu, L. Feng, L. Song, A DDoS attack detection method based on SVM in software defined network, Secur. Commun. Netw. (2018).

[30] F. Farahnakian, J. Heikkonen, A deep auto-encoder based approach for intrusion detection system, in: 2018 20th International Conference on Advanced Communication Technology (ICACT), IEEE, February 11, 2018, pp. 178–183.

[31] A.M. Vartouni, S.S. Kashi, M. Teshnehlab, An anomaly detection method to detect web attacks using Stacked Auto-Encoder, in: 2018 6th Iranian Joint Congress on Fuzzy and Intelligent Systems (CFIS), IEEE, February 28, 2018, pp. 131–134.

[32] M.Z. Alom, V. Bontupalli, T.M. Taha, Intrusion detection using deep belief networks, in: 2015 National Aerospace and Electronics Conference (NAECON), IEEE, June 15, 2015, pp. 339–344.

CHAPTER 10

E-CART: an improved data stream mining approach

Pardeep Kumar
Department of Computer Science and Engineering, Jaypee University of Information Technology, Solan, Himachal Pradesh, India

1. Introduction

Data stream mining is extensively used in applications like sensor data, image data, web data, and so on. Consider any satellite remote sensor that is constantly generating data. The generated data is massive, temporally ordered, potentially infinite, and fast changing. These features make data stream mining a challenging problem. Due to rapid generation and high volume of data, the stream has to be stored or processed immediately otherwise it is lost forever. It is very difficult to store such an overwhelming volume of data, thus effective mining of the data stream is required. The main research objectives in data stream mining are handling high volumes of data and the concept drift problem.Hence, data stream mining is defined as extracting the desired knowledge from the infinite streams of information in the form of models and patterns [1]. The data stream mining process can be figured out as shown in Fig. 10.1:

To limit the amount of processed data, the sliding window concept is used. There are various windowing models explained in [2], i.e., fixed sliding window, adaptive window, landmark window, and damped window. The number of examples within this window length is chosen for further processing. As the processing of an evolving stream as a whole is a very cumbersome job, many researchers have used the hoeffding bounds for mining data streams. In [3], the authors used the hoeffding bound to generate the decision tree, which is the mathematical tool of the hoeffding theorem [4]. The hoeffding bound ensures, with high probability, that the best splitting attribute chosen from the N examples is similar to the few samples chosen from infinite examples of the data stream. In [5], the authors introduced McDiarmid's inequality [6] to choose the best splitting attribute instead of using the hoeffding bound.

Trends in Deep Learning Methodologies
ISBN 978-0-12-822226-3
https://doi.org/10.1016/B978-0-12-822226-3.00010-6

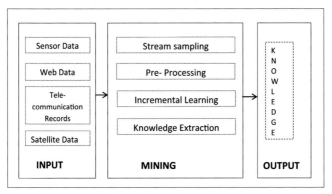

Figure 10.1 Data stream mining process.

Another research problem in data stream mining is concept drift, i.e., detecting promptly evolving concepts because of the highly dynamic nature of data streams. There are several approaches to handling the concept drift problem in data stream mining like Very Fast Decision Tree (VFDT) [3], Concept-adapting Very Fast Decision Tree (CVFDT) [7], and Efficient-Concept-adapting Very Fast Decision Tree (E-CVFDT) [8]. E-CVFDT will be used in this chapter. VFDT Learner is an incremental learning approach for stationary data distribution. CVFDT is an extension of VFDT that deals with the concept drift problem for high-speed data streams. In the traditional CVFDT method, with the change in concept, a new optional subtree is created and a splitting attribute is chosen on the basis of splitting function. It does not consider the type of concepts arriving at the data stream. The type of concept drift plays an important role in reducing the processing time and cost. Suppose the concept, arriving in a stream, is accidental like noise and disappears very quickly. In CVFDT, as this new concept arrives, a new subtree will be created. As this concept will disappear very quickly, after its disappearance the CVFDT algorithm will rebuild that subtree. Thus this affects the processing time as well as the cost. Gang Liu [8] proposed an improved CVFDT approach for mining data streams, i.e., the E-CVFDT. E-CVFDT considers the three types of concept instances, namely, accidental concept drift, gradual concept drift, and instantaneous concept drift. In accidental concept drift, the new concept will appear for a very short timespan and then the old concept will reappear. Suppose the sequence of the old concept is Seq_A and the sequence of new concept is Seq_b. Then, the accidental concept drift sequence can be represented as $S = \{A_1, A_2, A_3 \ldots A_n, B_1, B_2, B_3 \ldots B_r, A_P \ldots A_m\}$. In gradual concept drift, the new concept will evolve with the old concept. This can be shown as $S = \{A_1, A_2, A_3 \ldots A_n, B_1, B_2, B_3 \ldots B_r, A_P \ldots A_q, B_m \ldots B_s\}$. In instantaneous concept drift, the new concept will instantly appear and the old concept will disappear. This can be represented as $S = \{A_1, A_2, A_3 \ldots A_n, B_1, B_2, B_3 \ldots B_M\}$.

Here, a cached system is also used for storing the new concepts. As the new concepts arrive, the examples are stored in an array and if this concept seems to be useless, then these examples can be dropped. The appropriate sequence of examples is thus selected for the mining purpose. The number of examples is determined by the hoeffding bound. From these examples, the best splitting attribute is chosen and the corresponding decision tree will be created, i.e., incremental learning will be performed. Classification and Regression Tree (CART) decision tree induction is used for mining and classification purposes.

The rest of the chapter is structured as follows: Section 2 discusses the related state of the art. It explains the hoeffding bound CART decision tree induction approach and E-CVFDT algorithm. Section 3 explains the proposed approach, Section 4 shows the experimental results of the proposed work, and lastly Section 5 concludes.

2. Related study

For the last several years, classification has played an important role in data mining [3,9−11]. The data classification problem in data mining is a two-step process [9]. In the first step, a model is built by learning from the training dataset. And in the second step, the unclassified data is labeled by using the rules extracted from that model. Let X_i denote the set of possible values of attributes a^i where $i = (1, 2 \ldots D)$. The classification task is used to find a classifier that classifies an unlabeled set of attribute values A_i into labeled classes K, i.e., $H: \{A_1, A_2 \ldots A_d\} \rightarrow \{1, 2 \ldots K\}$. Classification is done with the help of the training set $S: (X_i, K_i) = \left(\left[X_i^1, X_i^2 \ldots X_i^D \right], K_i \right)$. Various algorithms have been proposed for classifying the static datasets in the literature. The most popular are neural networks [12,13], Bayesian classification, K-nearest neighbor classification [14], and decision trees [15−17]. As soon as the data streams came into the role, researchers adopted the data stream mining techniques. Decision trees are powerful tools for data stream mining. The main goal of the decision tree is to find the best splitting attribute at each node. The choice of attribute depends on some impurity measure. The split measure function for each attribute is calculated and the attribute with the highest measured value is chosen as the splitting attribute. There are various algorithms for building decision trees like ID3, C4.5, and CART [9]. The split measure function in ID3 is information gain, which is based on the information entropy, whereas gain ratio is used as a split measure function in C4.5. In CART, a binary decision tree is built by using the Gini index as a split measure function. But these algorithms cannot be applied directly for mining data streams because the data elements of the data stream come into the system at a very high rate. Moreover, concept drift also occurs in the data stream. Thus to handle these issues, various approaches have been discussed in the literature. In this chapter, we refer to the data stream-CART (dsCART, Descartes) algorithm [18] with some modification for improved performance and accuracy.

The main task in decision tree induction is to determine the best splitting attribute from the sample of data because it is impossible to get it from the infinite size of the stream. In the literature, there are various approaches that ensure that the best attribute chosen from the sample of data is the same as the best attribute chosen from the whole stream with some high probability.

In this context, P. Domingo and G. Hulten [3] introduced the commonly used algorithm the "hoeffding tree," which is based on the hoeffding theorem [4].

Theorem 1. If X_1, X_2 ... X_n are independent random variables and $a_i \leq X_i \leq b_i$ where $1 \leq i \leq n$, then:

$$P\{\overline{X} - E[\overline{X}] \geq \varepsilon\} \leq e^{-2\pi^2 / \sum_{i=1}^{n} (b_i - a_i)^2} \tag{10.1}$$

where $\overline{X}$ is the mean value of X_i and $E[\overline{X}]$ is the expected value of $\overline{X}$. This theorem states that after n observations the true mean of the random variable having range R must satisfy the equation:

$$R > \varepsilon \tag{10.2}$$

where $R = b - a \forall a_i = a$ and $b_i = b(i = 1, 2 \ldots n)$ and

$$\varepsilon_H = \sqrt{\frac{R^2 \ln 1/\alpha}{2n}} \tag{10.3}$$

But later on, researchers showed that this theorem violates the split measure function. In [5] Rutkowski et al. proposed McDiarmid's inequality instead of the hoeffding bound. McDiarmid's inequality states that:

$$\text{if } f(S) > \varepsilon_m \tag{10.4}$$

$$\text{where } f(S) = Gini_a x - Gini_a y \tag{10.5}$$

$$\text{and } \varepsilon_m = \sqrt[8]{\ln(1/\alpha)/2n} \tag{10.6}$$

then, with the probability $1 - \alpha$, attribute a^{axis} is better split than attribute a^y.

In this chapter, we refer to the dsCART algorithm [18], where the authors proposed a different theorem for making the best split attribute.

Theorem 2. If there are two attributes a^x and a^y, then let ΔG be the difference between the Gini gain function for a^x and a^y, i.e.:

$$\Delta G = Gini_a x - Gini_a y \tag{10.7}$$

If $\Delta G > \varepsilon_{G,K}$ satisfies for

$$\varepsilon_{G,K} = z_{(1-\alpha)} \frac{\sqrt{2Q(K)}}{\sqrt{n}} \tag{10.8}$$

Where $z_{(1-\alpha)}$ is the $(1-\alpha)$ th quantile of the standard normal distribution $N(0,1)$

$$\text{and } Q(K) = 5K^2 - 8K + 4 \tag{10.9}$$

then $Gini_a x$ is greater than $Gini_a y$ with probability $1 - \alpha$, i.e., a^x is a better split attribute than a^y.

Theorem 2 allows the authors to design CART for a data stream [18]. In this algorithm, the authors introduced a tie-breaking mechanism that depends on the parameter θ. It ensures the split of the node after some fixed number of examples even if the best two attributes do not satisfy Eq. (10.9). This mechanism is used to avoid the blocking of splitting the node permanently due to the comparable values of Gini gain for these attributes, i.e., the decision to split the considered node is determined by the conditions:

$$(\Delta G > \varepsilon_{G,K}) \text{ or } (\varepsilon_{G,K} < \theta) \tag{10.10}$$

After satisfaction of the foregoing condition, the node is split on an attribute having maximum gain value among the best two attributes a^x and a^y.

In the dsCART algorithm, the authors do not consider the concept drift issue. Thus we used the E–CVFDT approach [8] to the dsCART algorithm [18] to get much better results.

In E–CVFDT, the examples that will participate in the Gini gain calculation are cached. The caching system is helpful in reducing the cost required for the computation. E-CVFDT considers three types of drifts, i.e., accidental, gradual, and instantaneous concept drifts. In the case of an accidental concept drift where the probabilities appear small, a cache mechanism is used to increase the performance efficiency. This algorithm puts all the examples in an array "discard." When this array is full, then all the examples are sent back in the process of decision tree creation. In the case of gradual concept drift where the concept drift occurs in an evolving style, regrouping of the evolving data is done into the memory, i.e., the new concept examples are delayed while original concepts are used for the Gini calculation first. This classifies the same concept examples first and avoids the complex distribution of an evolving data stream. To handle the instantaneous concept drift where the new concept arrives instantaneously and the old concept disappears, the traditional CVFDT suits well (Table 10.1).

Table 10.1 Efficient-Concept-adapting Very Fast Decision Tree (E-CVFDT) algorithm [8].

Input:
    w: user–specified window size
    n: number of examples which have to be checked
    S: Sample of examples
    n_discard: maximum number of discarded examples
    discardArray: array of discarded examples
Output:
    acceptedArray: array of examples to be accepted
Let W be empty then return NULL
Let n(w) be the current number of examples in Window W
Let S (I) be an array of each example, initially set empty
If $|W| <$ w and n(w)$<=$n_discard
    for each example S(i) in w
      Add S(j) to acceptedArray
If $|W| <$w and n(W)$<=$ n* n_discard then,
    for each example in s(j) in w
      add S(j) to discardArray
    Remove this example from window of primary algorithm
    Let W be empty then return NULL
If $|W| <$w and n(W)$>=$ n* n_discard then,
    Remove this example from window of primary algorithm
Return acceptedArray

E-CVFDT is helpful in reducing the frequency of examples participating for the Gini calculation.

3. E-CART: proposed approach

There are various techniques for data stream mining as explained in the previous section. A new approach named E-CART, i.e., E-CVFDT-based CART algorithm, has been proposed, which is the combination of E-CVFDT and dsCART algorithms of data stream mining.

In E-CART, the sample of an example first checks for the type of concept drift. A similar type of conceptual data is mined first. Thus on the basis of type of concept drift, mining is performed. Three types of concept drift are taken into consideration, i.e., accidental, gradual, and instantaneous concept drifts. A sliding window concept is used. The sample of examples is collected within a window. The size of the window, i.e., the number of examples in a window, is specified by the user. When the sample arrives into the window, three possibilities could occur. If the stream is of accidental concept drift type, then the stream of new concept will be discarded because their occurrence probability was very low and the old concept stream is sent for the Gini calculation. If the stream is of gradual type, then the new concept is cached into another array and used for the Gini calculation after some delay. In case of instantaneous concept drift, the decision tree is built on the basis of the arrived concept.

Thus this algorithm is better than the Gaussian decision tree (GDT) [19], because in the case of GDT, for every new concept, a new decision tree is built, which is useless in case of noise, i.e., accidental concept drift. Thus it computes the stream in an efficient and effective manner.

The E-CART works as follows:

Instead of computing the splitting function for each and every example having a new concept, it checks the type of concept drift occurring in the data stream.

If the stream scenario belongs to an accidental concept drift like noise, then the computation will not be recomputed for this new concept. The decision tree will result on the basis of the old concept.

If the gradual concept drift occurs in the stream, then both the concepts are of importance. In that case, a cache system is used. The new concept is cached into an array and the size of the array is specified by the user. When the size fulfills the user-specified condition, then this new concept is encountered for the calculation of splitting attribute function.

In case of instantaneous concept drift, the algorithm simply builds the decision tree on the basis of a new concept arriving there. It works similar to the GDT data stream mining technique (Table 10.2).

Table 10.2 Efficient Classification and Regression Tree (E-CART) algorithm.

Input:
  S: a sequence of examples
  A: set of discrete attributes
  w: user-specified size of window
  cached_array: array of cached examples
  n: number of examples checked by the model
  n_discard: user-specified threshold for discarded examples
  Θ: tie-breaking parameter
  α: Fixed probability
Output: T: E-CART decision tree

Algorithm:
Procedure chooseSeq(S,w,cached_array, n_discard,n)

>   Let W be the window of examples of different concepts
>   Let S(i) be the sample-array of each example
>   If |W| > w then
> Add each sample S(j) to accept_array
> If |W| < w and n(w)<= n*n_discard then
>   Add each sample S(j) to cached_array and used later.
> If |W|<w and n(w)>=n*n_discard then
>   Remove this example from the primary processing.
> Return accept_array

Procedure E_CART(accept_array, A)

>   Let T be a decision tree with single leaf (the root node) X_0
>   Let $A_0 = A$
>   For each attribute $a_i \in A$
>   For each attribute value λ of class c
>   The number of examples are $n^c_{i,\lambda,0} = 0$
>   For each example e in accept_array
>   Sort e in leaf L_q
>   For each attribute $a_i \in A$
>   For each attribute value λ of class c
>   If value of $a_i = \lambda$ and class is c then
>   Increment $n^c_{i,\lambda,q}$
>   Label the leaf node L_q with majority class
>   If the examples at L_q does not belong to same class, then compute the
> splitting attribute
>   For each attribute $a_i \in A$
>   For each partition of A_i, i.e. left set A_i^L and right A_i^R

Compute $Gini_q\left(A_i^L\right)$ using $n_{i,\lambda,q}^c$
$$Gini_q^i = \max_{A_i^L \in A_i}\left\{Gini_q\left(A_i^L\right)\right\}$$
$$a_x = \arg\max_{a_i \in A_q}\left\{Gini_q^i\right\}$$
$$a_y = \arg\max_{a_i \in A_q/\{a_x\}}\left\{Gini_q^i\right\}$$

Compute $\varepsilon_{G,K}$ by using theorem 2

  $if\left(\left(Gini_q^{ix} - Gini_q^{iy} > \varepsilon_{G,K}\right)or\left(\varepsilon_{G,K} < \theta\right)\right)$then,

    Make a_x as an internal node by replacing L_q

    For both the branches left and right of the split

      Add a new leaf L_{end+1} and let $A_{end+1} = A_q/\{a_x\}$ at A_{end+1}

      For each value λ for attribute $a_i \in A_{end+1}$ and class = c,

$n_{i,\lambda,end+1}^c = 0$

      end=end+1

  Return T.

Here, $n_{i,\lambda,q}^c$ is the number of elements from the cth class of leaf L_q with attribute value λ for attribute a_i. $Gini_q\left(A_i^q\right)$ is the Gini gain computed for attribute a_i at leaf L_q.

4. Experiment

This chapter compares the E-CART with the E-CVFDT and CART decision tree with Gaussian approximation. The experiment is done by using a SEA concept generator and rotating hyperplane generator on Massive Online Analysis [20].

The data examples generated from the hyperplane generator are similar to the gradual concept drift data stream. By adjusting the data generation rate, the instantaneous concept drift stream is tested, whereas the examples generated from the SEA generator are similar to the instantaneous concept drift.

Computation time for building the decision tree by using the E-CART is calculated for the hyperplane generator and SEA generator and compared with the CVFDT algorithm. It is observed that the computation time for the SEA generator is very similar to the CVFDT approach, whereas in the case of the hyperplane generator, E-CART takes less computation time for building the decision tree classifier than CVFDT.

Table 10.3 represents the time taken by the CVFDT algorithm and the E-CART algorithm for the data examples generated by the SEA generator. The comparison is visualized in Fig. 10.2.

Table 10.3 Computation time comparison using the SEA generator.

Classification	SEA generator		
	$n = 1,000,000$	$n = 100,000$	$N = 10,000$
CVFDT	3.20 s	0.25 s	0.05 s
E-CART	3.37 s	0.32 s	0.06 s

CVFDT, Concept-adapting Very Fast Decision Tree; *E-CART*, Efficient Classification and Regression Tree.

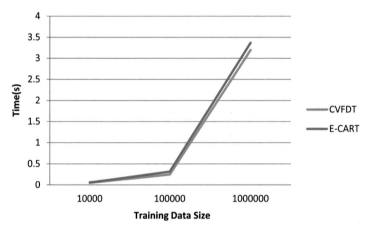

Figure 10.2 Computation time for the SEA generator. *CVFDT*, Concept-adapting Very Fast Decision Tree; *E-CART*, Efficient Classification and Regression Tree.

This graph shows that the performance of the E-CART is somewhat similar to the CVFDT approach given by G. Hulten and P. Domingos [7]. As said earlier, in the instantaneous concept drift data stream, the concept drift occurs instantaneously and then the older concept disappears immediately. When the new concept arrives in the stream, decision tree construction starts immediately rather than caching it as is done in the CVFDT approach to decision tree construction to mine the data stream.

Table 10.4 represents the comparison of E-CART and CVFDT approach in terms of performance efficiency on the dataset generated by the

Table 10.4 Computation time comparison using the hyperplane generator.

Classification	Hyperplane generator		
	$n = 1,000,000$	$n = 100,000$	$N = 10,000$
CVFDT	9.87 s	0.73 s	0.16 s
E-CART	7.30 s	0.34 s	0.15 s

CVFDT, Concept-adapting Very Fast Decision Tree; *E-CART*, Efficient Classification and Regression Tree.

Figure 10.3 Computation time for a rotating hyperplane generator. *CVFDT*, Concept-adapting Very Fast Decision Tree; *E-CART*, Efficient Classification and Regression Tree.

hyperplane generator. The computation time decreases with the proposed approach compared to the CVFDT.

The tabulated data shown in Table 10.4 is visualized in Fig. 10.3.

The graph represented in Fig. 10.3 shows that the computation time decreases by using the proposed approach compared to the CVFDT. This happens because the proposed approach E-CART takes the concept drift into consideration. Thus in case of accidental concept drift, it ignores the new concept because the probability of the new concept appearing is very small. Thus rebuilding the decision tree for such a new concept is totally inefficient. Generally, the accidental concept drifts result in case of any noise in the data stream. In case of gradual concept drift, the cached system is used by the proposed approach, which makes it more efficient. This proposed approach results in 93.23% accuracy with the data size of 1,000,000,000 examples as compared to the accuracy of the CART decision tree approach proposed by Rutkowski et al., which is 90%. Accuracy visualization is shown in Fig. 10.4.

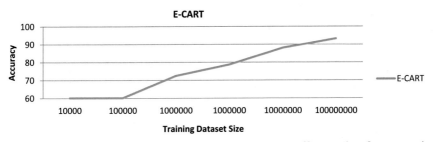

Figure 10.4 Accuracy of the proposed approach. *E-CART*, Efficient Classification and Regression Tree.

This graph shows an accuracy of 93.23%. It shows that the proposed approach for data stream mining is more efficient and better than the previous approaches.

5. Conclusion

Data stream mining is the process of extracting useful information from the continuous stream of information. The main issue in data stream mining is the concept drift. As a data stream is a continuous stream of data, concept changes dynamically, which must be dealt with during the mining procedure. This chapter mainly concentrated on the classification functionality of data mining. There are various approaches for the classification process like decision trees, Bayesian classification, K-nearest neighbor classification, and support vector machine classifiers. But the decision tree is considered to be the most popular tool for data stream classification. The CART algorithm, given by Rutkowski, was reviewed and it was found that the authors do not consider the concept drift aspect of the data stream. In this approach, with the change in concept in the data stream, a new decision tree rebuilds with this new concept. This results in more execution time. Thus, in the proposed approach, the concept drift scenario is added to the CART approach as applied by G. Liu [8]. Three types of concept drifts are considered in the proposed approach. These are accidental concept drift, gradual concept drift, and instantaneous concept drift. It is observed that the proposed approach performs better than the CVFDT approach and it is also observed that E-CART is more accurate than the CART decision tree without considering the concept drift. The computation time for the instantaneous concept drift scenario is similar to the CVFDT, whereas the computation time for the streams having gradual concept drifts and accidental concept drifts is less.

References

[1] M. Kholghi, M. Keyvanpour, An analytical framework for data stream mining techniques based on challenges and requirements, Int. J. Eng. Sci. Technol. 3 (3) (2011) 2507–2513.
[2] M. Matysiak, Data Stream Mining, 2012.
[3] P. Domingos, G. Hulten, Mining high-speed data streams, in: Proceedings of the Sixth ACM SIGKDD International Conference on Knowledge Discovery and Data Mining. ACM, 2000.
[4] W. Hoeffding, Probability inequalities for sums of bounded random variables, J. Am. Stat. Assoc. 58 (301) (1963) 13–30.

[5] L. Rutkowski, et al., Decision trees for mining data streams based on the McDiarmid's bound, IEEE Trans. Knowl. Data Eng. 25 (6) (2013) 1272−1279.

[6] C. McDiarmid, On the method of bounded differences, Surv. Comb. 141 (1) (1989) 148−188.

[7] G. Hulten, L. Spencer, P. Domingos, Mining time-changing data streams, in: Proceedings of the Seventh ACM SIGKDD International Conference on Knowledge Discovery and Data Mining. ACM, 2001.

[8] G. Liu, et al., E-CVFDT: An improving CVFDT method for concept drift data stream, in: Communications, Circuits and Systems (ICCCAS), 2013 International Conference on. Vol. 1. IEEE, 2013.

[9] J. Han, M. Kamber, J. Pei, Data Mining, Southeast Asia Edition: Concepts and Techniques, Morgan kaufmann, 2006.

[10] L. Rutkowski, New Soft Computing Techniques for System Modelling, Pattern Classification and Image Processing, Springer, 2004.

[11] D.T. Larose, Data Mining Methods & Models, John Wiley & Sons, 2006.

[12] R. Rojas, Neural Networks: A Systematic Introduction, Springer Science & Business Media, 1996.

[13] L. Rutkowski, Adaptive probabilistic neural networks for pattern classification in time-varying environment, IEEE Trans. Neural Netw. 15 (4) (2004) 811−827.

[14] T. Cover, P. Hart, Nearest neighbor pattern classification, IEEE Trans. Inf. Theory 13 (1) (1967) 21−27.

[15] L. Breiman, et al., Classification and Regression Trees, CRC press, 1984.

[16] J.R. Quinlan, Learning efficient classification procedures and their application to chess end games, Mach. Learn. (1983) 463−482. Springer Berlin Heidelberg.

[17] J.R. Quinlan, C4. 5: Programs for Machine Learning, Elsevier, 2014.

[18] L. Rutkowski, et al., The CART decision tree for mining data streams, Inf. Sci. 266 (5) (2014) 1−15.

[19] L. Rutkowski, et al., Decision trees for mining data streams based on the gaussian approximation, IEEE Trans. Knowl. Data Eng. 26 (1) (2014) 108−119.

[20] G.H. Brifet, R. Kirkby, B. Pfahringer, MOA: massive online analysis, J. Mach. Learn. Res. (2010). http://moa.cs.waikato.ac.nz/.

CHAPTER 11

Deep learning-based detection and classification of adenocarcinoma cell nuclei

G. Kalyani[1], B. Janakiramaiah[2]
[1]Department of Information Technology, Velagapudi Ramakrishna Siddhartha Engineering College, Vijayawada, Andhra Pradesh, India; [2]Department of Computer Science and Engineering, Prasad V. Potluri Siddhartha Institute of Technology, Vijayawada, Andhra Pradesh, India

1. Introduction

An aggregate term for uncontrolled threatening tumor development occurring in any tissue of the body is cancer. More than 100 kinds of tumors have been recognized to date. Some of them are explicitly based on gender, and others are not. Different types of malignant growth in the lungs, colon, and blood are commonly found in humans. Medical procedures like radiotherapy, chemotherapy, and surgery are the built-up procedures for treating cancer disease, but may also have critical symptoms as side effects. In any case, 100% healthy outcomes due to heterogeneity and immunity of tumor cells to available treatments of cancer disease have yet to be established. At the same time, tumors are known for their complex varieties that makes it hard for doctors to identify the strategy for treatment. Hence, it is progressively becoming an essential task to identify a given tumor and prove the location of the cancer and the phase it is at to continue "customized" treatment.

A carcinoid tumor is a well-separated neuroendocrine tumor that 55% of the time regularly starts in the gastrointestinal tract, or in different areas, for example, the lungs, kidneys, or ovaries. Tumors include a very high level of cell heterogeneity because of their capacity to inspire shifting degrees of fiery host reaction, angiogenesis, and tumor rot among different variables associated with tumor advancement [1]. The location of these various cell types has additionally been demonstrated to identify the malignant growth grades [2]. Subsequently, the subjective and quantitative examination of various kinds of tumors at a cell level not only helps to better comprehend a cancer but also to investigate different choices for the

Trends in Deep Learning Methodologies
ISBN 978-0-12-822226-3
https://doi.org/10.1016/B978-0-12-822226-3.00011-8

treatment of the disease. One approach to studying cell types is by utilizing various protein markers that identify multiple cells in malignant tissues.

Manual examination of microscopy pictures analysis by the manual process isn't just tricky and also costly but on the other hand, is biased with the inconsistencies based on the person who is examining the picture. Gurcan et al. [3] demonstrated that digitized example investigation could substantially make the objectivity and reproducibility of computer-assisted diagnosis better. In that type of case, programmed and robust cell identification are profoundly appealing and become essential for a wide assortment of ensuing tasks, for example, cell division and morphological estimations [4]. Also, the blend of cell recognition and a consecutive phase of classifying cells can give clinically relevant data about objects of intrigue, for example, the existence (or amount) of malignant growth in cells in a microscopy picture.

Cell detection is the process of discovering the presence of a particular sort of cell in a microscopy picture. Detecting cells is a noteworthy objective in a broad scope of applications with clinical images. Tumor development speed is a significant biomarker indication for detecting cancers. In most situations the most extensively accepted technique commonly applied by pathologists is observing tissue slides using a microscope and considering their observational evaluations. Observations by pathologists are precise in a few cases, yet for the most part they are less so and can lead to misinterpretation. Cell recognition and localization establish a few difficulties that require consideration. The initial challenge is that target cells are not simple structures but comprise complex structures such as vessels, collagen, and so on. The volume of the intended cell is tiny, and thus it tends to be difficult to identify cells from the previously complex structures. The other challenge is that objective cells can show up sparsely (in tens), modestly thickly (in several hundreds), or exceptionally thickly (in thousands) in a microscopy picture, as shown in Fig. 11.1 [5]. Furthermore, noteworthy varieties in the appearance of target cells can likewise be possible. These difficulties make cell identification/confinement/checking issues difficult to perform, regardless of notable advances in the research of computer vision.

After the success of deep learning, research has been conducted to detect objects in a picture. Nevertheless, the task of cell identification is not the same as general objects detection in a picture such as detecting persons and vehicles, which occupies a considerable space in the given image. Region-based convolution neural networks (CNNs) [7] and their variations [6] and

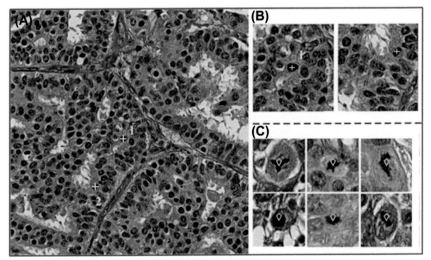

Figure 11.1 (A) Microscopy image with target cells marked at the centers. (B) Two target cells with nuclei in the mitotic stage. (C) Other examples of mitotic figures.

fully convolution networks with optimization [8] have become the best-in-class algorithms for the issue of object detection. However, these techniques are not meant for cell identification because of doubts and difficulties. For instance, for general objects, localization is viewed as fruitful if a recognition location box is half covered by the exact location region. For cell identification, tolerance is commonly required in a much tighter bound to make identification meaningful.

2. Basics of a convolution neural network

A CNN or ConvNet is an exceptional sort of multilayer neural network. CNNs mostly take images as input, which permits the user to encode a few properties of the network, thus dropping the number of parameters. Generally, there are three main layers in a simple ConvNet: convolution layer, pooling layer, and fully connected layer. The input layer holds the image data. Fig. 11.2 demonstrates the general structural design of a CNN with various layers.

2.1 Convolution layer

The principal layer in a CNN is the convolution layer, in which every neuron is associated with a specific region of the area related to the input called the receptive field. The main objective of convolution concerning

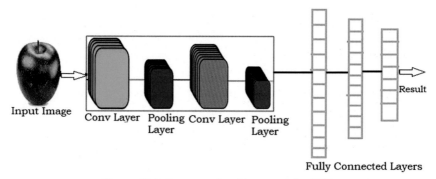

Figure 11.2 Conceptual architecture of a CNN.

ConvNet is to take out the features from the given image. This layer does most of the computation in a ConvNet. The result of every convolution layer is a set of feature maps, created by a solitary kernel filter of the convolution layer. These maps can be characterized as input to the following layer.

A convolution is an algebraic operation that slides a function over other space and measures the essentials of their location-based multiplication of a value-wise product. It has profound associations with Fourier and Laplace transforms and is intensely utilized in processing the signals. Convolution layers utilize cross-relationships, which are fundamentally the same as convolutions. In terms of mathematics, convolution is an operation with two functions that deliver another function—that is, the convoluted form of one of the input functions. The generated function gives an integral of the value-wise product of the two given functions as an element of the sum that one of the given input functions deciphered.

The architectural design of ConvNet enables the system to focus on low-level highlights first, and afterward collect them into more significant-level highlights in the following hidden layers. This type of various-leveled structure is regular in natural pictures, which is the reason for the functioning of CNNs for recognizing the images. A convolution layer in Keras has the following syntax:

Conv2D(filters, kernel_size, strides, padding, activation = "relu," input_shape)

Arguments in the foregoing syntax have the following implications:
- Filters: The number of filters.
- Kernel_size: A number specifying both the height and width of the (square) convolution window. Some additional optional arguments might be tuned.

- Strides: The stride of the convolution. If the user does not specify anything, it is set to 1.
- Padding: This is either valid or the same. If the user does not specify anything, the padding is set to valid.
- Activation: This is typically ReLu. If the user does not specify anything, no activation is applied. It is strongly advised to add a ReLU activation function to every convolution layer in the networks.

It is possible to represent both kernel_size and strides as either a number or a tuple. When using the convolution layer as a first layer (appearing after the input layer) in a model, you must provide an additional input_shape argument—input_shape. It is a tuple specifying the height, width, and depth (in that order) of the input. Make sure that the input_shape argument is not included if the convolution layer is not the first layer in the network. Fig. 11.3 illustrates an example of convolution with filter size 2×2 with a stride of 2.

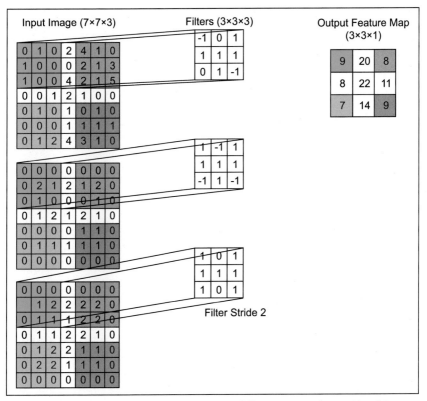

Figure 11.3 An example of convolution of filter 2×2 with a stride of 2.

In CNN, the behavior of the convolution layer is controlled by specifying the number of filters and dimensions of each filter. The number of nodes in a convolution layer is increased by enhancing the quantity of filters. Dimensions of the filters are to be enhanced to enlarge the size of the pattern. There are also a few other hyperparameters that can be tuned. One of them is the stride of the convolution. Stride is the amount by which the filter slides over the image. The stride of 1 moves the filter by 1 pixel horizontally and vertically. Here, the size of the convolution becomes the same as the width and depth of the given input image. The stride of 2 makes a convolution layer half the given input dimension. If the kernel filter moves outside the image, then we can either ignore these unknown values or replace them with zeros.

2.2 Pooling layer

As we have seen, a convolution layer retrieves the feature maps, with one feature map for each filter. More filters increase the dimensionality of convolution. Higher dimensionality indicates more parameters. So, the pooling layer controls overfitting by progressively minimizing the spatial size of the feature map to reduce the quantity of parameters and calculations. The pooling layer often takes the convolution layer as input. Every neuron of the pooling layer is linked to a few neurons of the preceding layer, which is positioned in a receptive field, i.e., specified as a rectangular region. However, size, stride, and type of padding are specified for that region. In other words, the aim of using pooling is to reduce a load of computation, usage of memory, and the number of parameters by subsampling the input image. It helps the model from overfitting in the phase of training. Lessening the image size of the input additionally causes the neural system to endure a slight picture shift. The spatial semantics of the convolution operations rely upon the scheme of padding picked.

The operation of padding is to expand the size of the information. On account of 1D information, a constant is added to the array; in 2D information, the constants are used surrounding the input matrix. In n-dimensional data, the n-dimensional hypercube is surrounded by a constant. To a maximum extent, the constant used in the padding is "0." Hence, it is called zero padding. There exist other types of padding techniques like "VALID" padding and "SAME" padding. "VALID" padding drops the rightmost columns or bottom-most rows. In the case of "SAME" padding, data is padded evenly on the right and left. If the padded columns are odd, then an additional column is appended to the right.

Selecting the operation for pooling plays a significant role in the pooling layer. The pooling operation is like the filter applied to the feature map. Hence, the filter size should be less than the feature map size. Explicitly, it is quite often 2 × 2 size, with stride 2. This implies that the pooling layer will consistently diminish the size of every feature map to half of its original size. The most generally utilized pooling approach is max pooling. Along with max pooling, pooling layers can also implement other pooling operations like mean pooling and min pooling.

The most extreme pooling, i.e., max pooling, considers the most significant pixel value in each filter patch of the feature map. The outcomes are downtested or pooled maps that feature the brightest element in the filter patch. Max pooling selects the bright features in the given image. For the task of classifying the images in the domain of computer vision, max pooling presents the enhanced results when contrasted with the other pooling operations. Max pooling provides improved results if the image is white on a black background. Fig. 11.4 illustrates the operation of max pooling.

Average or mean pooling performs the calculation of the mean of all the values in a filter patch, which are applied to the feature map. This implies that each 2 × 2 square of the filter is examined to the usual incentive in the square. The mean pooling technique smooths out the picture, and thus the sharp highlights may not be recognized. Fig. 11.5 illustrates the operation of mean pooling.

The minimum pooling or min pooling operation considers the minimum or smallest value in every patch of the feature map. Min pooling presents enhanced results in the case of images on a white background. Fig. 11.6 illustrates the operation of min pooling.

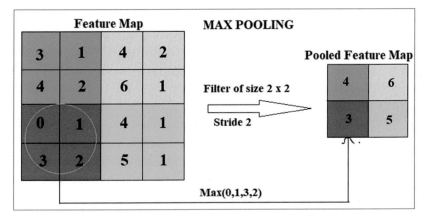

Figure 11.4 Illustration of max pooling.

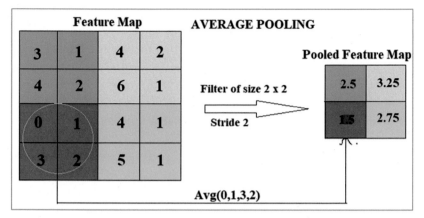

Figure 11.5 Example of average or mean pooling.

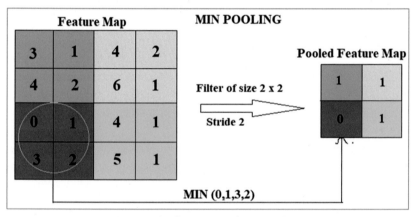

Figure 11.6 Illustration of min pooling.

Fig. 11.7 shows the difference between these three pooling methods with an example picture resulting in max pooling, average pooling, and min pooling for a given original picture.

2.3 Fully connected layer

The set of convolution and pooling layers acts as the feature extraction part in the CNN. The retrieved features are processed to classify or detect the objects in the image. The final few layers of the ConvNet are fully connected layers for detection purposes. Fig. 11.8 illustrates the fully connected layers.

(A) Original Image   **(B)** Max Pooling

(C) Average Pooling   **(D)** Min Pooling

Figure 11.7 Comparison of the different pooling operations results.

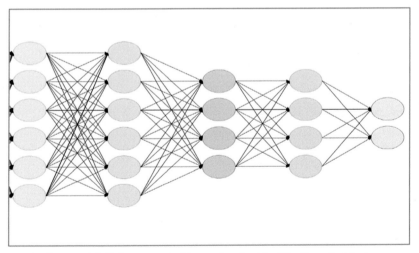

Figure 11.8 Fully connected layers for the identification of objects.

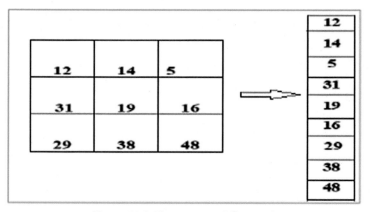

Figure 11.9 The process of flattened.

Fully connected layers simply work as a feed–forward network. The result of the last pooling is in the form of a matrix. It is converted into a vector with a technique called "flattened" and is considered as input to these layers. The process of flattened is shown in Fig. 11.9.

Fully connected layers compute the mathematical operations as follows:
$(W*X+b)$
where:

A stands for activation function

W indicates weight matrix of dimension $M \times N$

M indicates neurons of the preceding layer

N stands for neurons of the succeeding layer

X represents the input vector obtained from the flattened process of size $N \times 1$

b denotes the vector of bias.

The computation is carried out in every layer. All the fully connected layers make use of ReLu as the activation function. After processing through fully connected layers, in the final layer instead of ReLu a function called softmax function is implemented. This function gives probabilities of the input related to every label. The utmost probability node indicates the label of the considered input.

3. Literature review

Identifying objects in a familiar scene generally yields a set of rectangular boxes to specify the position and volume of recognized substances. R-CNN [9] and YOLO [10], along with their variations, use the aforementioned rectangular box indication. Some of the broadly utilized methods for object detection utilize marking in boxes, such as OTB [11] and COCO [12]. Indicating an entity with a carton of four boundaries, the quantity of yield hubs in entity identification has decreased. For marking the cells, the spots at the center of the cell and the curved outline shape of cells are generally used. The curved outline shape incurs additional time when compared to center dot labeling; the latter is the widely used marking strategy for detecting cells. In cell identification strategies that rely on learning, initial labels are preprocessed and then only used as data to train the model. Dividing the entire image into little fixes [13] and changing the dots into a density indication [14] are two standard methodologies.

Over the last couple of decades, various methods for cell detection have been proposed [15]. Cell detection methods based on computer vision use basic techniques for processing images, such as thresholding on intensity, identification of features, morphological separating, accumulating the regions, and model fitting. In these cases, conventional approaches for cell detection based on architecture comprise significant feature determination followed by a classifier. In the first phase, the system disengages one or more highlighted features as the picture representation. Conventional methods for processing the images offer scope for the selection of highlighted feature extraction techniques. Later on, machine learning was developed, which works as a classifier, feature selector, and identifies the regions that contain identified cells. However, the aforementioned conventional approaches have limitations. The first one is that manually selecting the essential features is a difficult task. Much of the time this requires critical information about the targeted cells in advance. The second is that features may contain numerous parameters that have a significant role in the performance of a task. Hence, users have to spend more time with trial and error methods to tune those parameters. The third one is that all the features will not play the same role on the targeted cells, i.e., the essential features may change from one target cell to another. The most important limitation is that the accuracy of the classifier selected with the manually selected features may not always be better when compared to accuracy with all the input features.

To overcome these limitations, cell detection based on deep learning has been proposed. In the computer vision domain, the best-in-class strategies in cell identification depend on deep neural systems. The primary thought behind these techniques is that models are prepared as a classifier in picture space as a pixel-naming [16] or as a region [17] network. Therefore the strategies anticipate the horizontal and vertical directions of cells legitimately on a 2D picture. Nowadays, deep neural systems are used for an extensive range of problems in computer vision and have accomplished better accuracy on benchmark datasets in the corresponding domain [18]. The most convincing benefit with deep learning is the usage of an advanced form of fixed component plan methodologies toward automatic learning of issue-explicit highlights simply from training information [19]. By providing vast amounts of images and related labels as the training data, clients do not need to pay much attention to the detailed strategy for the retrieval of highlights. As an alternative, the deep neural system is developed by applying the gradient descent technique on the training data, so the deep neural systems facilitate the autonomic learning of associations in the information. For instance, upper layers of deep neural systems concentrate on adapting low-level highlights, while deep layers of deep neural systems concentrate on progressively dynamic elevated-level semantic portrayals.

Cires et al. [20] introduced a methodology based on CNN for detecting cells. The anticipated network consisted of a 12- and 10-layer network, and in detection attained a computation speed of 0.01 and 0.03 megapixels per second. Another way of classification with CNN consists of 8 layers. AlexNet [21] was utilized by Janowczyk et al. [22] to identify lymphocytes in the images related to breast cancer. Khoshdeli et al. [23] utilized a five-layer deep network for identifying the nuclei in hematoxylin and eosin (H&E)-marked metaphors of a variety of tissue types. They filtered the given images by extorting the hematoxylin based on a Laplacian or Gaussian filter, and the outcome was subsequently given to the network.

Cell checking and recognition are executed by a CNN pursued by a compressive detecting module [24]. An image of size 200×200 pixels containing dissimilar cells was given as input to the CNN. The outcome was a vector "z" that included compacted focus area data. The compressed area data was estimated by framing a matrix "S" with "$z = S * x$," in which "x" is an input vector. The size of "z" should not be more than the size of the "x". Previously, compressed sensing based output encoding was used along with the predictors of linear and non linear type. The idea of coding the basic cell locations was addressed in [24], by using compressed sensing which is not exactly the same as spatial channel coding. To begin with, the detecting framework S was an additional mapping connection by the neural system. Due to the size of S, much preparing of information was required to avoid overfitting and maintain exactness. Second, recouping the area data from the compacted vector can be tedious.

Henning Höfener et al. [25] trained CNN to create a PMap, which was considered as either a classification or a regression task. Taking into consideration the classification task, two classes existed, i.e., nucleus center and background. In the training phase, the classes were considered as discrete values 1 and 0. The probabilities corresponding to the class nuclei center were considered as values of the PMap. Later, location of the nuclei centers was identified by calculating the local maxima of PMap that go beyond a certain threshold. An area of identical values in which the entire adjacent pixels contain reduced values compared to other areas was considered as local maxima. The local maxima may be as small as a single point. The fundamental PMap approach was managed with the number of parameters. The authors concentrated on efficient listing, estimation, and comparison of those parameters. The effect of individual parameters concerning accuracy of detection, efficiency, and effort required for training was assessed. Finally, the authors merged individual parameter settings, which achieved ideal results in the experimentation for final evaluation.

Chowdhurya et al. [26] used a pretrained AlexNet network, trained on the ImageNet dataset, for retrieving the features based on which colon cancer can be detected. The extracted features were united with the manually selected features by particular persons who were the feature extractors. They used a support vector machine for the detection of colon cancer. Kashif et al. designed a model with CNN based on spatial constraints for the identification of tumor cells in histology images [27]. By applying the spatial constraints, two layers were included in the general CNN architecture, which were designed for extracting color characteristics and texture information. The automatic extraction of features with deep learning was proposed by Xu et al. [28]. Two frameworks based on CNN were introduced for learning the features, which were fully supervised and unsupervised, respectively. Haj-Hassan et al. [29] projected a method by training a CNN using segmentation results. The trained CNN was used to classify the colorectal cancer tissues from multispectral images [29]. Table 11.1 summarizes the work reviewed in this section for adenocarcinoma detection.

4. Proposed system architecture and methodology

The outline structural design of the methodology is illustrated in Fig. 11.10. The proposed architecture comprises mainly two phases: (1) cell detection

Table 11.1 Comparison of related work.

References	Application	Architecture used	Learning type
Hao Chen [17]	Cell detection	Deep neural network	Design and training
Cires et al. [20]	Cell detection	CNN	Design and training
Janowczyk and Madabhushi [22]	Identifying lymphocytes in breast cancer images	CNN	Transfer learning
Khoshdeli et al. [23]	Checking nuclei in hematoxylin and eosin marked metaphors	Deep neural network	Design and training
Y. Xue [24]	Cell checking and recognition	CNN	Design and training
Henning Höfener et al. [25]	Identification and classification of nuclei	CNN	Design and training
Chowdhurya et al. [26]	Grade classification in colon cancer	CNN	Transfer learning
Kashif et al. [27]	Detection of tumor cells	CNN	Design and training
Xu et al. [28]	Feature learning with minimum manual annotation	CNN	Design and training
Haj-Hassan et al. [29]	Classification of cells corresponding to colorectal cancer	CNN	Design and training

CNN, Convolution neural network.

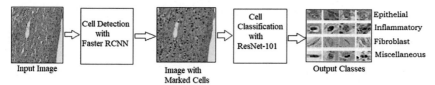

Figure 11.10 Architecture of the proposed methodology.

with Faster R-CNN and (2) cell classification with ResNet101. H&E-stained images are taken as input images. The output is whether the image contains cancerous cells or not. Hence, the final task is a binary classification task of having cancer cells or not having cancer cells.

The algorithm of the proposed methodology consists of the following steps:

Step 1: Load the image dataset

Step 2: Adjust the training and test sets

Step 3: Detect the cells with Faster R–CNN

Step 4: Prepare training images and test image sets

Step 5: Load the pretrained ResNet-101 model

Step 6: Train the ResNet-101 with the training data

Step 7: Evaluate the classifier

Step 8: Apply the trained classifier to test images

Step 9: Evaluate the accuracy

4.1 Cell detection using faster R-CNN

The Faster R–CNN algorithm efficiently detects the cells in an image. The architecture of Faster R–CNN is shown in Fig. 11.11. The outline of Faster R–CNN is explained in the following steps:

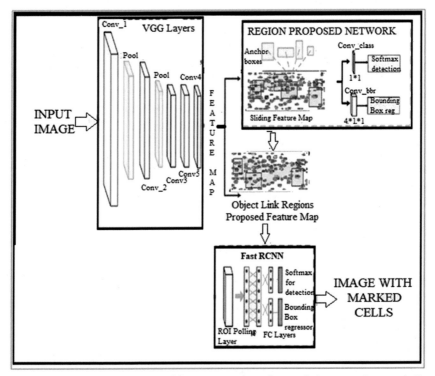

Figure 11.11 Structural design of faster region-based convolution neural network (R-CNN) for cell identification. *FC*, Fully connected; *RoI*, region of interest.

Step 1: Pass an input image to the convolution net of Faster R-CNN, which retrieves the feature map in the given input.

Step 2: The identified feature map is the given to the region proposal network (RPN) of Faster R-CNN. The RPN receives the object proposals.

Step 3: The identified object proposals are given to the region of interest (RoI) pooling layer to convert the object proposals of varying sizes into a uniform size.

Step 4: The uniformly converted object proposals are passed onto the fully connected layers of Faster R-CNN. The fully connected layers place bounding boxes if the object proposal contains a cell that is different from the background.

The input for Faster R-CNN is an image and it is processed with four modules. It consists of a feature extraction network, RPN, RoI pooling layer, and R-CNN. RPN aims to adjust anchor boxes with the original bounding boxes. The R-CNN for calculating the bounding box regression values and classifying the bounding box as the box that contains cells or the box does not contain the cells. RPN and R-CNN share convolution layers to save time.

For extracting the original features in the given input image, we used a VGG16 network to attain better feature extraction performance. VGG16 is a CNN model presented by the University of Oxford [30]. VGG16 is a convolution layered model to extract the sophisticated features even though the training dataset consists of smaller instances. The outline architecture of VGG16 is shown in Fig. 11.12. VGG16 is used because the network will use fewer hyperparameters. The convolution layers are based on filters of size 3 × 3 with a stride of 1. The pooling layers are implemented with the SAME padding and filters of size 2 × 2 with a stride of 2.

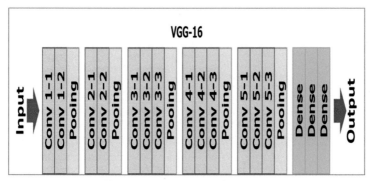

Figure 11.12 VGG16 architecture.

The features extracted by the VGG16 are used in RPN to produce the object proposals. The idea for obtaining the region proposals of the objects is the concept of anchor boxes. Anchor boxes are the bounding box assigned for every pixel in the feature map, and the network will try to search for the best counterbalance from the coordinates of the anchor box to fit the nearest enclosing object directed by a loss function. The output of RPN is a set of boxes that are checked by a classifier to confirm the incidence of objects, i.e., cells eventually. To be exact, RPN forecasts the likelihood of an anchor box as a background or foreground, and refines the anchor.

After RPN, the marked regions are available with varying sizes. The regions of varying sizes imply CNN feature maps with varying sizes. It is difficult to make a productive structure with feature maps of various sizes. RoI pooling solves the issue by converting all the feature maps into a similar size. RoI pooling divided the highlighted feature map as a predetermined number (supposedly k) of regions with equal size and afterward used max pooling for each part separately. Hence, the result of RoI pooling does not depend on the input feature map size.

After RoI pooling, the similarly sized regions are given to the R-CNN classifier to categorize them as either the foreground, i.e., containing cells, or the background of the image. In the medical images, the foreground means the presence of cells in that part of the medical image.

4.2 Cell classification with ResNet-101

The detected cells are classified by using a deep network, which is meant for classification. Here, we use the ResNet-101 network for classification [31]. The pretrained net is adjusted with our training data. ResNet-101 is a residual network that solves the problem of vanishing gradient, which arises in deeper networks. With ResNets, the gradients can flow directly through the skip connections. The architecture of ResNet-101 is shown in Fig. 11.13. ResNet-101 consists of mainly five types of convolution blocks called conv-1, conv-2, conv-3, conv-4, and conv-5. Conv-5 is succeeded by a fully connected layer and softmax layer for output classification. Each convolution block makes use of three convolution layers of size 1 × 1, 3 × 3, and 1 × 1. ResNet-101 was able to classify images into 1000 categories, but we fine-tuned the model to classify the images into four categories.

5. Experimentation

This section elaborates on the dataset used for experimentation of the proposed algorithm and the results with the experimentation completed.

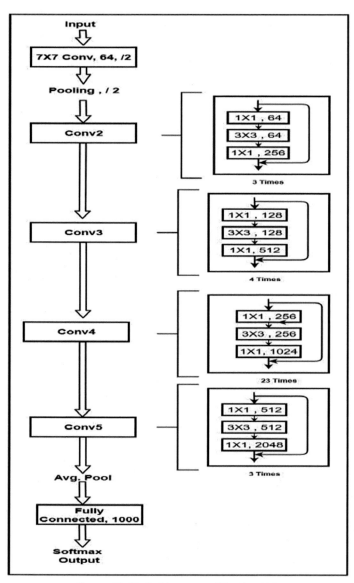

Figure 11.13 Architecture of ResNet-101.

5.1 Dataset

Experimentation of the proposed methodology was done by considering an adenocarcinoma dataset, which is openly accessible by the Tissue Image Analytics Lab at Warwick, UK [32]. The dataset comprises 100 H&E images of adenocarcinoma tissues. The given input pictures have a

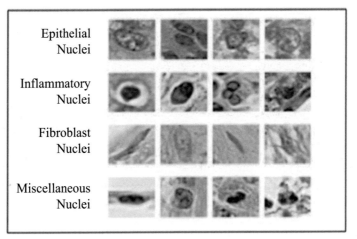

Figure 11.14 Sample images of four different nuclei in the dataset.

resolution of 500×500, which corresponds to $20\times$ visual magnification. Center marker indications exist for every nuclei in all the images. A skilled pathologist authenticates the marked observations of the images. A total of 29,756 nuclei is indicated for detection purposes. Among 29,756 nuclei, 22,444 nuclei have a related class label. The leftover 7312 nuclei are not labeled. The marked nuclei are classified into four classes. Fig. 11.14 shows samples of nuclei from the dataset related to four class labels [32].

5.2 Discussion on results

For robustly validating the proposed algorithm, the experimentation was carried out with the cross-validation technique. The dataset was partitioned as five disjoint folds. All the folds were of the same size. In every experimentation, the network was trained with four folds and validated with the remaining one fold. Hence, 80 images were considered for training the network, and 20 images were used for testing in every run of the experimentation. After testing, the values related to TP, FP, TN, and FN were added with respect to the complete test data in all the experiments, and the measure F1-score was evaluated:

$$F1 - Score = 2 * \frac{Precision * Recall}{Precision + Recall}$$

$$Precision = \frac{TP}{TP + FN}$$

$$Recall = \frac{TN}{TN + FP}$$

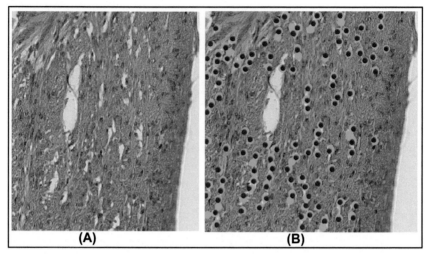

Figure 11.15 (A) Original image. (B) Image labeled by faster region-based convolution neural network (Faster R-CNN) (manual labeled is in green color and labeled by Faster R-CNN is in red color).

where TP is the number of properly classified nuclei, TN indicates the correctly identified normal nuclei, FP is the number of infected nuclei recognized as normal nuclei, and FN is the number of normal nuclei recognized as infected nuclei.

In the proposed algorithm, the first part of Faster R-CNN first marks the nuclei in the given test image. Fig. 11.15 illustrates the result of the cell detection part of the projected methodology using Faster R-CNN. The left part of the figure, i.e., (A), demonstrates the original image given as an input, and the right side (B) is the image marked with the cells detected.

Later, the second phase of the proposed algorithm, the identified nuclei in the first step with Faster R-CNN, was given as input to the network, i.e., ResNet-101 network, to classify the patches and have the cells marked at the center as four classes: epithelial, inflammatory, fibroblast, and miscellaneous. To evaluate the efficiency of the classification phase, we calculated the F1-score measured by using the measures precision and recall. The outcomes of the proposed algorithm were evaluated with two of the existing methods called spatial constrained convolution neural network (SC-CNN) and stacked sparse autoencoder (SSAE) [32].

Comparison of the precision parameter is shown in Fig. 11.16. Fig. 11.16 demonstrates clearly that the precision has the values 0.617,

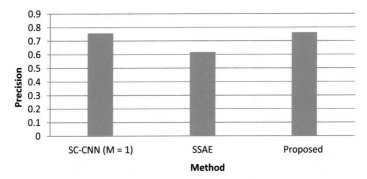

Figure 11.16 Comparison results of precision for stacked sparse autoencoder (SSAE), spatial constrained convolution neural network (SC-CNN), and the proposed method.

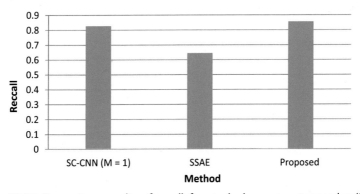

Figure 11.17 Comparison results of recall for stacked sparse autoencoder (SSAE), spatial constrained convolution neural network (SC-CNN), and the proposed method.

0.758, and 0.762 for SSAE, SC-CNN, and the proposed method, respectively. Comparison of the recall parameter is shown in Fig. 11.17. Fig. 11.17 demonstrates clearly that the recall has the values 0.644, 0.827, and 0.855 for SSAE, SC-CNN, and the proposed method, respectively. Comparison of the F1-score parameter is shown in Fig. 11.18. Fig. 11.18 demonstrates clearly that the F1-score has the values 0.63, 0.791, and 0.805 for SSAE, SC-CNN, and the proposed method, respectively. Table 11.2 shows the outcomes of the precision, recall, and F1-score for the existing SC-CNN, SSAE, and the proposed algorithm, respectively.

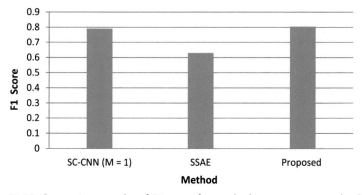

Figure 11.18 Comparison results of F1-score for stacked sparse autoencoder (SSAE), spatial constrained convolution neural network (SC-CNN), and the proposed method.

Table 11.2 Comparison of the experimental results.

Method	Precision	Recall	F1-score
SC-CNN ($M = 1$)	0.758	0.827	0.791
SSAE	0.617	0.644	0.63
Proposed	0.762	0.855	0.805

SC-CNN, Spatial constrained convolution neural network; *SSAE*, stacked sparse autoencoder.

6. Conclusion

We demonstrated an automatic cell identification and classification framework using deep learning for processing medical images. The framework was mainly intended to resolve complex imaging scenarios concerning classification problems with multiple class labels, in which the cells in the input image can overlap with each other. For detecting the cell, we used the Faster R-CNN architecture, which involved feature extraction, region marking, and a classifier to classify that either the marked regions had cells or they were associated with the background of the picture. The second phase of the proposed framework was cell classification. We used the ResNet-101 framework by fine-tuning with our training data. The experimental results proved that Faster R-CNN with VGG16 efficiently detected the cells in the medical images. ResNet-101 classified the cell patches identified by Faster R-CNN efficiently.

References

[1] A. Magen, N. Jia, T. Ciucci, S. Tamoutounour, Y. Zhao, M. Mehta, B. Tran, D.B. McGavern, S. Hannenhalli, R. Bosselut, Single-cell profiling defines transcriptomic signatures specific to tumor-reactive versus virus-responsive CD4+ T cells, Cell Rep. 29 (10) (2019) 3019—3032, https://doi.org/10.1016/j.celrep.2019.10.131. ISSN 2211-1247.

[2] A. Basavanhally, M. Feldman, N. Shih, C. Mies, J. Tomaszewski, S. Ganesan, A. Madabhushi, Multi-field-of-view strategy for image-based outcome prediction of multi-parametric estrogen receptor-positive breast cancer histopathology: comparison to Oncotype dx, J. Pathol. Inf. 2 (2011).

[3] B. Kong, Z. Li, S. Zhang, Chapter Thirteen - toward large-scale histopathological image analysis via deep learning, in: Biomedical Engineering, Biomedical Information Technology, second ed., Academic Press, 2020, pp. 397—414, https://doi.org/10.1016/B978-0-12-816034-3.00013-4. ISBN 9780128160343.

[4] S. Saxena, M. Gyanchandani, Machine learning methods for computer-aided breast cancer diagnosis using histopathology: a narrative review, J. Med. Imag. Radiat. Sci. 51 (1) (2020) 182—193, https://doi.org/10.1016/j.jmir.2019.11.001.5. ISSN 1939-8654.

[5] Y. Xue, N. Ray, Cell Detection in Microscopy Images with Deep Convolutional Neural Network and Compressed Sensing, 2017 arXiv preprint arXiv:1708.03307.

[6] G. Ross, Fast r-cnn, In Proceedings of the IEEE international conference on computer vision (2015) 1440—1448.

[7] Y. Cao, G. Fu, J. Yang, Y. Cao, M.Y. Yang, Accurate salient object detection via dense recurrent connections and residual-based hierarchical feature integration, Signal Process. Image Commun. 78 (2019) 103—112, https://doi.org/10.1016/j.image.2019.06.004. ISSN 0923-5965.

[8] R. Joseph, F. Ali, Yolo9000: Better, Faster, Stronger, 2016 arXiv preprint arXiv:1612.08242.

[9] R. Girshick, J. Donahue, T. Darrell, J. Malik, Rich feature hierarchies for accurate object detection and semantic segmentation, in: CVPR, 2014, pp. 580—587.

[10] J. Redmon, S. Divvala, R. Girshick, A. Farhadi, You only look once: unified, real-time object detection, in: CVPR, 2016, pp. 779—788.

[11] W. Gan, M.-S. Lee, C.-H. Wu, C.-C. (Jay) Kuo, Online object tracking via motion-guided convolutional neural network (MGNet), J. Vis. Commun. Image Represent. 53 (2018) 180—191, https://doi.org/10.1016/j.jvcir.2018.03.016. ISSN 1047-3203.

[12] T.Y. Lin, M. Maire, S. Belongie, L. Bourdev, R. Girshick, J. Hays, P. Perona, D. Ramanan, C.L. Zitnick, P. Dollar, Microsoft COCO: common objects in context, in: ECCV, 2014, pp. 740—755.

[13] Y. Xie, F. Xing, X. Kong, H. Su, L. Yang, Beyond classification: structured regression for robust cell detection using convolutional neural network, in: MICCAI, 2015, pp. 358—365.

[14] J.P. Cohen, G. Boucher, C.A. Glastonbury, H.Z. Lo, Y. Bengio, Count-ception: counting by fully convolutional redundant counting, in: ICCV Workshop, 2017, pp. 18—26.

[15] M. Erik, Cell segmentation: 50 years down the road [life sciences], IEEE Signal Process. Mag. 29 (5) (2012) 140—145.

[16] C. Arteta, V. Lempitsky, J. Alison Noble, A. Zisserman, Learning to detect cells using non-overlapping extremal regions, in: International Conference on Medical Image Computing and Computer-Assisted Intervention, MICCAI), 2012, pp. 348—356.

[17] H. Chen, D. Qi, X. Wang, J. Qin, P.-A. Heng, Mitosis detection in breast cancer histology images via deep cascaded networks, in: Proceedings of the Thirtieth Conference on Artificial Intelligence, AAAI), 2016.

[18] A. Krizhevsky, I. Sutskever, E. Geo rey, Hinton. Imagenet classification with deep convolutional neural networks, Adv. Neural Info. Proc. Sys. (2012) 1097−1105.

[19] Y. LeCun, Y. Bengio, G.rey Hinton, Deep learning, Nature 521 (2015) 436−444.

[20] D.C. Cireş an, A. Giusti, L.M. Gambardella, J. Schmidhuber, Mitosis detection in breast cancer histology images with deep neural networks, in: MedicalImage Computing and Computer-Assisted Intervention 2013, Springer, 2013, pp. 411−418.

[21] A. Krizhevsky, Convolutional Deep Belief Networks on Cifar-10, 2010.

[22] A. Janowczyk, A. Madabhushi, Deep learning for digital pathology image analysis: a comprehensive tutorial with selected use cases, J. Pathol. Inf. 7 (2016) 29, https://doi.org/10.4103/2153-3539.186902.

[23] M. Khoshdeli, R. Cong, B. Parvin, Detection of nuclei in H E stained sections using convolutional neural networks, in: 2017 IEEE EMBS International Conference on Biomedical Health Informatics (BHI). Presented at the 2017 IEEEEMBS International Conference on Biomedical Informatics (BHI), 105−108, 2017, https://doi.org/10.1109/BHI.2017.7897216.

[24] Y. Xue, N. Ray, Cell Detection with Deep Convolutional Neural Network and Compressed Sensing, 2017 arXiv 1708.03307.

[25] H. Höfener, A. Homeyer, N. Weiss, J. Molin, C.F. Lundström, H.K. Hahn, Deep learning nuclei detection: a simple approach can deliver state-of-the-art results, Comput. Med. Imag. Graph. 70 (2018) 43−52.

[26] A. Chowdhury, C.J. Sevinsky, A. Santamaria-Pang, B. Yener, A computational study on convolutional feature combination strategies for grade classification in colon cancer using fluorescence microscopy data, Proc. SPIE 10140 (2017) id. 101400Q 5 pp.(2017). 140.

[27] M.N. Kashif, S.E.A. Raza, K. Sirinukunwattana, M. Arif, N. Rajpoot, Handcrafted features with convolutional neural networks for detection of tumor cells in histology images, biomedical imaging (ISBI), in: IEEE 13th International Symposium on, IEEE 2016, 2016, pp. 1029−1032.

[28] Y. Xu, T. Mo, Q. Feng, P. Zhong, M. Lai, I. Eric, C. Chang, Deep learning of feature representation with multiple instance learning for medical image analysis, acoustics, speech and signal processing (ICASSP), in: IEEE International Conference on, IEEE 2014, 2014, pp. 1626−1630.

[29] H. Haj-Hassan, A. Chaddad, Y. Harkouss, C. Desrosiers, M. Toews, C. Tanougast, Classifications of multispectral colorectal cancer tissues using convolution neural network, J. Pathol. Inf. 8 (2017).

[30] K. Simonyan, A. Zisserman, Very Deep Convolutional Networks for Large-Scale Image Recognition, 2014 arXiv preprint arXiv:1409.1556.

[31] K. He, et al., Deep residual learning for image recognition, in: Proceedings of the IEEE Conference on Computer Vision and Pattern Recognition, 2016.

[32] K. Sirinukunwattana, S.E.A. Raza, Y.W. Tsang, I.A. Cree, D.R.J. Snead, N.M. Rajpoot, Locality sensitive deep learning for detection and classification of nuclei in routine colon cancer histology images, IEEE Trans. Med. Imag. 35 (5) (2016) 1196−1206.

CHAPTER 12

Segmentation and classification of hand symbol images using classifiers

Jatinder Kaur[1], Nitin Mittal[1], Sarabpreet Kaur[2], Rajshree Srivastava[3], Sandeep Raj[4]

[1]Department of ECE, Chandigarh University, Mohali, Punjab, India; [2]Department of ECE, Chandigarh Group of Colleges, Mohali, Punjab, India; [3]Department of CSE, DIT University, Dehradun, Uttarakhand, India; [4]Department of ECE, IIIT Bhagalpur, Bhagalpur, Bihar, India

1. Introduction

Hand symbols commonly act as a bridge for communication balance when interacting with mute people, and as a supporting tool for those in difficult conditions. To ensure a balance in terms of communication there is a need to keep a check on the requirements of the mute fraternity to help them at the early stages of their development [1]. The delay in the advancement of mute people-supporting systems results in a huge loss in their early growth as it can make them unable to express their views and ideas. Hand gesture recognition studies concern the observation of hand symbols that can be used with artifacts that mainly include hand occlusion or light conditions [2]. Regular development of the sign recognition system is crucial for its sustainable development. The efficient recognition of hand symbols is very difficult to maintain as it depends on accuracy and precision. A lot of expertise is required for manually performing all stages of a hand symbol recognition system. Hence, the trends for detection are moving toward automating the process and replacing the traditional manual methods with smart detection [3].

Image processing techniques are gaining importance with the automation of detection techniques. There are numerous reasons why it is necessary to recognize hand gestures. Knowledge of the extent of symbol datasets is required for making decisions at management level because it is directly linked to special category people [4].

Although a significant level of accuracy of hand symbol classification has been attained by using these existing methods, there is a large margin in terms of the following issues:

Trends in Deep Learning Methodologies
ISBN 978-0-12-822226-3
https://doi.org/10.1016/B978-0-12-822226-3.00012-X

265

- The sample dataset input being used must be valid.
- The dataset must consist of samples of every alphabet to make sentence formation easy.
- There must be optimum segmentation.
- Adequate feature extraction and selection for making a feature matrix are necessary.
- Efficient classification is required for hand symbols.

The aim of this work is to apply an appropriate algorithm to the detection of hand gestures through image processing. Optimality can be carried out by using more advanced and appropriate algorithms of image processing at different stages for the achievement of an accurate system. The algorithm thus developed can act as an efficient alternative for application to a practical scenario. Utility of the algorithm depends on efficient training of the classifier, which in turn depends on the availability of a dataset as per the requirements just stated (Fig. 12.1).

2. Literature review

Khan and Ibraheem [5] researched the essential parts of communication via hand gestures and distinguished the methods that could be helpful to structure sign language vocabulary arrangements for gesture-based communication. The main aim was to report the significance of unaddressed problems, related difficulties, and likely arrangements in the practical implementation of sign language translation.

Mohandes et al. [6] presented a sign language recognition system for Arabic sign language. An effort was made to use a color-based approach where the subject wore colored gloves. A Gaussian skin color model was used to detect the face. The centroid of the face was taken as a reference point to track the movement of hands. The feature set included geometric values such as centroid, angle, and area of the hands. The recognition stage was implemented using the hidden Markov model.

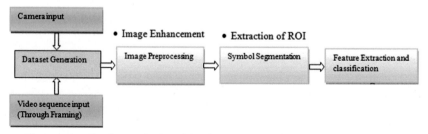

Figure 12.1 The layout for hand symbol recognition. *ROI*, Region of interest.

Ross and Govindarajan [7] utilized fusion based on feature level and evaluated on two biometrics systems such as face and hand biometrics system. The data related to the feature level and match level was consolidated. The strategy was examined by combining two types, i.e., intermodal and its fusion scenarios of the classifier such as strong and weak classifiers.

Jiang et al. [8] used RGB and depth image datasets for extricating shape features of input images. The size of the shape features vector was reduced with the application of discriminate analysis, which upgraded the discriminative capacity of the shape features by selecting an adequate number of features. The concepts of multimodal and method of image extraction were thoroughly explained.

Zhu [9] provided a two-phase strategy of feature fusion for bimodal biometrics. During the first phase, linear discriminant analysis was performed to measure the transform features. In the subsequent stage, complex vectors were considered as a transform feature and had the flexibility to add more input compared to the regular fusion method.

3. Hand symbol classification mechanism

The classification mechanism of hand symbols starts with acquisition of a sample image. The sample input taken with the help of a camera or the inputs available in the dataset can be used. This symbol input needs to be processed through a preprocessing operation before passing onto preceding stages.

The following are the stages of hand symbol classification:
- Symbol image acquisition
- Preprocessing of hand symbol image
- Segmentation
- Designing of the feature matrix of the hand symbol image for feature extraction and selection
- Classification of hand symbol image

3.1 Image preprocessing stage

The main objective of the preprocessing stage is to enhance the visualization effect of an input image by applying various image enhancement techniques and to smooth the image through noise removal techniques if required. At this stage the image is converted into color space as per the requirement of segmentation.

3.2 Segmentation stage

The preprocessed image samples are then transferred as an input to the segmentation stage [10,11]. The main goal of segmentation is to extract a region or area of interest from the problem image. The result thus created contains subsets that collectively make a complete image [12].

Researchers have explored various strategies for image analysis [13]. A few strategies are general purpose and some are application explicit. The proficient segmentation method has an effect on the overall efficiency of the system [14]. A few segmentation techniques are based on a clustering mechanism [15]. Region-based segmentation methods have also been proposed in the literature [16]. Segmentation-based method classification is called either region-growing or region-splitting segmentation [17].

3.2.1 Thresholding methods

These strategies change a range of colors of gray image into two colors, i.e., black and white. This works by picking an estimation of threshold. The pixels grouping into two clusters depend on the intensity value of the pixel. The value belonging to one cluster will be all pixels having a gray value less than threshold and the second cluster will consist of all pixels having a gray value greater than threshold:

$$\text{A pixel} = \text{White if gray value} > T$$
$$= \text{Black if gray value} < T$$

3.2.2 Histogram-based image segmentation

The histogram-based technique is used to calculate a histogram from all the pixels of an image. In this method, clustering of the image is based on the peaks and valleys but this method is not easy since it is difficult to identify significant valleys and peaks of an image.

3.2.3 Feature extraction and selection for making a feature vector

Feature extraction is one of the most significant parts of the strategy of classification. It has gained a vital role in the fields of computer vision and pattern recognition tasks. The selection of features is completely based on the quality of the segmented image. The extracted features are sorted into a codebook for reference to a classifier [18]. The extracted features must be selected in such a way to minimize the redundancy of the parameters.

3.2.4 Types of features

1. **Color features:** To extract this feature set the required image is provided by the preprocessing stage. These are the global parameters of

the enhanced image and are important because the lesions differ in color from the rest of the image. For extraction of these features, different color spaces are required. The examples of color spaces include hue, saturation, value and Lab color space. Examples of color features include entropy, skewness, mean, and standard deviation.

2. **Geometric features:** These belong to the lesion-segmented area. The lesion area is the most prominent feature in the classification of diseases. These features are local area features. Examples of these features include area, aspect ratio, orientation, etc.

3. **Zernike moment features:** These polynomials are orthogonal to each other. Zernike moments can depict properties of an image without redundancy or overlap of information between the moments. Thus they can be used to extricate features from images that describe the shape attributes of an object.

3.3 Classification stage

An appropriate feature vector is the basic need of a classifier. Classification requires a wide range of decision theoretical approaches to object recognition [19]. The classification process consists of assemble and allocate labels to each group of pixels. The classification method works on the principle of training through certain indices of image data. Initially, the classifier analyzes the statistical values of various image features and then arranges the data into categories [20].

3.3.1 Classification phases
- Training phase
- Testing phase

The training phase is the learning phase of the classifier. At this stage the classifier network is trained for the features of the image training class [21]. The testing phase of the classifier makes use of decision strategy, which helps the classifier to make decisions about the samples of image provided at its input [22,23].

4. Proposed work

This chapter proposes a complete process of an application of classifiers on hand symbol images. The hand symbol image from the dataset is preprocessed to enhance its visualization effect. In our proposed methodology, various alternatives of classifiers in terms of accuracy are tested on an input image.

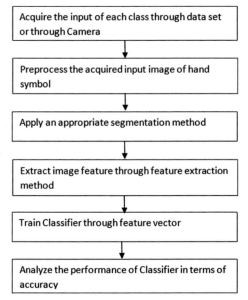

Figure 12.2 Flow chart of the proposed method.

Image segmentation is used for extraction of the region of interest. The hand symbol image is segmented using the color-based segmentation method. Through this proposed methodology, three classes of features are extracted from the acquired input. The extracted features belong to the classes of color feature, Zernike moment feature, and geometric feature (Fig. 12.2).

5. Results and discussion

The proposed method is tested on the images database that includes various static gestures acquired through a Creative Senz3D camera as mentioned in literature and in [24]. Implantation is done in MATLAB and the performance evaluation is done at two stages. First, the performance is tested for the preprocessing stage in terms of performance metrics, and then at the final stage of classification [25]. The dataset includes hand gestures performed by four different people, each making 11 different hand symbols repeated 30 times each, a total of 1320 image samples. The color, confidence, and depth frames are available for each dataset sample. Intrinsic attributes for the Creative Senz3D are also prepared.

A number of segmentation algorithms are proposed in the literature for a variety of applications. The choice of segmentation technique depends on the type of application and region of interest for further processing. The main goal is to select the region of interest and separate the background. The color-based image segmentation method is applied to the images. RGB color images are converted into YCbCr image space, which is further transformed into a binary image. Furthermore, background subtraction is applied to the binary images to finally segment the images.

The segmented image will thus serve as input to the feature extraction stage.

Feature extraction is done with the segmented image of all three gestures. From the selected segmented image and enhanced image, appropriate feature extraction is done. This feature extraction brings out a feature vector that helps in the training of a classifier.

For the training of a classifier, a set of 18 images belonging to three hand symbols is selected out of a complete alphabet set. The performance of four classifiers is tested in terms of accuracy on extracted features of three sets of sample inputs to compare their performance (Fig. 12.3).

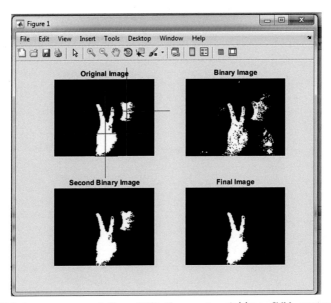

Figure 12.3 Image segmentation. *KNN*, K-nearest neighbor; *SVM*, support vector machine.

Table 12.1 Execution setup for classification of features.

Image class	Number of samples for training	Feature vector
Class 1	6	Zernike moment features + geometric + color features
Class 2	6	Zernike moment features + geometric + color features
Class 3	6	Zernike moment features + geometric + color features

Table 12.2 Accuracy-based performance comparison of classifier.

Classifier type	Accuracy
Support vector machine	94.4%
K-nearest neighbor	88.89%
Decision tree	66.7%
Naïve Bayes	88.2%

The feature execution arrangements as shown in Table 12.1 are used on a classifier and the accuracy results of each classifier are listed in Table 12.2.

From the data comparison in Table 12.2 it may very well be envisioned that the support vector machine (SVM) classifier is the most optimal choice for classification of features extracted from the image data–set of six samples of three hand symbols. The decision tree classifier performance is very low for the applied feature matrix of the test dataset (Fig. 12.4).

Figs. 12.5 and 12.6 depict the performance of the SVM classifier in the form of a confusion matrix and receiver operating characteristic curve of the SVM classifier.

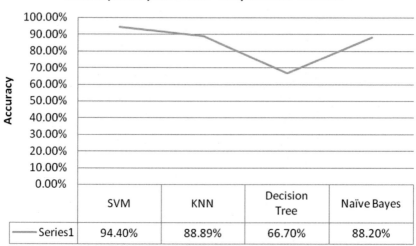

Figure 12.4 Comparison of classifier.

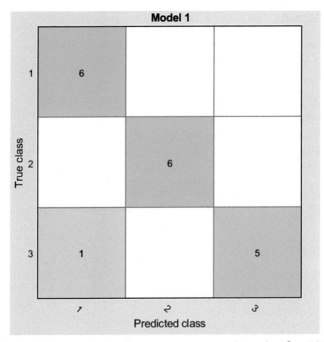

Figure 12.5 Confusion matrix for the support vector machine classifier. *ROC*, Receiver operating characteristic.

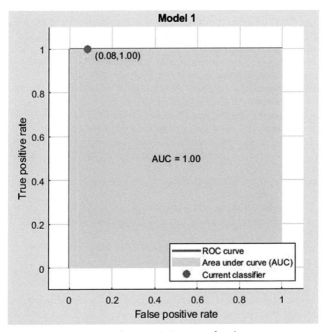

Figure 12.6 Receiver operating characteristic curve for the support vector machine.

6. Conclusion

In this research work, a complete and effective mechanism for hand symbol recognition was proposed. The image processing-based model reduced human effort and minimized the problem related to hand symbol recognition. A preprocessing stage served for the enhancement of visualization of the acquired input image. Furthermore, this preprocessed image went through the segmentation and feature extraction stage and then classification was done. In this execution, the classifiers were tested on 18 sample inputs and the optimum results were achieved for the SVM classifier. This work could be extended by implementing optimization and decision-making algorithms for selection of features and classification.

References

[1] A. Fornés, J. Lladós, G. Sánchez, D. Karatzas, Rotation invariant hand-drawn symbol recognition based on a dynamic time warping model, Int. J. Doc. Anal. Recogn. 13 (3) (2010) 229–241.

[2] L.B. Kara, T.F. Stahovich, An image-based, trainable symbol recognizer for hand-drawn sketches, Comput. Graph. 29 (4) (2005) 501–517.

[3] J. Lladós, E. Martí, J.J. Villanueva, Symbol recognition by error-tolerant subgraph matching between region adjacency graphs, IEEE Trans. Pattern Anal. Mach. Intell. 23 (10) (2001) 1137–1143.

[4] A. Delaye, E. Anquetil, HBF49 feature set: a first unified baseline for online symbol recognition, Pattern Recogn. 46 (1) (2013) 117–130.

[5] R.Z. Khan, N.A. Ibraheem, Survey on gesture recognition for hand image postures, Comput. Inf. Sci. 5 (3) (2012) 110–121.

[6] M. Mohandes, S.I. Quadri, M. Deriche, Arabic sign language recognitionan image-based approach, in: 21st International Conference on Advanced Information Networking and Applications Workshops, 2007, pp. 272–276.

[7] A. Ross, R. Govindarajan, Feature level fusion of hand and face biometrics, Biom. Technol. Hum. Identif. II 5779 (1) (2005) 196–205.

[8] F. Jiang, C. Wang, Y. Gao, S. Wu, D. Zhao, Discriminating features learning in hand gesture classification, IET Comput. Vis. 9 (5) (2015) 673–680.

[9] Q. Zhu, Using linear discriminant analysis to fuse bimodal biometrics traits in complex space, in: International Conference on Computational Intelligence and Communication Networks, 2012, pp. 770–773.

[10] W. Khan, Image segmentation techniques: a survey, J. Image Graph. 1 (4) (2013) 166–170.

[11] B.N. Li, C.K. Chui, S. Chang, S.H. Ong, Integrating spatial fuzzy clustering with level set methods for automated medical image segmentation, Comput. Biol. Med. 41 (1) (2011) 1–10.

[12] S.M. Bhandarkar, H. Zhang, Image segmentation using evolutionary computation, IEEE Trans. Evol. Comput. 3 (1) (1999) 1–21.

[13] E.A. Anjna, R.K. Er, Review of image segmentation technique, Int. J. Adv. Res. Comput. Sci. 8 (4) (2017).

[14] F. Albregtsen, Statistical texture measures computed from gray level coocurrence matrices, Image Process. Lab. 5 (2008). Department of Informatics, University of Oslo.

[15] K. Sarabpreet, J.S. Sahambi, Curvelet initialized level set method for touching cells in low contrast images, Comput. Med. Image Graph. 49 (2016) 46−57, https://doi.org/10.1016/j.compmedimag.2016.01.002.

[16] S. Kaur, J.S. Sahambi, A framework for segmentation of inhomogeneous live cell images using fractional derivatives and level set method", Int. J. Comput. Appl. 127 (3) (2015) 1−8, https://doi.org/10.5120/ijca2015906357.

[17] S. Kaur, J.S. Sahambi, Cell detection in very low contrast images using discrete curvelet transform and radon transform with morphological operations, in: IEEE International Conference on Recent Advances in Engineering and Computational Sciences, UIET, Chandigarh ,pp. 1−6, 21−22 Dec, 2015, 2015.

[18] A. Al-Badarneh, H. Najadat, A.M. Alraziqi, A classifier to detect tumor disease in MRI brain images, in: 2012 IEEE/ACM International Conference on Advances in Social Networks Analysis and Mining, IEEE, 2012, pp. 784−787.

[19] Y. Tian, C. Zhao, S. Lu, X. Guo, Multiple classifier combination for recognition of wheat leaf diseases, Intell. Autom. Soft Comput. 17 (5) (2011) 519−529.

[20] R. Pydipati, Evaluation of Classifiers for Automatic Disease Detection in Citrus Leaves Using Machine Vision, PhD diss., University of Florida, 2004.

[21] A. Devi, A. Misal, A survey on classifiers used in heart valve disease detection, Int. J. Adv. Res. Electr. Electron. Instrum. Eng. 2 (1) (2013).

[22] M. Gandhi, R. Dhanasekaran, Diagnosis of diabetic retinopathy using morphological process and SVM classifier, in: 2013 International Conference on Communication and Signal Processing, IEEE, 2013, pp. 873−877.

[23] B. Kaur, R. Sharma, Image segmentation using RGB decomposition and modified bacterial foraging optimization, Int. J. Comput. Eng. Res. 3 (5) (2013) 50−55.

[24] A. Memo, L. Minto, P. Zanuttigh, Exploiting silhouette descriptors and synthetic data for hand gesture recognition, STAG: Smart Tools Apps Graph. (2015) 1−9.

[25] A. Memo, P. Zanuttigh, Head-mounted gesture controlled interface for human-computer interaction, Multimed. Tools Appl. 77 (2018) 27−53, https://doi.org/10.1007/s11042-016-4223-3.

Index

Note: 'Page numbers followed by "*f*" indicate figures and "*t*" indicate tables.'

Printed in the United States
By Bookmasters